D060025b

Tell me a Story in the Dark

Tell me a Story in the Dark

A GUIDE TO CREATING MAGICAL BEDTIME STORIES FOR YOUNG CHILDREN

JOHN OLIVE

Copyright © 2015 by John Olive

All rights reserved.

Published by Familius LLC, www.familius.com

Familius books are available at special discounts for bulk purchases for sales promotions, family or corporate use. Special editions, including personalized covers, excerpts of existing books, or books with corporate logos, can be created in large quantities for special needs. For more information, contact Premium Sales at 559-876-2170 or email specialmarkets@familius.com

Reproduction of this book in any manner, in whole or in part, without written permission of the publisher is prohibited.

Library of Congress Catalog-in-Publication Data

2014959239

Paperback ISBN 978-1-939629-58-6
Hardcover ISBN 978-1-942672-74-6
Ebook ISBN 978-1-942672-01-2

Printed in the United States of America

Edited by Brooke Jorden
Cover design by David Miles
Book design by Brooke Jorden

10 9 8 7 6 5 4 3 2 1

First Edition

For Michael, who heard it first.

Contents

Author's Note

Do you want to experience primal parenting?

Tonight at bedtime, instead of reading a story to your child, tell it. Dim the light, lie down next to her, and begin:

"In a faraway land, a long, long time ago . . ."

Or: "I'm gonna tell you about a crazy thing that happened to my great-grandpa."

Or maybe, simply: "It was a dark and stormy night."

And then, weave a spell.

You will connect with your child, or children, in ways you never thought possible. Images will blossom. Characters will grow. Plots will evolve.

Your children will listen to you. They will hang onto your every word. So fervently believe that you are the most creative and entertaining person it's been their privilege to encounter.

And maybe, if you're lucky—cross your fingers—you'll hear the most wonderful sound ever, the sound that signifies the bedtime storyteller's triumph:

Snoring.

This book will provide you with every tool you need to explore this wonderful—ancient and yet fresh—form. Part I: The Shimmering Dark is introductory. It details the benefits, or bennies, accruing to tellers of bedtime stories. I'll supply you, the reader, with performance tips: how to set up the room, how to prepare the story, and how to tell the story effectively.

Part II: The Sea of Stories. This is the meat of the book. Here, I'll share stories of all kinds, starting with simple nonsense stories; moving on to myths, legends, tall tales, stories from religious and historical sources, and stories from family history; ending with examples of the most important, most powerful type of story in the dark: the fairy tale. I'll present these tales to you as vividly as possible with, where appropriate, story points — or the skeletons of stories in bulleted lists — allowing you to make the tales your own.

Some of these stories are "standards," — oft told, ancient, and wonderful, though created in this book with much originality. "Jack and the Beanstalk," "Prometheus and the Stealing of Fire," and "City Mouse and Country Mouse" (from Aesop's Fables) are examples. Some are less known: e.g., "A Huron Creation Myth." Some stories are based on popular works of literature: *Great Expectations* or *The Secret Garden*.

And many others are completely original: "Ralph, the Sad, Sad Ghost," "Big Bertha," "Stacy, the Cowardly Crocodile," "Sophie and the Unicorns," et al. In all cases, I have adapted stories and made them my own.

Finally, in Part III: The Greatest Gift, I explore the process of creating original, never-before-heard stories, giving the reader an easy "1-2-3 Method" for doing so.

I urge you to use these tips, tricks, and tales to make this ancient and marvelous art form part of your regular family life.

Part I

The Shimmering Dark

Bedtime

Scenario Numéro Uno

I t's bedtime plus thirty minutes, and the Essence of Sweetness, the Center of the Known Universe—for now, let's call her Natalie—is drawing a line in the proverbial sand:

"I'm not tired. It isn't even dark. I can hear kids playing outside. No fair!"

"Natalie, you should have been in bed a half hour ago."

"I'm not going to bed." She faces you, wearing her patented make-me smile. "No way, José."

You groan inwardly. Not again.

Ah, but this time you have a card to play, and it's an ace. "Natalie," you say in your patented calm-but-stern voice, "if you put your jammies on, brush your teeth, and get into bed like a good girl, I'll tell you a story in the dark."

"Okay!"

And off she rushes, quickly donning PJs, brushing teeth, and leaping into bed.

You enter Natalie's room. She's in bed, but the light's still on. It's one of those dreadful overhead units, bright and garish. The place feels like an operating theater.

You turn off the light.

Boom.

The room changes. What had been familiar and dull is now charged with possibility, with imagination. New shapes appear. Moon-driven shadows emerge. Strange, moving wedges of light from passing cars cross the walls. It's not scary, though. Not really.

Why?

Because you are there. So, yes, the room bristles with potential, but not with demons and scream-producing monsters. Your presence makes it safe.

You settle yourself in. Perhaps you sit on the floor or pull a chair up close. Or maybe you get into the bed. Get comfortable.

"Tell me a story."

"Shhhhhhhh." You pause for effect. This is it. Storytime.

You're a touch nervous. Who wouldn't be? You have a basic story in mind—maybe you've recently read a book or seen a movie that you want to share, or perhaps you've downloaded and read *Tell Me a Story in the Dark* (bless you), and you've found a story you want to try out. But you certainly haven't memorized the story. A lot of it will be semi-improvised.

It's even possible that you have no idea at all what you're going to say.

Natalie grows impatient. She starts shifting around in the bed, adjusting her blanket and stuffed animals.

Not to worry. You and Natalie have experience with stories in the dark. (That's why she's suddenly so cooperative; she loves these bedtime tales.) You know what a piece of cake this is going to be. You know that as soon as you install yourself in the dark bedroom, next to your child, the story will flow.

Easy.

Easy? Really?

Well, okay, I can't absolutely guarantee this. I can't offer you your money back. But I'll bet you a nickel—heck, I'll bet you a whole quarter—that with a little practice and a lot of love, you'll become a maestro of the bedtime story. Inside everyone lurks a master teller of bedtime tales.

Scenario Numéro Dos

I remember the first time I told my son Michael a story in the dark.

It was a sticky-hot night in the middle of a brutal Minnesota heat wave. We lived in an apartment without air conditioning before we moved to our current home with (ahhhhhhhh) central air. Michael (who was two and half years old) was suffering—tossing and turning, sweating and moaning. I stood in the bedroom door, listening to the rattling window fan and my unhappy son, wondering what to do.

Then, without really thinking about it, I went in and knelt down next to his crib.

"On a hot night like this, Micky . . . "

He jumped. The loud fan had prevented him from hearing my approach.

" . . . what we need is a ghost story to send shivers up and down our spines."

He listened. I'll never forget it: he lay on his tummy, bediapered butt sticking up, eyes round pools of wonder.

This story happens in one of those modern housing developments at the very edge of the city. You know: cheap houses and no trees. Parks where nobody goes. At the edge of the development is a cornfield. Beyond that, a valley, filled with trees. And an old rundown house.

This story's about a guy named . . . Chuck. Chuck? Sure, why not? Chuck.

> And one day, Chuck leaves his air-conditioned house and heads out across the cornfield.

Thus began the story that became known as "Ralph, The Sad, Sad Ghost." I ahemed and stumbled, took lots of lengthy pauses, and made up the story *in situ*, not at all sure of where it was going. I had only one clear idea: a ghost. Apart from that, I was working with, telling from, whole cloth.

I told myself that there was no way the little dude would remember my story. *He's only two and half. He has the attention span of a grasshopper.* But the next morning, as I served Michael his nutritious cereal, I asked him if he had any memory of the previous night's story.

"Ralph the ghost," he said, eyes shining.

And thus, with Michael to lead the way, I became a master of what I now believe is a unique (and ancient) art form: the story in the dark. I've created dozens of stories (many of which are included with this book). I've begun teaching a seminar: "Tell Me a Story in the Dark." I am bedtime stories. Bedtime Stories "R" Me.

And bedtime stories are you, too. You can, I'm convinced, become a master, too.

Read on.

The Bennies

A Story in the DErk Why-To

Why become an expert at telling bedtime stories? After all, aren't we living in the high tech twenty-first century? Isn't there an exciting new paradigm? Hasn't the Digital Revolution altered everything and rendered oral storytelling hopelessly passé? Why become conversant in an art form invented by Neanderthals?

Here's why.

Yes, storytelling goes back many thousands of years, but the tradition retains astonishing power. You'll feel this when you enter a darkened bedroom and lie down next to a small child or children. Your voice will shine with power. All the frou-frou of civilization will disappear—cars and trucks and loud motorcycles, electronic devices, and (most significantly) artificial light. You and your children will find yourselves in a primordial campsite. The primal power of the story will beat back the frightening dark. The young listeners will rest secure in the warmth of clan and family.

In what other sphere of life can you do this for your child? Strip away the demanding jobs, the competitive schools, rehearsals, and practices, the sleep deprivation, and say, "We're human beings. Tonight, let's celebrate it. Let's slow down. Take some deep breaths. Relax. Let's do what our species has done for ages: listen to a story."

Ahhhhhhhh, yes.

Become a Master Storyteller

When you spin a bedtime tale, it's possible — indeed, probable — that you will become a master storyteller.

Oh, no, I hear you say. I can't do this. I'm no storyteller. I'm a product of Hollywood, TV and video games, and the all-powerful computer. I can't act; I can't perform; I freeze up whenever I have to talk to a group; there's no way I can convince my sharp-as-tacks kid that I have anything resembling talent.

Well, I say, as politely as possible, you're wrong. Storytelling is bred in your human bones.

Language, by its very nature, spins a narrative. When you talk, you're telling a story. "I'm fine," is a story. Granted, it's not terribly original. Instead, you could say, "I'm great! I just discovered the joy of telling my kid a bedtime story, and it's revolutionized our life!"

Or: "See you later," could become, "My life-journey today is taking me to the office, and then out to dinner with friends, but the good Lord willing and the creek don't rise, I'll see you at bedtime."

Those are stories. You may not know it, but you are already a master storyteller.

And remember: you're not telling a story to harsh critics like Roger Ebert or Gore Vidal. This is [insert your child's name here], and she loves and trusts you completely and unreservedly. You know her better than you know anyone. This familiarity both intensifies the story and makes it easier to tell.

You can do this. Definitely.

Enter the Creative "Zone"

Many artists describe a state of mind as they work, in which their connection to their creative subconscious is heightened. Some refer to this as a waking dream, a creative trance.

Dream-storming.

For me, the best analogy is athletic: you get in a zone. Time slows. You feel inspired (the artist's version of an athlete's heightened reaction time). You're smarter — literally. Ideas come more rapidly. Character dialogue has vibrancy. Sentences have power.

I bet you've experienced something akin to this. At work, maybe, or when you're enjoying a hobby. I'm the family cook, and there are moments when I have three or four dishes working, and I know they'll be great, and I know they'll be ready at the same time. I'm in a zone, a whirligig of calm, energized, focused action.

This can happen, beautifully, when you tell your child a bedtime story. Your love will create a "zone" of amazing intensity and depth. This makes stories in the dark uniquely satisfying. Both you and the listeners enter a unique space. It's great fun, but there are several secondary benefits, as well.

Stories Counteract the Pernicious Influence of Glowing Screens

You know what I mean: the isolation, the lack of meaningful social interaction, the passivity, the dreary mediocrity of so many

TV programs and video games, the fake stimulation. When you tell a story, all this goes away, replaced by imagination, narrative vibrancy, touch, warmth—the ancient power of storytelling.

I'm by no means an anti-tube Luddite, scowling into my cowboy coffee and mumbling about the growing influence of the screens. One very excellent result of TV watching (and one which positively affects the telling of bedtime stories) is that contemporary children are very adept at following complex narratives. They understand rising and falling action, reversals versus complications, climaxes, etc. Children learn many of these concepts from schoolwork and reading, but a lot of it comes from Hollywood—from the TV shows and the movies they watch. Thus, when you settle in to tell a child a complex story, he is right with you.

And video games: the probe—reward—reprobe vibe of video games makes a child very patient with repetition, very likely to want to explore the world of a story with video game-like thoroughness.

Ultimately, it comes down to balance. TV, gaming, texting—all that stuff can be dangerous if it's not properly offset with a sense of family, mystery, wonder, and imagination. Without these, the screens can indeed be creepy, isolating, and deadening.

Stories in the dark provide much-needed balance, in addition to building other skills.

Stories Build Vocabulary

We don't have to sit down and teach our children to use language. They teach themselves.

But we are responsible for building their vocabularies, for teaching them complex words with varying shades of meaning. Schoolteachers do much of this work. The authors of the books they read are a huge influence. They pick up words from their peers, their siblings, and the TV. And, of course, from us. To quote the great Stephen Sondheim, "Children may not obey, but children will listen," and indeed, they do.

One of the best ways to expose our children to new words, to expand their vocabulary, is by telling stories in the dark. After all, when else will our dear darlings be so language-focused?

A child has two types of vocabulary. First, there are the words she is able to use herself: the working vocabulary. This vocabulary is often quite limited, particularly when it comes to very young, and very shy, children. Kids permit themselves to use words only when they are absolutely sure of the meaning.

And then there are the words that the child understands, but hasn't yet made part of her regular usage. This roster of words is much, much bigger than the working vocabulary. Indeed, I would bet that you would be amazed at how extensive this vocabulary is. Your child can very likely understand many, many more words than she uses.

Children become experts at context. They might not recognize every word they hear, but based on the context, children can create for themselves a tentative meaning. They will file a word away, and the next time they hear it, it's less exotic and more understandable.

For example, if in a bedtime story you say, "A luminous moon burned in the night sky, and the air was still and crisp," Your child might not understand *luminous* or *crisp,* but I bet she will understand "moon" and "sky," and there's a pretty good chance she will know what "still" means in this context. She will grasp the overall meaning of the sentence. She'll put "luminous" and "crisp" into her (robust) memory bank. The next time she hears these words, she'll have a better idea of what they mean. And pretty soon, sooner than you might expect, she'll move these words into her working vocabulary.

Moreover — and this is crucial — she will appreciate that you're not condescending to her, that you're using grown-up words and treating her like she's intelligent — like a big kid. She will love you for this, and that strengthened relationship can yield a number of unexpected benefits.

Stories End the Battle of Wills at Bedtime

You work hard. Your job gets more demanding every day. You come home to an equally tired and cranky spouse. Then you have to prepare an edible meal, and now your kid refuses to go to bed. Is anything more frustrating and exhausting?

Well, here's your chance to transform bedtime into a highlight of the day, to send your child scampering off to the bathroom to brush his teeth, wash his face, empty his bladder, etc., with genuine enthusiasm.

All you have to do is promise him a story in the dark.

Now, granted, it does take energy to tell a bedtime story. You won't always have it. Don't make a promise you don't have the wherewithal to keep. (Plus, you want Billy to fall asleep; you don't want to be snoring yourself.) Still, the energy required to tell a story is often less, much less, than that required to combat spirited defiance. Stories in the dark have the potential to make bedtime a special time, a time of joy and love.

Stories Create Wonderful Parenting Moments

You know what these are, those ineffably wonderful moments when your child really and truly listens to you. Maybe she asks you a question, out of the blue, on the way to school.

"Does time go faster when you get older?" my son once asked

me. What a marvelous question, and when I answered, taking my time, thinking through the implications, my son stayed with me, listening. Wow.

Or maybe your daughter comes into your office and shares something with you, unbidden, something wonderful. "I cried at school today."

"You did? Why?"

And then she tells you about a dream she had at nap time—innocuous, but tear-producing nonetheless.

It's impossible to force these magical moments. My dear son Michael has been known to cover his ears and chant, "Blah, blah, blah, blah," whenever I try to impart one of my many pearls of fatherly wisdom. I get a lot of heavy sighing. Gee-I'd-really-prefer-to-be-watching-TV. Let me know when your lips stop moving.

I suspect you know what I mean.

Unless I'm telling him a bedtime story. Then, Michael listens, asks pithy questions, giggles at my jokes, and oohs and aahs at my oh-so-inventive stories.

Parenting moments are often preceded by that question all parents love to hear their children ask:

"Why?"

For example, as you will see, in "Ralph, the Sad, Sad Ghost," I created a character, Madeleine, a young girl at school who I described as being "different." Unkempt hair, food stains on her shirt, too-bright eyes: she's a Special Ed kid. Madeleine becomes Chuck's partner in adventure. I guess in clinical terms she might be called "high-function autistic," though I didn't get into that in my story. What I did mention was that a lot of the kids at the school either made fun of Madeleine or they ignored her.

Michael asked, "Why, Dad?" and this served as an opportunity for me to launch into an eloquent discourse on our unfortunate tendency to categorize people—by race, religion, nationality, and socioeconomic status. I told him how, when I was growing up in small-town Minnesota, we used make fun of kids who were farmers. I quoted (well, paraphrased) Martin Luther King: we must judge people by the content of their character.

Michael listened.

These priceless moments are one of the grand pay-offs of this art form.

A big caveat, though: don't push it. Don't make your bedtime stories preachy. Though they can't articulate it, kids sense when they're being manipulated in this way, and they don't like it. The last thing you want your child saying to herself is, "Oh no, another condescending, sanctimonious story. Zzzzzzzzz." Stories in the dark should be 99.5 percent entertainment. If an opportunity to create a parenting moment arises, by all means go for it, but don't consciously create it.

Address a Child's Need for Stories

Children adore stories in the dark for many reasons: they're entertaining; they provide some sweet and wonderful attention from their often busy and distracted parental units; they're a great way to fall asleep; there's real magic in the air, and the bedroom is transformed.

But underlying all this is an instinctive sense that they are getting something they really need. Once a child develops a taste for stories, he becomes insatiable. The darkened bedroom is transformed into a primal environment, and important work — the proper word — gets done here.

Young children need, at all ages, guidance. Infants need to be assured that a parent is present. They need to feel their physical presence, to hear their voice. Why not tell them a bedtime story? They may not understand a word, but they will feel your protective presence.

Toddlers, as indicated above, need to develop language skills. And, of course, they continue to need the reassuring presence of a parent.

A child between the ages of four and eight begins to understand that she exists as an individual separate from her parents. She begins to recognize sexual and racial differences. She becomes aware of class. She senses that the world is vast, stretching far beyond the tiny boundaries of home, school, and park. She grasps that bad things can sometimes happen. The world contains great beauty and love, but also crime, poverty, dysfunctional families, violence, war, and deadly illnesses. Endings in this life are not always happy.

But a child lacks the cognitive tools to make rational sense of this. She's at sea.

This is where bedtime stories come in. Young children immediately identify with "ordinary" heroes: dumb-but-sweet Jack, who spontaneously climbs up the beanstalk; quiet-but-brave Little Red Riding Hood making her way through the scary woods; shy Chuck compelled to explore the haunted house in "Ralph, the Sad, Sad Ghost." Heroes who live by their wits and conquer adversity are thrilling.

Stories in the dark take on a vital role, providing meaning, a tool for dealing with this wonderful but bewildering world. They connect a child to the rich tapestry of the imagination. Listen to this story. The dorky heroes are confused, at sea—just like you. Lost—just as you are. Frightened—like you.

But do they give into this terror? Hesitate? Dither and blather? They do not. They forge forward. They discover that they possess unimagined resources of courage and resourcefulness—just as you do. This is who you really are: confused but focused; scared yet brave at the same time. You can defeat these ogres and orcs. You have people who love you—parents and grandparents, siblings and friends, teachers and preachers. We will guide you, protect you. You can count on us.

Nothing reinforces this message like a well-told story in the dark.

This book will address this issue in much more detail when it deals with the primary type of bedtime story: the fairy tale. For now, suffice it to say that when you tell a child a bedtime story, you are giving him a priceless and desperately needed gift.

How to Prepare a Bedtime Story

L et me begin here by saying:

Don't memorize it! Never, never, never memorize a bedtime story!

Even if you had the time (and the brain capacity) to sit down
with a text and incorporate it word-for-word into your memory,
it wouldn't work. You would be reciting and picturing words on
paper, not the vivid reality of the story. Even if you happen to be
a gifted and trained actor, reciting memorized text simply will
not cut the bedtime mustard. You would be acting, pretending to
be someone you are not—in this case a person with a memorized
story. It's unnatural.

More to the point: what separates oral storytelling from acting
is that storytelling is personal. A storyteller, whether performing
on *A Prairie Home Companion* for a radio audience of millions or
for an audience of one in a child's shadowy bedroom, is saying, "I
have something special to share with you, something that comes
from me. No one else will ever hear this story in quite the same

way as you will tonight." If you've memorized the story, there is a third, and foreign, personality in the room: the author of the text. You can't have that. It has to be just you and your child.

But, I hear you say, the tales in this book are fully developed. Don't you intend for me to memorize them, to give them to my child word-for-word?

I don't. In this book, I present the tales as vividly as possible in hopes that they will come alive for you, so that you'll get a clear sense of how they will work. But I certainly wouldn't want you to memorize the material. Certain phrases, if you find them sufficiently memorable, might be used, but not, by any means, the entire text.

Here's what you should do when you tell your child a bedtime story: read through the material a few times (depending on length and time available). Incorporate the basics of the story into your imagination, fill it with vivid sensual details, and let the story go organically where your imagination takes it.

Story Points

Once you have the basics of a given story in mind, you should create, for each telling, a set of story points. These are, simply, a list of things that you're pretty sure will happen in tonight's story. There may be a dozen of these points or as few as four or five. You may not get through all of them. Maybe your little beauty will drop off to sleep instantly. Or maybe other story material will suggest itself. The magic of the wild, dark bedroom can spark new ideas. If a new direction emerges, follow it.

Remember, it's quite acceptable for these stories to be free form, improvised, and repetitive. This will often get the child involved in the story, cause increased concentration, and induce sleep.

Indeed, often the unexpected material will come from the young listener: "What's behind that tree?"

Or: "I don't wanna hear about the crocodile. Tell me the one about the sled dogs."

Don't become overly fond of your brilliant story points.

Make them concrete. "Joe feels depressed," "Carmen is confused," or "Molly is happy," won't get you very far. A detail like "Molly is happy. She dances and skips," is helpful to a point, but, again, we soon get bogged down in vagueness.

But how about this: "Joe, depressed, gets in his car and starts driving. He drives and drives."

Much better. Useful questions come up: Why is he depressed? Did he have a fight with his dad? Where's he going? Will he get lost? Where might he end up?"

Or: "Carmen is confused. She finds herself in strange woods. Could this be a dream? How did she get here?"

These are great story-driving questions.

It might be useful to write these points down. I often find that the physical act of writing can help get my creativity juiced. If this is true for you, spend a few minutes jotting your stories points down. It's certainly not necessary to spend a great deal of time doing this. You may not need to do it all. You may simply want to go over them in your mind so that you're prepared, at least on some level, when you enter your child's dark room.

Let's continue this "exercise" (perhaps an overstatement) with the story points I created for an original story, "Ricky Fred and His Flying Bed," a story not included in this book:

★ Small town in the Midwest.
★ Beautiful summer evening—endless twilight.
★ Ricky Fred is sweet and shy. His mother tells him she has to go away for a few days.
★ He'll be staying with a very weird family, the Kadiddlehoffers, in a huge Victorian house with 50 plus Kadiddlehoffers living there, etc.
★ They put him in the attic, in a huge bed, under an enormous

skylight. The attic is filled with shadowy corners and strange knick-knacks.

★ That night, as Ricky sleeps, the roof opens up, and the bed rides. Soon it's flying over an endless forest.

And that was it. Thus armed I went into Michael's bedroom, and a story emerged. Of course, the story I told my son was much more detailed. My "Ricky Fred and His Flying Bed" is a multi-nighter, detailing the adventures Ricky Fred has in the enchanted forest. I described the smell of the pine trees, the chilly night air, and the way Ricky Fred's hair whipped around as he flew. Part of the story even takes place on the moon. No doubt these points would suggest something completely different, and maybe better, to you.

Sensual Detail

Let's quickly define this term. Sensual detail refers to the five senses: what the world of your story looks like, feels like, smells like—whether it's hot or cold, night or day, a forest or city, etc. The term does not in any way refer to eroticism, what we grown-ups often call sensuality.

Children enjoy fast-moving plots, for sure, with plenty of action and nifty story ins and outs and ups and downs. They adore fully rendered characters, people they can readily identify with.

But what they want, what they really desire, more than anything is to be transported; to enter the world of the story, to be taken out of their humdrum existence and allowed to live purely in the realm of imagination. This is what they want, and this is what you, the storyteller, must provide.

How do you do this?

Easy: use rich sensual detail.

Take your time. These details may seem peripheral to the plot (they are), but your young listener will revel in them. If they are truly entranced, they may ask you to repeat the world-spinning detail every night. "Talk about the forest."

Indeed, extensive use of sensual detail is a major reason that these yarns are so easy to spin. For example:

What is the weather like? When Jack (in "Jack and the Beanstalk") leads Harriet the cow to town, is he sweating in the harsh August heat? Shivering in an unusual cold snap? Is the sun shining? Is the sky filled with ominous low scudding clouds? Is the air crisp? Hot and muggy? Or does Jack revel in the perfect warm weather?

Probably the latter (it reinforces Jack's goofy dreaminess), but this is your choice to make, and you should definitely make it. Don't be vague.

What does the world look like? Is the forest Nordic, filled with stately spruces and crunchy pine needles? Or is it a jungle, dense with wild tropical undergrowth, moss dripping off the canopy-creating trees?

What can you hear? Wind in the treetops? Screaming monkeys? Hooting birds? Buzzing insects? Something in the distance? Are the sounds human? From friends? Enemies? Can you smell woodsmoke? Rotting vegetation? Or something even worse?

Is that distant firelight? A campfire! Or is something on fire? A town burning? Oh, no!

Crunch, crunch, crunch. Who's there? Is he friendly? It's hard to tell. His clothes are ragged, and he smells like he needs a shower. But that doesn't necessarily mean anything. Then look into his eyes . . . is he a friend or foe?

He's a monster! His sharp teeth gleam, and his mouth drips strings of stinky saliva. He's ten feet tall if he's an inch, and that laugh! It sounds like he comes from the fires of Inner Earth.

Or maybe she's beautiful, with braided hair, a sweet smile, and a blue dress—look at those gleaming ruby slippers!

You get the idea.

Let me provide you with a quick example: the following comes from the always-popular (because it's terrific) "Jack and the Beanstalk":

Jack got out of bed. He stretched. Then he noticed that the light in his room was different. He ran outside and saw an enormous beanstalk, stretching up, up into the clouds. "Wow," said Jack. "I'm gonna climb it."

He jumped onto the stalk, and started up.

There's nothing wrong with this. There's some nice detail: the altered light in Jack's room and the beanstalk reaching high into the sky. These details are excellent story devices — the first time we really come up against genuine magic.

But let's try it again, with more compelling, sensual detail:

Jack jumped out of bed. "What a great day! Man, I'm hungry. I hope Mom isn't mad at me anymore."

He started pulling on his scratchy homespun clothes: first his shirt, then his overalls. He sat down and tied his boots. "Maybe she made some pancakes. Yum. Hey."

Jack looked out the window. The sun was shining, but there was a curious shadow over the window.

"Did Mom build a new henhouse or something?"

He ran into the kitchen. "Mom? Mom, are you here?!"

"Out here, Jack."

Jack went outside.

"Whoa."

Outside the kitchen window, right where his mother had thrown the seeds, a beanstalk had grown — an enor-

---

mous beanstalk, thick as an oak and reaching, up, up, up into the sky. It was a sunny day, but at the top of the beanstalk there were clouds, swirling and twisting, swirling and twisting.

"Wow . . ."

Jack touched the stalk. It was woody—strong. He could feel a strange power coursing through it. There were branches growing out of it at regular intervals, like it had been built for climbing.

"What are you going to do?" his mom asked.

Jack looked at his mom, and then up at the beanstalk. "I'm gonna climb that sucker."

He jumped onto the stalk, and started up.

I've stacked the deck here, but I think you get the point: the second example is more vivid, for two reasons. First, it uses richer and more exciting sensual imagery. Jack jumps out of bed, pulls on his rough clothes, sees the weird shadow, rushes outside, sees the clouds swirling around at the top of the beanstalk, and decides to climb the sucker.

Second, the latter example is longer and much less rushed. It gives the young listener the chance to savor detail, to really experience the action of the story. Your child, in a real way, becomes Jack and experiences the story close up. This will make it all the more thrilling, funny, scary, etc.

And more sleep inducing.

Here's one specific tip that works well for me: use the ceiling as a canvas on which you, often with your hands, paint the scenery.

"We're deep, deep in a swamp—the kind of place where lots of people get lost. Can you see the big swamp birds? They're flying up. What are those eyes? A crocodile. Ooh."

In other words, the ceiling functions as a blank canvas on which you, the storyteller, can paint vivid detail. The child, as she slips into the imaginative world you create, can actually see the story unfold!

Dialogue and Vocalized Thoughts

Everyone likes dialogue. Maybe it's because we've been conditioned by Hollywood; dialogue is what we associate with well-written material. Beyond that, though, dialogue makes a story real, giving characters immediacy and presence. Remember the old creative writing saw: show, don't tell. Dialogue shows.

For example, you could say:

Cinderella's Step-Mother was nasty and shrewish. She made poor Cinderella do degrading tasks — just because she enjoyed it.

The same with Cinderella's step-sisters. Poor Cinderella was the family goat, the one blamed for everything and punished severely.

Again, nothing wrong here. It's valid, and it portrays Cinderella's pathetic situation vividly. But see how a little dialogue can spice things up:

Cinderella!" Step-Mother was livid. "Cinderella!"

Cinderella stuck her head up from the cellar. She had been working on the laundry. "Yes, Step-Mother?"

"There is dust in the kitchen."

"Dust?"

"Dust!"

"That's not possible. I cleaned the kitchen this morning."

"See for yourself!"

Cinderella followed the angry step-mother into the kitchen. She pointed a shaking finger at some white stuff, behind a jar.

"That's not dust—it's flour. I made some bread. I must have missed that spot."

"You will clean the entire kitchen again. The counters, the shelves, the floor!"

"The whole kitchen?"

"Yes!"

The step-mother marched off. Cinderella got out the mop and pail. She worked slowly, feeling woozy—she hadn't had any breakfast.

The ugly step-sisters appeared, smiling.

There is another kind of dialogue. This occurs when a character speaks to him or herself. No doubt you've heard the expression, "He gave himself a good talking to." When a character deals with a quandary, as they often do in these heightened stories, there is often an important decision to be made. When this happens, dialogue-with-oneself can be very useful:

Jack looked up at the beanstalk, rising up, up, up into the clouds. He hesitated. "Wow," he said to himself, a big grin forming on his face, "I'm gonna climb that sucker!"

Or:

> Little Red Riding Hood suddenly stopped. She listened. *Crunch, crunch, crunch.* "Could that be a . . . ? A . . . ?" She heard it again. *Crunch, crunch, crunch.* Even closer. "I bet it's a wolf!" Little Red Riding Hood hurried down the path, her heart pounding.

Internal dialogue brings characters to life. Use it liberally.

Dialogue is, in itself, a sensual detail. When you give the characters a voice, you are appealing to a very powerful sense: hearing. This kind of sensual detail, the use of external and internal dialogue, plays a central role in every yarn in this book. As you read, you will, I trust and hope, emphatically get the idea.

The Rule of Threes

The Rule of Threes is a useful and powerful structural device. Often things happen three times. Jack climbs the beanstalk thrice. Dorothy has three allies in *The Wizard of Oz*: the Scarecrow, the Tin Man, and the Cowardly Lion. She taps the ruby slippers together three times. Cinderella has three family members: two ugly stepsisters and an even uglier stepmother. There are three blind mice, three bears, three stooges, three musketeers, three little pigs, etc. When Chuck goes back to the haunted house for the third time, all heck breaks loose. That things happen three times isn't inevitable, but it's common, especially in stories as short and pithy as bedtime tales.

Be aware of the progression: narrative tension is established in the first iteration, intensified in the second, then released in the third, in a way that feels logical and satisfying. The use of this device can make a story feel polished and dramatic, even when it's largely improvised, made up on the spot.

Winging It

Now that we've gone over some story prep tools, I should mention another crazy possibility: you can, if you wish (and if you possess the intestinal fortitude), wing it. This is an old theatre term. It means to take the stage with no idea at all of what you're going to do or say. Your performance will be improvised, made from whole cloth. You could, if you have the confidence, march yourself into Joey's room without the first idea of what the story might be.

Can you? Really?

I don't recommend it for everyone, but it's possible. Winging it has several clear advantages. For a start, prep time is zero. Also, it's fun. You're flying (well, telling) by the seat of your pants, as caught up in the suspense as your kid. What's gonna happen next? You better figure it out ASAP.

Winging it may not be as nerve-racking as it sounds. The darkened bedroom and the larger-than-life presence of the child can inspire you. The ideas that come unbidden into your mind can be quite good.

The first story I told Michael, "Ralph, the Sad, Sad Ghost," was completely off-the-cuff. When I went into his room, I didn't even know I was going to tell a story, much less what the story might be.

But something happened that night between Michael and me. The darkness of the room, Michael's wide-eyed attention, the intense connection taking place between us—whatever it was, it made the story flower. Ideas flowed. I saw that strange house by the overgrown apple orchard, the "wisps of sadness" floating in the air. The characters, Chuck, Madeleine, and Nancy, came alive for me.

I was inspired, and I mean that quite literally.

So, consider winging it. After all, you love Junior with an intensity that reaches deep into the core of your being. And when you feel her there, waiting, expectant, wanting to listen to you, looking to you for guidance and story material that will help her make sense of the scary world she lives in, you will instinctively and immediately understand that you are engaged in an ancient and vital exchange. You will rise to the challenge. You may not be an experienced and polished storyteller, but you are a committed parent (or family member or family friend), and this will make you a wonderful storyteller.

Inspiration happens. Trust it.

Make a Bedtime Story an Occasion

No doubt you're aware that that many young children develop going-to-bed rituals: books read out loud, singing, backrubs, music playing softly (and often children are very specific about what music they want; nothing but Raffi will do), night lights, glasses of water, etc. Once these rituals are established, it can be difficult to vary from them without provoking angry dissension.

Be very careful, then, not to let bedtime stories become part of the regular night-time protocol. Stories in the dark should always be special. They require energy that you won't always have.

You might establish them as a privilege, a reward you offer in return for positive behavior. "Thank you for helping me put your toys away. Tell you what, if brush your teeth and get into your jammies, I'll tell you a story in the dark."

Manipulative? Sure. But like many—most—parents, I've become quite shameless in my use of the few carrots (as opposed to the sticks of punishment) that I have available.

Setting Up the Room

Darkness is essential. So turn out the lights. Draw the blinds, and shut the door. Do all this slowly—in other words, turn the preparation into a ritual. This is a special time.

If your child is used to a night light, that's okay (though you might bargain to turn the light on after the story—"I'll be here with you, sweetie, there's no reason to be afraid."). Make the room as dark as possible.

And as quiet as possible. Again, strike a bargain: Raffi will play after the story. No distractions. The only artistic sensibilities in the room should be yours and your child's.

I would guess that after you tell a few stories, all this negotiation will prove unnecessary. The tellee will want to enter storyland as soon as possible, and you won't need to argue about minor matters like lights and music.

Consider making a Grand Entrance.

One way to do this is to let your partner get the child ready for bed: jammied, snacked, and well-tucked in. Lights out.

Then you enter the room—slowly.

"Ready?"

You will want to be as physically close to your child as you can get. The ideal way to achieve this is to actually lie down in bed next to your child. It puts you on the same level. You're saying, in effect, that we will explore this story world together, as collaborators.

If, however, it is not possible for you to get in bed with the child—if he's in a crib, for example, or if the bed is too small or too flimsy—then you should endeavor to get as physically close as you can. Pull up a chair, or kneel on the floor. However you manage it, make sure that you are comfortable. Use a cushion or two. The last thing you want to be thinking about is your own physical discomfort. You want your mouth to be as close to the child's ear as possible so you can speak in a low yet expressive voice.

Touch is vital. When you tell a story, you should constantly be stroking the listener's forehead, rubbing her back, holding her hand, punctuating the story with kisses. It's essential.

It's also good for the child to be under the covers. It's like swaddling a colicky baby; it creates sleep-inviting stillness. Even in hot weather, a light sheet is helpful.

And make sure all pre-sleep business is taken care of. It's time for a story.

Rules

There aren't many rules, but they're important. The most important one is "Head On Pillow": no stories get told unless the child's head is resting on the pillow.

And the corollary: if the child's head leaves the pillow, the story stops.

Be firm here. Friskiness happens — we all know this — but you can keep things well reigned in if you rigidly enforce the Head-on-Pillow rule. After a while, once the tellee has some experience with bedtime stories, all you will have to do is stop talking. She will realize what is happening and settle herself down.

I have, on several occasions, even staged mock-outraged exits from Michael's bedroom. "If you can't be quiet, I can't tell a story — I will leave. Okay, here I go," and I do, in fact, go.

And then, after a moment, I hear, from the bedroom, a plaintive, "Okay. I'm ready."

Another important rule: we have to be quiet. Stories are very shy. Easily spooked. If we're carrying on, not paying attention, making noise, we can easily frighten the story. This has the virtue of being true. "Oops," I often say, "we just scared the story away. Let's be quiet and see if it wants to come back. Shh."

Performance Tips

- ★ Use a lot of pauses for effect.
- ★ Take your time.
- ★ Don't rush.
- ★ Maintain a slow, easy-going pace.
- ★ Really?

You'll recall our discussion of sensual detail, the heavy use of internal and external dialogue and action-oriented plots. Don't stories in the dark thus require over-the-top energy, boffo characterizations, lively gesticulation, and hopping around the room?

They do not.

Yes, the stories will be entertaining. Often, they will be melodramatic, filled with physical action. But there is always one clear goal: sleep. So keep the plot lively (otherwise your listener will get bored and develop a severe case of the friskies), but keep the telling quiet and low-key.

Shoot for a "telling voice." This voice should be quiet, restful. It should also be supple and expressive. If there's exciting action in the story, and often there will be, let your voice—quietly—reflect that. If characters in the story are speaking, then let your voice take on their vocal characteristics—but, again, without full characterization. Do them at, roughly, ten percent. You might be surprised at how far a little quiet flavor of the character will take you.

Take "Cinderella," for example. Your portrayal of the nasty step-mother is likely not going to have Paltrovian intensity or Clooneyesque imagination. You likely lack (nor do you need) this kind of talent. Just pitch your voice up a notch or two when step-mom speaks, and then down a bit for Cinderella. Anyone can do this, and it will work wonders.

Aim to create a storytelling convention: you can't expect these scenes, you are saying to your child, to have the same kind of flair and passion that they would have onscreen or onstage. I'm just going to give you a flavor. You will have to fill in the rest, imaginatively. Your child will be up to this task, and the collaboration between teller and tellee will make the stories come alive, thrillingly.

Alright. We have finished the intro material. Time to forge forward will-nilly into the wonderful sea of stories.

Part II
The Sea of Stories

Types
of Stories

There are two basic categories of bedtime stories.

The first, one-nighters, are designed, obviously, to be rendered in a single telling. Then there are multi-nighters, longer stories intended to be told over a series of nights; you could call the latter "long-form" bedroom stories. The following chapters give examples of each type.

However, one can say that some stories are "one-nighters," but it may not work out that way. Your child might fall asleep before the story ends. She might insist that you explore the world in greater detail than you had intended: "Let's go in that house." Or she may ask, "Why, Mom?" thus prompting a discourse on a subject you weren't expecting. You may not get through the whole story, even though it's short. A one-nighter may thus become a two-or-even-more-nighter.

Remember, always, that flexibility is key. If sleep happens before you finish a one-nighter, well, you'll just have to tell it in two.

This is where repetition comes into happy use. Most children will not object if you retell material they've already heard. Indeed, they may very well like it if you do. This means that you can, if you wish, go back to the very beginning the second (or third) time through. Or you can start halfway. It's your call.

Multi-nighters are designed to be told over a number of nights, so they feature more complexity and a more fully rendered journey. They are thus most appropriate for somewhat older children, those who are able to follow and respond to longer material. Multi-nighters create an intricate and special world, which you and the child can revisit night after night. The worlds grow and become more elaborate—more special—as the stories progress. Multi-nighters are, in my opinion, the best kind of story in the dark.

When this book presents a multi-nighter, the material is divided into "nights": Night One, Night Two, etc. These divisions are entirely arbitrary. You can break the story at other places, later or earlier, as you prefer. If your child starts sawing logs before you get to the place where you'd planned to break the story, then stop. There's no point in yakking at the ceiling while Junior snores. The next night, you can go back (to the beginning, if that seems like it would work) and pick up material he might have slept through. If, on the other hand, your listener is still awake—still into the story—when you approach a breaking point, by all means, soldier on.

Let's go!

Nonsense Stories

N onsense stories tend simply to be words and images twisted around so that the teller can hear herself talking and the listener can become used to the teller's physical presence, the sound of her voice, the magic generated by the darkened bedroom, and the rarified atmosphere of a bedtime story. Thus, often, nonsense stories are intended for the youngest listeners, kids who might lack the patience and the attention span required for a coherent narrative. They are often very short.

These stories are also partly, or sometimes wholly, improvised, just words spun around a silly idea. Because of this, nonsense stories can be good practice for tellers intending to, later on, make up their own stories. Like young listeners, tellers can become comfortable with the darkened bedroom, the feeling of being in charge. Tellers can sense how relaxed the atmosphere is, how the presence of the child makes it simple to create compelling material.

Finally, nonsense stories require heightened involvement from the listener. In the example below, the child supplies the organizing trope: "And then he . . . ?" You could almost see the resulting story as a piece of music, with the listener "playing" the continuous drone and the teller spinning melodic variations around it.

In any event, the improvised nature of many of these stories makes them great fun.

Here's an example of a nonsense story, based on the old typewriting exercise: "The quick red deer ran through the rough wet woods." Given the shoot-from-the-hip nature of these stories, there's no reason to prepare story points.

Teller: The quick red deer ran through the rough wet woods. And then he . . . ? Go ahead, ask.

Tellee: And then he . . . ?

Teller: Slipped on some wet leaves.

Tellee: And then he . . . ?

Teller: Bonked his head on a tree branch.

Tellee: And then he . . . ?

Teller: Had a dream.

Tellee: And then he . . . ?

Teller: Ran. In the dream he ran, and he ran, and he ran. Until he came to a hidden cave.

Tellee: And then he . . . ?

Teller: Pushed aside the branches hiding the cave. It was huge and dark. But something was glittering, deep in the cave.

Tellee: And then he . . . ?

Teller: Went in.

Tellee: And then he . . . ?

Teller: Saw gold, jewels, and rich silks, piled high, all the way up to the ceiling.

Tellee: And then he . . . ?

Teller: Wanted to grab some. But he couldn't. You know why? He had no hands. Then he heard something. "What's that?" *Crunch, crunch, crunch.* A noise. Ohhhhhhhh . . .

Storytelling Tip:

Here's an example of how some quiet – i.e., not startling, completely sleep-inducing – sounds can pull your listener into the story.

Tellee: And then he . . . ?

Teller: He ran. He ran, and he ran, and he ran.

Tellee: And then he . . . ?

Teller: Ran and ran and ran.

Tellee: And then he . . . ?

Teller: Came to a cliff. He tried to stop himself, but he was going too fast. He fell.

Tellee: And then he . . . ?

Teller: He fell, and he fell. He saw the ground rushing up. Up, up, up. He closed his eyes. Said his prayers.

Tellee: And then he . . . ?

Teller: Flew.

He opened his eyes, and he found that he was soaring, just above the treetops. He looked in one direction, and he was flying that way. He looked up, and he flew up. Up, up, up.

Tellee: And then he . . . ?

Teller: Looked around. The whole forest was stretched out before him. It was enormous. Look, there. A clearing. He flew down toward it.

Tellee: And then he . . . ?

Teller: Hovered over the clearing. He saw other animals: Squirrel, Rabbit, Porcupine. "Hey." The animals looked around. "Up here."

Tellee: And then he . . . ?

Teller: Landed in the clearing. "Hop up on my back." They did. And then the deer took off flying. "Whoa!" the animals said. "Hang on." They all flew.

Storytelling Tip:

Room for SFX (sound effects) here: Whooooooo, zooooooom, etc. Again, create the reality of the story world, while at the same time keeping your voice soft.

And so on. This story can go on, as long as you want. Maybe one of the animals gets scared;, maybe they meet Porcupine's mortal enemy, Bear; and maybe the Quick Red Deer sets up a rapprochement between the two. Or maybe they visit a human village.

There are no rules. Be sure to watch your child closely. If he seems to be drifting off to sleep, allow the narrative to resolve itself, and leave your child to his dreams.

An Improvised Story

Nonsense stories can be entirely improvised. One sure-fire option is to let your child decide what the story will be about. For example:

Teller: Give me three items, and I'll make up a story featuring all of them. Three things.

Tellee: Okay. A . . . cloud. A watch. And a . . . school.

Teller: A cloud, a watch, and a school. Okay. One day, Harriet the Cloud was zipping through the sky. Back and forth, back and forth. The other older clouds said, "Harriet, why do you behave like that? Can't you see we're all moving in the same direction? C'mon, stop messing around."

"I just gotta be me!"

So, one day, Harriet was flitting through the sky—bored, probably. She happened to look down. Below her was a school. And there, in the school parking lot, was a . . . Harriet squinted. She couldn't quite see it. "What is that thing? Is that a . . . ?"

Can you guess?

Tellee: It's a watch.

Teller: How did you know? You're amazing. It's a watch. And you know what else?

Tellee: What?

Teller: It's a magic watch.

Storytelling Tip:

You may recall the explication of the Rule of Threes. When you're improvising stories, this can be extremely helpful. It automatically provides structure and build.

Storytelling Tip:

These stories will inevitably involve talking objects. How else can you spin a coherent story around three otherwise unrelated items?

Of course it's magic! Again, how else can you come up with story material from three small objects? Does this watch stop time? Give its wearer the power to disappear? Make people do whatever he wants them to (small children would adore this idea)? Become older?

And here (if you'll permit me a brief aside), we're borrowing freely from a certain very popular movie from the 1980s, starring a prominent actor, in which a twelve-year-old becomes very grown up. Don't be ashamed (or afraid) to borrow (make that "steal") material like this. It makes the telling easier. And one of the grand aspects of this form is that material that feels old-hat to you is fresh and original to your young tellee(s). Besides, those nasty movie studio attorneys can't reach all the way into your kid's bedroom. At least, not yet.

I won't take this any further because, after all, how likely is it that your kid will come up with "a cloud, a watch and a school"? But I think you get the idea: freely use talking objects and lots of magic, and there's a good chance that you'll come up with something captivating.

Indeed, it might be possible to come up with a generic story to fit almost any combination of objects. Here are some ideas:

★ Make sure that one of the objects enjoys the magical power to fly.
★ Let another object be running away from home.
★ Maybe the third object is evil, trying to make the runaway object believe he can live on his own.
★ Fashion a chase.
★ The flying object stops the runaway and exposes the evil object as a fraud.
★ Mr. Runaway goes home, where he is greeted with joy and love.

Depending on how elaborate you make these on-the-spot stories, a single telling might involve several improvs. Three might be nice — the Rule of Threes once again coming to the fore.

Nonsense Poems

This is the only time in this book that I will present works by other writers word for word. But given the introductory purpose of nonsense stories—that is, establishing your presence in the dark bedroom as a way to educate your very young children, letting them know that this will be an arena for story magic—these poems are entirely appropriate. I've had great luck with them. I used them often and memorized them thoroughly. I can still rattle them off.

Jabberwocky

"Jabberwocky," written by the great Lewis Carroll, is the most astutely brilliant nonsense poem ever penned. I like to perform this piece in a gruff, hoarse, world-weary, masculine voice—against the sweet grain of the text. But it will stand up to many different interpretations. Carroll included the poem in *Through the Looking Glass*:

> 'Twas brillig, and the slithy toves
> Did gyre and gimble in the wabe;
> All mimsy were the borogoves,
> And the mome raths outgrabe.
>
> "Beware the Jabberwock, my son!
> The jaws that bite, the claws that catch!
> Beware the Jubjub bird, and shun
> The frumious Bandersnatch!"
>
> He took his vorpal sword in hand:
> Long time the mansome foe he sought—
> So rested he by the Tumtum tree,
> And stood awhile in thought.

And as in uffish thought he stood,
The Jabberwock, with eyes of flame,
Came whiffling through the tulgey wood,
And burbled as it came!

One, two! One, two! and through and through
The vorpal blade went snicker-snack!
He left it dead, and with its head
He went galumphing back.

"And hast thou slain the Jabberwock?
Come to my arms, my beamish boy!
O frabjous day! Callooh! Callay!"
He chortled in his joy.

'Twas brillig, and the slithy toves
Did gyre and gimble in the wabe;
All mimsy were the borogoves,
And the mome raths outgrabe.

The Owl and the Pussycat

Written by Edward Lear, "The Owl and the Pussycat" is another masterpiece. Is there a lovelier image than a small owl and a tiny cat, holding hands and dancing on the beach as the moon smiles down? Note that this poem reads like song lyrics, and indeed, there are a number of musical settings of the poem. Research this if you have talent, and you might end up with a lovely song to sing to your earnest young charge.

The Owl and the Pussycat went to sea
In a beautiful pea green boat.

They took some honey
And plenty of money
Wrapped up in a five-pound note.
The Owl looked up to the stars above
And sang to a small guitar:
"O lovely Pussy, O Pussy, my love,
What a beautiful Pussy you are,
You are,
You are,
What a beautiful Pussy you are."

Pussy said to the Owl, "You elegant fowl,
How charmingly sweet you sing.
O, let us be married;
Too long have we tarried.
But what shall we do for a ring?"
They sailed away, for a year and a day,
To the land where the bong-tree grows.
And there, in a wood, a Piggy-Wig stood,
With a ring at the end of his nose,
His nose,
His nose,
With a ring at the end of his nose.

"Dear Pig, are you willing to sell for one shilling
Your ring?" Said the Piggy, "I will."
So they took it away, and were married next day
By the Turkey who lives on the hill.
They dined on quince and slices of mince
Which they ate with a runcible spoon;
And hand in hand, on the edge of the sand,
They danced by the light of the moon,
The moon,
The moon,
They danced by the light of the moon.

Myths

Myths are stories about gods.

For example, Zeus—the Greek god-of-gods—lived on Mount Olympus, high in the sky, looking down on the pathetic struggles and tribulations of men. Zeus and his cohorts (e.g., gorgeous Athena, zippy Hermes, sexy Aphrodite, party-hearty Dionysus, et al.) used their powers to intervene in men's affairs, often to work out their own petty jealousies and selfish ambitions. The Greek gods led thwarted and often bizarre love lives.

Then there's Odin, the Norse god, living in huge Valhalla, engaging shape-shifting Loki in constant battle. Odin presides over the "Nine Worlds": the worlds of the Elves, Dwarves, Men, the world of the Dead, etc.

Then we have the fragmented and incomplete Egyptian myths of Isis and Osiris.

Or the even more fragmented world of Celtic, Gaulish, and Germanic mythology, which comes to us through a Christian filter.

Some myths concern themselves with human beings who have godlike qualities. The Viking warrior Beowulf does battle with vile Grendel, and then with Grendel's even nastier mother, capping it off with a struggle with a fire-breathing dragon.

This kind of mythology — Greek, Norse, Celtic, etc. — is ancient. Its origins go back thousands of years, into the mists of recorded history. Initially, these myths were religious in scope, intended to tell listeners who the gods were, how they lived, what their personalities were like, how they intervened in the human world, and how they expected us to behave. There are still a few people who worship Isis, Zeus, or Odin today, but statistically speaking, as religious instruction, myths no longer have much power.

But as bedtime stories? They are boffo.

It would well behoove tellers of stories in the dark to read mythic literature extensively in order to find stories that will live on in the story-wild bedrooms of our children.

Prometheus and the Stealing of Fire

The following story (much of which I made up) derives from the mythological tale of Prometheus, who steals fire from Zeus and gives it to humans, thus imparting to them a revolutionary power which Zeus never intended for them to have. Armed with fire, humans begin what we now call civilization.

Cool.

But the myth goes on: Zeus, steamed about Prometheus's temerity, punishes him by chaining him to a cliff where a giant eagle eats his liver. A god, the immortal Prometheus's liver grows back within 24 hours and the ever-ravenous eagle eats it again. And again, and again. Thus begins an endless cycle of unspeakable horror for our fire-giving hero.

Gee, I wonder if this might be a bit much for impressionable young minds. Let's leave this tidbit out.

"Prometheus and the Stealing of Fire" is our first multi-nighter. Again, please note that the breaks — Night One, Night Two, etc.—are entirely arbitrary. Feel free to place them elsewhere, or to ignore them altogether.

By way of a disclaimer, this story has lots of action-packed melodrama. Hawks soar through the night sky, angry Zeus makes storms, Prometheus takes fire from under the sleeping Zeus's nose and gets chained to a volcano, etc. Zeus gets hugely angry and creates—kaboom!—a huge thunderstorm, but there is no overt violence. Still, given the complexity of the tale, the appeal here might be to children who are slightly older, and a bit more mature.

Night One

The ancient Greeks believed in a "pantheon"—a bunch—of gods. Or maybe they just liked to tell the stories. The stories are terrific.

Greek gods were human, with human personalities and weaknesses. They looked like us. They possessed gender—some were men, and some were women. They got jealous of each other. They fell in and out of love with each other. They spent a lot of time gossiping and trying to undermine each other.

Each god had a specialty that they guarded jealously. Poseidon was the god of the sea; Hermes was the god of travel; Dionysus was the god of celebrations and rituals; Aphrodite was the goddess of love; Apollo was the god of music, etc.

The god in charge—the big kahuna god—was Zeus. Zeus was the god of the sky, of storms and thunder. Zeus ruled, and many of the other gods resented his power. This resentment figures greatly in the story I'm going to tell you tonight.

Storytelling Tip:

I'm starting here with a discourse on Greek mythology, in the belief that a parent has a duty to educate his child. But maybe your kid is too young, or on this night too wiggly and uninterested. You could certainly leave the educating out. Personally, I find it interesting, but that's me. Just don't get carried away.

All the gods lived in a place called Olympus. Sometimes it's called Mount Olympus. It's above us, in the sky. The gods could sit up in Olympus and look down on us humans below, struggling and striving.

Now, the gods might have looked like us, but there were some big differences. For one thing, they were all good looking — they had no scars, no wrinkles, no flab, and no gray hair. They were all perfect.

And they were big. One of the stories describes a god as being hundreds of feet tall. They didn't eat human food; they ate something called nectar and ambrosia. They had no blood. They were also shape-shifters, which means that they could take on the forms of animals, and other humans, as they wished. This ability figures in tonight's story, too, as you are about to see.

And here's the big thing: the gods never died. They never aged, they had no sickness; physically, they never changed. They were immortal.

Maybe they're still up there.

Now. There was a god, Prometheus. Prometheus was the god of craftiness — slyness. Not to beat round the bush, but Prometheus was sneaky. He was also, as we'll see, a big friend of human beings.

One night, Prometheus got bored. Things around Olympus were quiet. All the gods were snoring, the cattle were dozing, and even Hermes's trusty wingèd horse was sawing logs. Zeus was curled up next to the fire.

Zzzzzzzzz.

Prometheus went for a walk. He looked down from Olympus and saw the land below sweeping away in all directions. It was completely dark. "Is anyone down there?" he asked himself.

Storytelling Tip:

Now the "story proper" starts. This might be a good place to touch base with the tellee(s): "Are you comfy?" "Keep your head on the pillow. Remember, that's the rule." Maybe you can get a sense of the state of squirreliness, how close sleep might be, etc.

He decided to go look. He changed himself into a hawk—gods could do this—and down he swooped, down to the earth below, sailing, wheeling, riding the thermals, up and down—he was a hawk after all, and hawks can fly like nobody's business. Must've been great fun!

Prometheus was swooping and spinning, back and forth, back and forth, until he was gliding just over the treetops. He kept gliding, every now and then using his wings to keep his speed up.

There, set in the side of a cliff, he saw something.

A cave.

A dark cave.

Prometheus landed in a tree just outside the cave entrance. He peered with his hawk eyes into the cave. He listened with his hawk ears.

Nothing.

Then he heard it.

You know what it was?

Snoring. There were humans in that cave.

You wanna go inside? Check it out? Careful, it's rocky, and the rocks are sharp. Deeper into the dark cave. Be careful.

Ooh. It's damp in here. Ick. Deeper and deeper, darker and darker. Why don't they light a torch or something?

I'll tell you why: they don't have any fire.

Can you imagine what it would be like to live without fire? All light bulbs are made of fire. Cars run on fire. We cook with it. Even computers run on tiny little bursts of electricity: fire.

But this story happens before humans had fire at all. This was a scary time. They had nothing. All they could do was cower in an ice-cold cave.

Storytelling Tip:

You'll recall the emphasis on sensual detail, creating a vivid world to which your listener(s) can be transported. Well, here's a shot at it. Create the sensation of flying, of soaring, and then riding up on thermals. Use your hands. Use SFX (sound effects) freely. Describe what Prometheus (the hawk) is seeing. Take your time, and don't worry that the story isn't being developed.

Storytelling Tip:

Maybe your child will answer, "What?" This will indicate that she's into the story. Or, even better, maybe she won't answer at all, indicating that sleep is on its way. In any case, touch base regularly with the child. Keep apprised of what's going on with her.

Storytelling Tip:

Here's an example of a scene that fleshes out the characters and adds nifty detail. It makes the world come alive. Again, you don't need to be a polished actor. Just do the characters as simply as possible, at, say, ten percent. Your child will love it.

But there was one guy. A kid, named Heracles. Heracles was fearless.

That night, Heracles couldn't sleep. He decided to go outside. He wanted to look at the stars—the burning stars.

He got up and started making his way to the cave entrance.

A little kid called out, "Heracles! Where are you going?"

"Shh."

"Where are you going?"

"Outside."

"It's dark out there."

"I wanna see the stars. You wanna come?"

"Too scary."

Heracles made his way to the cave entrance. He was trembling.

But then he looked up at the stars.

Ohhhhhhhh . . .

The sky was alive with stars.

"That's where I want to live."

"You can," said a voice.

"Who's there?!" Heracles frantically looked around.

"Up here."

"Where?"

"Up here."

Heracles saw a hawk sitting in the tree branches. "Please don't eat me."

"You humans are such scaredy-cats," the hawk—Prometheus—said. "Except for you, Heracles."

"Hey, how'd you know my name?"

"Never mind that. You came outside. I wonder why."

"I like to look at the stars."

"You like stars?"

"Oh, yes. When I look at them, I feel like I'm looking at . . . the future."

Prometheus jumped down to a rock right by Heracles. Heracles backed away. "Don't worry. I won't hurt you. Ever wonder what the stars are made of?"

Heracles shook his head.

"Fire."

"What's fire?"

"Fire is hot—very hot. It's made of flames, and the flames dance and flicker, rising off glowing coals. Some flames are yellow, some blue, and some white. Fire is beautiful."

Prometheus looked at Heracles. An idea was forming in his mind. He thought of Zeus, snoring and giving out little belches from his ample dinner of nectar and ambrosia.

"Hmm. Heracles, I want you to wait here. I'm going to bring you something—something special. I'll be right back."

With that, Prometheus flapped his hawk wings and took off, flying and soaring, up, up, up, back to Olympus.

Night Two

Prometheus flew back to Olympus.

When he got there, he turned himself back into Prometheus. He moved very slowly, making sure no one woke up. He was a sneak. A nice guy, but sneaky. *They'll pay attention to me after tonight,* he thought to himself. *Ha!*

Zeus was sleeping, giving little nectar-burps. And snoring. Hmmmmm-zzzzzzzzz. Hmmmmm-zzzzzzzzz. Hmmmmm-zzzzzzzzz. Prometheus knew that Zeus didn't want the humans to have fire, but they looked so cold and scared; Prometheus wanted to help.

Storytelling Tip:

I'll end Night One here. Feel free to carry on if your child is still awake and into the story.

Storytelling Tip:

You may—assuming this is a new night—want to go back a bit here and remind your sweet girl or boy how you got here: maybe a shortened version of Prometheus, restless and bored, looking down onto the world, becoming a hawk, soaring, and finding the cave and young Heracles, etc. Remember, young listeners greatly appreciate repetition.

Storytelling Tip:

I know what you're thinking: a fennel frond? But that, according to the myth, is what Prometheus used. However, since we're radically changing the myth to suit our bedtime purposes, we could easily change this detail as well. Maybe Prometheus scoops the hot coals into . . . a golden nectar-cup. Whatever Prometheus uses – cup or frond – the important thing is that the fire is almost out. Suspense ensues.

He looked at the fire. It looked black. *Is it out? Oh, no, this is terrible.* He grabbed a stick and started poking at it.

There.

At the very bottom. A small glowing coal. Prometheus blew on it, trying to get it hot. *I better hurry.*

He saw the garden. There were all kinds of plants growing in it. Zeus did like his flowers.

Prometheus saw the fennel plant. He looked at the base of it. The plant was thick there, thick leaves growing into a bulb. Prometheus thought, *Perfect!* He ripped a fennel plant out of the earth, threw away the top, and opened up the frond.

Prometheus ran with the fading coals to the edge of Olympus. He turned himself back into a hawk and leapt into the night.

The wind! It's gonna put the fire out! Prometheus blew to keep the fire going. Phew! Phew! Phew! *Please don't go out!* Prometheus, a hawk now, was hurtling downward, fast, fast, faster. Phew! Phew! Phew! Finally, he landed in the lone pine tree.

No sign of Heracles.

Oh, no.

"Heracles!"

Heracles came out from behind a rock. "Here I am. You were gone so long. I got really scared."

"Quick! Dead wood!"

"What do you need dead wood for? It's no good for anything."

"For the fire!"

"The fire?"

"Hurry!"

Heracles disappeared into the woods. It seemed like he was gone forever.

"Hurry, hurry, hurry."

Finally Heracles emerged from the forest pulling on a branch from an old dead oak.

"Perfect!"

And now, Prometheus turned himself into a young man. Heracles saw him and went, "Aaaaaaagh!" in pure terror.

"Sorry," Prometheus said. "I need hands for this."

Prometheus tore the ends of the oak branch into kindling. He put the dying coals under the kindling and started blowing. Phew. Phew. Phew. "Come on. Burn." Phewwwwww . . .

Then a flame leapt up. Then another one, and another one. "More dead branches. Hurry!" Heracles went off into the woods for more wood as Prometheus fed the growing fire with branches. The fire got bigger and bigger. Soon, it was a raging bonfire. "Look what we've done. Go get everyone."

Heracles ran to the mouth of the cave, shouting, "Look! Look what I've done!"

Soon, the other people started stumbling out of the cave, staring at the bonfire. They were astonished. "It's hot," one of them said.

"What is it?" an old man asked.

"I call it fire," Heracles replied, very proud of himself. "Fire."

Prometheus, meanwhile, turned himself back into a hawk. He rode the hot air from the bonfire upward, up, up, until he was soaring high above the cave. The fire was a beacon, beating back the night — for the first time in human history. He looked down and saw the people dancing and whooping for joy. He knew their lives would be altered forever. He smiled.

"Fire."

Storytelling Tip:

Things are getting high-energy, story-wise. Does this mean that the story no longer works as a bedtime story? Not at all. I'm using exclamation points here to facilitate your reading of the story, not to suggest that the teller needs to be shouting and frenetic. Keep your voice soft, and don't forget: an exciting story creates more concentration and focus, and is thus more likely to induce sleep, than a boring story.

Do you think Zeus was happy about all this when he found out? That Prometheus had stolen fire—as he was specifically and explicitly told not to? That he had given the fire to the humans, changing their lives forever? Do you think Zeus liked behavior like this?

Zeus did not. He was unhappy. In fact, Zeus was pretty seriously ticked off: boom, crash, kapow, thunder.

After all, Zeus was the god of the sky, and he could make a storm whenever he wanted: kazap, kabuzz, kawhump, lightning. The sky was black with seething, roiling clouds, all rolling right toward the humans, and the lightning was eye-searingly bright. The people had never seen a storm like this, and they were frightened. They ran back into the cave to hide.

Only Heracles understood.

"The fire!" he cried. "We can't let it go out!"

He ran back though drenching rain to the bonfire. He grabbed a burning branch—the last one. Rain hissed down. Psst. Psst. Psst. Heracles ran back into the cave. He blew on the branch. The fire flamed up. "More wood! We need more wood!" He looked at the cave dwellers. They stared at him blankly. Heracles ran out into the pelting rain to get wood.

Meantime, Prometheus, still a hawk, was trying to fly back to Olympus, but the fierce wind from the Zeus-storm wouldn't let him.

"Prometheus! What have you done?!" Zeus thundered.

"Nothing."

"How did those cavemen get fire?"

"Oh, that. Well, yeah, I thought a little fire would jolly things up."

"You gave the humans fire?!"

"I did, yes."

"I'm going to snuff it out!"

"You can't."

"I can do anything I want!"

Back to the cave: Heracles ran inside, dripping wet, with more wood. He dropped to his knees and carefully put the wood on the fire. At first, it hissed because it was wet. Sssssssss. But then it caught. Flames danced upwards. Heracles heaved a sigh of relief. Whew. The fire was saved.

The sky: "You can't undo what I've done."

Prometheus pointed out. "I'm a god, and whatever a god does stands. Ha."

"Arrrrrrgh!"

And now, a cloud began twisting and spinning, turning itself into a huge hand, a Zeus-hand. As soon as the hand grasped him, Prometheus turned back into Prometheus. Writhing and squirming, he stammered, "What, what are you going to do? Where are you going to take me?"

The hand lifted Prometheus away, away into the clouds.

Night Three

The next day was clear and bright. Heracles sat outside the cave, looking at the sky. Something was wrong; he could feel it in his bones. But he didn't know what the problem was.

A girl brought him some cooked meat. "Try this, Heracles."

"What is it?"

"It's fish."

"It doesn't look like fish."

"That's because we . . . on the fire, we put it into the

Storytelling Tip:

This is a nice ending: the humans dancing around the raging bonfire, celebrating while Zeus is about to punish Prometheus. If this is too much of a cliffhanger, you could stop with the humans and begin Night Three with the angry-Zeus material.

This next section is a bit more challenging. You may decide it doesn't work and since the above is such a natural ending, you could easily declare Prometheus over. Or you could carry on. It's your call.

flames, and we, we . . . "

"You cooked it?"

"Yeah, we cooked it."

Heracles took the fish and tasted it. It was good. "Yum," he said, and then he ate it all. "That was real good. Thanks."

"What's wrong?"

"I think something has happened to Prometheus." Heracles pointed at a distant volcano. "I think he's up there."

"How do you know that?"

"I just sense it. Maybe because volcanoes are made of fire."

"It's a long way away."

But that night, Heracles couldn't sleep, and so the next day, he set out for the distant volcano. He brought a stout walking stick and a pouch full of cooked squirrel meat. The nights were scary—dark and filled with strange noises. Heracles kept thinking a saber tooth tiger was going leap out of the shadows and eat him up.

Heracles missed fire.

After a week, he reached the base of the volcano. He started climbing. Up, up, always up. He reached the tree line. He kept climbing. Up, up, up.

Finally, he came to the lip of the volcano. There, in the middle of the cone, surrounded by acrid volcano smoke hissing out of the earth, was Prometheus. Prometheus was chained to a rock. He was coughing, and tears were streaming down his face. The lava fumes were terrible.

Heracles slid down to Prometheus "Prometheus! Who did this?"

Prometheus could barely talk. "Zeus. He . . . chained me here. I made him angry when I . . . when I gave you people fire."

"We've got to get you out of here."

Heracles looked at the thick chains holding Prometheus down. He yanked at them. Solid.

"It's no use," Prometheus said. "Zeus put those chains there. You'll never budge them."

"Never say never."

"Never?"

"Never." Heracles looked at the chains. Then he had an idea. "Wait here," he said to Prometheus.

"I'm not going anywhere."

Heracles ran down the mountain, back to the tree line. He found wood—kindling, sticks, and big pieces. He carried it all back up the mountain to Prometheus. When he got there, he was exhausted. It was getting dark and scary, and the fumes seemed to be worse.

Heracles built a fire under the chains. "There," he said. He waited. And waited.

But nothing happened.

How does this fire thing work? Heracles wondered. *Don't you just put some wood in a circle, and then . . . fire? Hmm.*

"Ohhhhhhhh," moaned Prometheus.

Heracles had an idea.

Who knows where these ideas come from? Maybe it was because Prometheus was there. Maybe just being close to a god made Heracles smart.

But maybe Heracles just figured it out. Sometimes people get inspired.

However it happened, Heracles took a strong stick and a flat piece of wood. He spun the stick in between his hands. He noticed that it got hotter. He spun it faster—hotter, faster, smoke!

"Smoke!"

Heracles found some dried lichen and put it around the stick. This time, when the spinning stick got hot, a fire started.

"Flames!"

Heracles fed the fire more lichen, then some sticks, some larger sticks, and finally some big chunks of wood. The fire roared. Heracles put the chain through the fire. He blew and blew. Whoo. Whoo. Whoo. Harder and harder. Whoo! Whoo! Whoo!

The chain was melting. It started to sweat tears of red-hot steel; it stretched.

And then, finally, it fell apart. Heracles ripped it out of the chainstay. "Let's get you out of here." He picked Prometheus up, and the two of them staggered up the volcano to the lip of the cone. Away from the nasty lava fumes, Prometheus started to revive.

They started down the mountain.

As the air got fresher, Prometheus got bigger. He was a god, after all. By the time they had reached the tree line, he was himself again. "I'm free! Free!" He looked at Heracles. "C'mon, I'll give you a ride home."

"You'll . . . give me a ride?"

With that, Prometheus turned into a giant hawk. "Hop on."

Heracles did, and the two of them took off, soaring and gliding above the moonlit land.

"Prometheus!" Zeus's voice boomed.

"I escaped! And whatever a god does can't be undone! Ha!"

Story Points: "Prometheus and the Stealing of Fire"

Night One

★ Intro material: the Greek gods lived on Olympus and had some human and some God-like attributes. Hermes, Dionysus, Athena, Aphrodite, et al. Zeus, the god of thunder, was in charge. The gods were jealous and quick to fall in love, etc. This all can be expanded if the tellee gets into it.

★ Prometheus: sneaky and ambitious, looking over the dark land. Turns himself into a hawk and soars, swooping and gliding.

★ Story shifts to Heracles, sleeping in the dark, dank cave. Makes his way outside to look at the stars: "The Future." Meets the hawk (Prometheus). Scene: stars are made of fire. "What's fire?"

★ Prometheus gets an idea and heads back to Olympus.

Night Two

★ Prometheus takes an almost dead coal from Zeus's fire, puts it into a fennel frond (or something), transforms himself back into a hawk, and heads back to Heracles, frantically blowing on the coal.

★ Prometheus turns himself into young man and commands Heracles to get kindling and wood. He blows on the coal. A flame jumps up—fire!

★ Heracles invites the other humans outside. They dance around the bonfire.

★ Prometheus, a hawk again, watches as he soars in the updraft from the fire.

★ Zeus is angry: thunder storm. Heracles leads the effort of the humans to save the fire, and they succeed.

Night Three

★ A girl offers Heracles cooked fish. He looks at a distant volcano. "I think Prometheus is there."

★ Heracles hikes to the volcano. This is hard. The nights are scary. The volcano is high. Heracles climbs and climbs.

★ He finds Prometheus in chains. He figures out how to make his own fire. Melts the chains, freeing Prometheus. They make their way down the volcano.

★ Prometheus exalts, "Whatever a god does stands!"

A Huron Creation Story

Native American mythology is a rich source of "creation stories." These describe how this wonderful world we inhabit came to be. Native myths boast a depth, a range, and a richness that reflects the many tribes, languages, cultures, and religions that go into the tradition.

One of the most remarkable aspects of Native American stories is that they were, until the mid-19th century when they began to be collected, completely oral, part of a living (and evolving) story-telling tradition. This oral tradition continues to this day, as shamans, elders, etc., tell (and change) the old stories and make up new ones. This ensures that their cultures remain alive and vital.

It's worth emphasizing that these storytellers, with good reason, dislike the term "mythology," with its connotations of a dead culture, with cynical know-everything scholars holding forth on an "old" tradition's vaunted "beauty." "Myth" implies an ancient, quaint, and false belief, whereas these tellers believe passionately in the truth of the stories they tell.

Really? Do they literally believe the world began on top of a turtle shell? Well, perhaps not. But they do believe that we live in a world suffused with magic, a world shared equally by all living beings, where wild and beautifully crazy things can happen. I believe that, too.

As the old southern preacher once said, "It may not have happened this way, but this is a true story."

This story is very sweet and gentle. There are a few possibly scary segments, but these can be modified or eliminated altogether. Thus, the story is a one-nighter, and would work well for younger children.

Storytelling Tip:

Is your family religious? If so, this would be a logical place to elaborate on "What We Believe." But don't get carried away. You're telling a bedtime story, and that's where the emphasis should be.

I'm going to tell you a Native American creation story. There are many creation stories like this one.

Are these stories true?

Factually? No. We know that this planet earth is five billion years old (give or take), that it was originally a ball of seething molten rock until it cooled, and slowly, over many eons, the earth's oxygen-rich atmosphere formed. And then, after uncounted eons, Life began.

But are these native stories poetically true? Yes, indeed.

Native Americans believe that the earth is alive and that we are part of the earth, just like the other animals. The Earth nurtures us and keeps us close. I believe that, too.

Here's the story.

At first, the earth was made of water.

Think of it: water everywhere, flat, no hills, and wet. All the animals were drenched all the time, coughing and struggling with awful, water-borne illnesses. Squirrel, Rabbit, Bear, and Fox were all miserable—even Duck. Duck spends a lot of time in water, but occasionally he wants to walk on dry land and stretch his muscles. Only Fish was happy.

So the animals decided they had to make some dry earth; their lives depended on it. So they dove down into the water. They swam down, as far as they could. Down, down, down, until they reached the muddy bottom. Then they tried to bring up some of the mud, but they couldn't. Every time they tried, they found that the bottom was too far down, and to keep from drowning, they had to swim

Storytelling Tip:

In the original story, some of the animals actually die in this attempt. This may be a touch too scary, especially for young children. But it does lend the story intensity, and it raises the stakes. Gauge your child's ability to deal with this.

up, up, up, as fast as they could.

And they couldn't hold on to the mud. They dropped it, and it slowly settled back down to the bottom.

Finally, Toad gave it a shot.

Little Toad.

Up to that point, everybody had ignored Toad. He was ugly, for one thing, full of knobs and warts. His feet looked silly, and his voice was weird. Toad croaked whenever he tried to talk.

"I'll try it," he croaked.

Everyone laughed. "Ha, ha, ha. Silly Toad."

Ah, but there was something about Toad they didn't know: he could hold his breath, really hold his breath.

Toad got ready. He breathed hard, panted, and then he sucked in a great breath of air and dove. Down, down he went. The bottom was so far away! But Toad kept on going, even though his little toad lungs were about to burst. Down, down, down. He was afraid he was going to black out.

But his lungs held out. He reached the bottom. He grabbed a big scoop of mud in his webbed hands. He pressed the mud close as he paddled as hard as he could to get to the air. Up, up, up, up, and boom! Toad broke the surface and sucked in a huge breath of air. Ahhhhhhhh!

"Where's Turtle?" he demanded.

"Here I am," Turtle replied.

And Toad slapped the scoop of mud onto Turtle's shell: the first earth ever.

And you know what? The turtle grew. It grew and grew and grew until the mud and the turtle reached as far you can see. It covered the whole earth. Hills formed, and rivers and lakes—even mountains.

And that's why the earth we live on is called Turtle Island.

One day, way up in the Sky Kingdom, the Great Mother was walking along, thinking about the two babies growing in her belly — twins! — and she wasn't looking where she was going.

You know what she did? She fell through a hole in the sky and hurtled toward Turtle Island, far, far below.

"Help me!" she cried. "Help! Help!

Ah, but two loons heard her cries and flew under her and stopped her from squishing herself on the hard ground. The loons flew along, supporting the Great Mother. They were strong loons. They called out in their wonderful loon voices for all the animals to come to a great pow-wow — a meeting. Slowly, the loons landed on Turtle Island with the Great Mother. They gently set her down.

She was the first human being ever to set foot on Turtle Island!

The animals didn't know what to do. A person on Turtle Island? What will happen to us? Is there room? What if she turns out to be fierce and mean? What if she eats us all up? They were scared.

And then one animal — it was Toad, the guy they were always underestimating — figured out that Great Mother was pregnant.

"She's pregnant," Toad said, "and she has twins."

Well, that did it. The animals let the Great Mother stay. And sure enough, two boys were born.

The first boy came out quietly, with hands folded in front, like he was praying. Even when he was born, he was smiling. He made the animals laugh because he was so sweet. They called him, naturally, Sweet Boy.

Turtle Island is a name that has been woven into the American fabric. In Minnesota, where I live, there is a town named Turtle Island, as well as a holistic healing center and a TV production company. There's even Turtle Island beer. I bet there are Turtle Islands near where you live. This would be a natural place to end the story, if Mr. or Ms. Wonderful is approaching sleep. Check in with her and find out. If she's still wide-awake, you can go on.

Storytelling Tip:

You could describe this battle in technicolor detail. The battle can rage all across the North American continent, from the mountains, to the desert, to the Great Plains; there can be herds of buffalo facing swarms of snakes, panthers, and nasty skeeters, etc. Older children might thoroughly adore this; younger children might not. So, again, gauge your child's ability to handle scariness, and tell the story accordingly.

But then the second boy was born. He came out fighting and crying, angry. Whenever someone got near him, he swung at them. The animals called him Flint Boy, because his head was so hard, and he was so mean.

What do you think happened to Great Mother? She didn't die, but she became part of the earth. She grew things: plants, grass, vegetables, and trees. Every spring, when the plants come surging back in all their green nurturing glory, it's because of Great Mother.

The animals raised Sweet Boy and Flint Boy.

The boys were powerful. They created animals. Sweet Boy made wonderfully useful animals, like Buffalo, Partridge, Horse, and Turtle. They were all gentle, and he made Turtle Island ring with laughter. Sweet Boy created rivers that ran both upstream and downstream. That way you could travel the river and always go downstream.

But Flint Boy — yikes. He made angry animals, animals that roared their fierceness and hated the world: rattlesnakes, panthers, nasty crows, smelly skunks, and mosquitoes the size of turkeys. He made impassable waterfalls and tornados and blizzards and scary windstorms.

Well, Turtle Island wasn't big enough for them all. There had to be a battle.

The day came. The two boys faced each other, with the animals they had created.

I wish I could say that this story has a happy ending, but it doesn't. For Flint Boy, with his powerful animals — the snakes, the mountain lions, the skeeters — drove Sweet Boy out of Turtle Island. And that's why there are snakes and panthers and mosquitoes. That's why rivers only run in one direction. Sometimes we have to go upstream.

But Sweet Boy didn't disappear altogether — not at all.

Sweet Boy lives on, inside us. And when we die and go up to be with the Great Mother in sky, Sweet Boy is up there with her, waiting for us.

Story Points: "A Huron Creation Story"

★ Intro: the nature of Native American mythology and what the stories say about Native beliefs.

★ In the beginning there was only water. The animals want to create land, so they dive down to get some mud. All fail, except Toad. He slaps his mud on the turtle's back. It grows, and the earth becomes Turtle Island.

★ Earth Mother falls through a hole in the sky. Two loons save her. The animals debate what to do with her. Toad reveals that she is pregnant with twins.

★ The twins are born: gentle Sweet Boy and angry, harsh Flint Boy. Sweet Boy creates useful animals and Flint Boy creates harsh ones: panthers, snakes, mosquitoes, etc.

★ Earth Mother dies and becomes plants and trees. Animals raise the two boys.

★ Finally, there is conflict between the boys. The battles rages across Turtle Island. Flint Boy wins, but the animals created by Sweet Boy live on—and so does he, along with Earth Mother, in the sky and in us.

Legends

Similar to myths, legends are about larger-than-life individuals, epic heroes, and people with seemingly super-human power. But there's one enormous difference: these heroes really lived.

George Washington, Ben Franklin, Paul Revere, Abe Lincoln, Davey Crockett, Crazy Horse, George Armstrong Custer, Sitting Bull, Geronimo, Wyatt Earp, Billy the Kid, Annie Oakley, Will Rogers, Martin Luther King Jr., et al., (the list is long) really did do many — but by no means all — of the things attributed to them. Many wonderful stories about them have sprung up. Many of these stories are embroidered and embellished. Often, they are utterly fictitious. These exaggerated and occasionally entirely made up tales are legends.

"My son," asked George Washington's father, "did you cut down the cherry tree?"

"Oh, Father dear, I cannot tell a lie. Yes, I did cut down the cherry tree."

Was George Washington an honest man? Most definitely. Was his father strict? Certainly. Is there a scintilla of historical evidence that George felled a cherry tree against his father's wishes? There is not. The story is entirely legendary.

Did Paul Revere cry, as he galloped through the Massachusetts night, "The British are coming, the British are coming!" Probably not. When Abe Lincoln died, did someone intone (per the legend), "Now he belongs to the ages." Maybe, but probably not. Was Martin Luther King Jr. just a young assistant pastor, asked to make a brief speech, and did he then electrify the congregation and seize control of the Civil Rights movement? Yes.

When dealing with legendary figures, we're constantly asking ourselves: did this really happen? Did it happen this way? This delicious quandary gives legends zest.

And this predicament drives the following story:

Legend or History?

This is a long story. Feel free to do it in several nights, or just leave one (or several) stories out.

The material is appropriate for any age.

I'm gonna try something different tonight for our story. I'm going to tell you some stories, and then we'll decide together whether you think they tell historical facts (meaning they really happened) or whether they're legends (meaning somebody just made the stories up).

Okay?

George Washington

George Washington. Do you know who he was? People call him the father of our country. He was the military leader of the colonies during the Revolutionary War. And then he served two terms as our first president. After that, he walked away, said good-bye, and went back to his estate called Mount Vernon.

Washington owned hundreds of slaves. They worked in

Storytelling Tip:

In the interest of historical verisimilitude and political correctness, I feel obligated to mention this. But you could leave it out.

his fields and as servants in his house. But you know what he did? In his will, he freed them all. Washington was the only slave-owning founding father to do this. Even Thomas Jefferson, the man who wrote the great Declaration of Independence, didn't do this.

Here's the story:

George Washington was a good boy. He was a rich kid. He grew up on a plantation in Virginia in the eighteenth century. But he didn't just lie around and let the field hands do everything — not George. He worked hard at school and on the plantation. He read as much as he could and did his homework. When he wasn't studying, he was working, planting tobacco. To do this, you had to make a mound of soil, and then put the tobacco plant in a hole at the top — thousands of times. He also planted corn, pumpkins, and vegetables.

Then George Washington turned fourteen. It was a big day for him. But you know what? His father didn't say a word. George was sure he'd forgotten. After school, he went to work in the fields, as always. Then he went inside, washed up, and sat down with his family for dinner. And still, his father didn't say anything. George was crestfallen. *I bet Dad forgot.*

Then, suddenly: "Happy birthday to you! Happy birthday to you! Happy birthday, dear Georgie! Happy birthday to you!"

His mother brought in a present.

George was sure it would be a toy. That's what he always got.

He held this present. It was heavy. In fact, it was very heavy. What could it be?

He ripped it open.

You know what it was?

It was a hatchet. You know what a hatchet is? It's a kind of axe, but it's smaller; you only need one hand to use it. Sometimes people wear hatchets on their belts. You take them camping for when you only need to chop up a little bit of firewood.

George's new hatchet was nestled in the wrapping paper. George picked it up. It gleamed in the candlelight, sharp.

Wow.

George looked up at his beaming parents. "Thanks."

George could barely sleep that night, and the next day he was up at dawn. He took his new hatchet outside. It fit perfectly into his hand. It seemed like the perfect weight. He chopped at the air. *Whiff! Whiff! Whiff!*

But it wasn't enough. He needed to really feel his hatchet bite into something, something real. He was excited, feeling something, a power, something he'd never felt before. He looked around and saw that he was in the orchard. There were apple trees, pear trees, almond trees.

And cherry trees.

You know what he did? He chopped down one of the young cherry trees. *Chop, chop, chop. Wham, wham, wham. Bang, bang, bang.* It felt really good! To feel that sharp hatchet clad biting into the wood. The way it smelled, the way pieces of the tree flew off.

And the noise when it fell: *whooooooo-BOOM.*

Uh-oh.

George looked at the fallen tree and remembered: these cherries were his father's favorites. *What have I done? What am I gonna do? Oh no!*

George ran off to the barn. *I'll, I'll say it wasn't me. I'll blame it on one of the farm hands, yeah. I'll swear up and down that it wasn't me.* He stayed in the barn all morning, telling himself that he'd blame one of the slaves.

"George?" His father's voice was unmistakable: stern and quiet. "Are you in here?"

"I'm over here."

His father walked to the far end of the barn where George was. He looked at him. "George. Did you cut down that cherry tree?"

Lie! Go on, lie. Blame it on someone else.

George stood up. *Lie.*

He looked his father in the eye.

And then he said, "Father, I cannot tell a lie. I did cut down that cherry tree."

George's father looked at him for a long while. Then he said, "George, I'm proud of you for telling the truth." George looked down, filled with regret. "But I'm going to have to take the hatchet away from you."

And George handed it over.

Did this happen? What do you think?

That's right. This is a legend. It has a lot of truth: George Washington's father was stern, and George himself was very honest. But there's no evidence that George ever cut down a cherry tree.

Abe Lincoln #1

Here's another one, about Abraham Lincoln. Many people consider Abe our greatest president. He guided the US through the horrifically violent Civil War. He gave the Gettysburg address. This is one of the most important events in our history: "Four score and seven years ago, our forefathers brought forth upon his continent a new nation, conceived in liberty and dedicated to the proposition that all men are created equal." Actually, our forefathers didn't do that. According to them, it was okay to own slaves and it was fine that women couldn't vote. But Lincoln said everyone is equal, and he made it true. He was a great man.

Lincoln is also known as the Great Liberator. You know why? Because he freed the slaves. He issued the Emancipation Proclamation, and then later, he made the end of slavery permanent by fighting for the Thirteenth Amendment to the Constitution. All his life, Lincoln hated slavery. He hated the injustice of it. He thought it put a blight on this country. He wasn't sure what to do about it, but all his life he struggled against slavery.

In 1858, Abe participated in the "Lincoln-Douglas debates," the most famous political debates in history. Stephen Douglas was the Senator from Illinois, and even though Illinois was what they called a free state—no slavery was allowed—Douglas was pro-slavery. He sponsored laws that in Illinois no free black person could settle there, it was illegal for blacks and whites to intermarry, and that no black person could be a citizen. He was running again for the Senate, and he was traveling around the state giving speeches—he was a very good speaker.

Well, Abe Lincoln showed up, and he wanted to speak, too. He was running for the Senate, too. Douglas said no. He wanted all the attention. Douglas was short, like a little bulldog, and Lincoln was tall and lanky.

What happened is that Douglas would speak in some town, and the next day, Lincoln would show up and give one of his famous anti-slavery speeches. Lincoln was an excellent speaker. So Douglas gave in. And that's how the

Lincoln-Douglas Debates happened. There were seven debates, as the two men traveled around Illinois speaking in front of thousands of people. Newspaper writers from all over the country came. The Lincoln-Douglas debates were one of the premiere events in the history of slavery.

Lincoln took the texts of the debates and turned them into a book. The book was hugely popular — it sold like hotcakes — and even though Lincoln lost the election, the book helped Lincoln become president two years later.

Fact or legend? What do you think?

It's a fact. It really happened. Lincoln was a rube from what they called the "West" — Illinois was on the frontier in those days. But he had passion and presence, and these debates proved it. They helped him become the president.

Abe Lincoln #2

Here's another cool Abe story: he was good with an axe — really good. This was a result of his upbringing on the frontier, where Lincoln felled trees in the forest and built fences and cabins. He was so good that he often hired himself out as an axe-man. Know what he worked for, sometimes? Not money, no — books. Abe was a voracious reader.

Anyway, when he was running for president, they called him Honest Abe Lincoln, the Rail-Splitter.

Why? Well, once, Abe was in a rail-splitting contest against a big, strong man. All the smart money was bet on the other guy. On your mark, get set, go! Both guys started chopping trees, lopping off the branches, debarking the trees, cutting them into the right lengths, splitting them, notching them, and building a fence. They worked like devils! They were rail-splitting blurs! *Chop chop, bing bang, fence fence.* They got to a cliff, and the other guy started to make his fence curve around, but you know what Abe did? He built his fence straight up the cliff! *Chop chop, bing bang!*

And he won. Know what he spent the money on? A set of the *Complete Works of William Shakespeare.*

The end.

Truth or legend? What do you think?

Okay, it's a legend. Sure, Abe was a voracious reader, he was good with an axe, and he did build a lot of fences, but he couldn't build one straight up a cliff.

Harriet Tubman

Here's a cool story. It's about Harriet Tubman. Harriet was born in 1822—as a slave, and she lived in Maryland. Lots of people don't realize that Maryland was a slave state because it never seceded, like the Confederate states. But slavery was permitted, and Harriet was born into bondage, like millions of her fellow Americans.

As happened with a lot of slaves, Harriet was hired out. This meant she had to go to other places, other farms, and do odd jobs. She had to work hard, and she didn't get paid a penny. The man who owned her got all the money. After all, Harriet was his property.

Here's what happened: one day, a slave was escaping, and he ran past Harriet. A white man was chasing him, and this man was angry and frustrated. Harriet tried to back away, but it was too late: the white man threw a huge rock at the runaway. He missed him.

He hit Harriet instead—in the head. Harriet always said that her hair, which was wild and thick, probably saved her life. But even so, Harriet nearly died. They took her back to her owner's house, and they just laid her out on her cot and walked away. They didn't call a doctor, give her any medicine, or do anything. Why should they have? She was just a slave, and they figured she was done for.

But she wasn't done for. She lived, even though she had a serious head injury, and it really affected Harriet. For the rest of her life—and Harriet lived a long time—she had headaches and seizures.

And visions, incredible visions. She became very religious. She believed that God had something important for her to do, something crucial.

And whatever God had in mind, it didn't involve being a slave. So one night, Harriet escaped—just walked away.

This was dangerous. People who owned slaves put ads in the paper with descriptions of runaways. They offered rewards. There were men, called slave catchers, nasty men who made a living chasing runaways and bringing them back.

But Harriet's luck held. Being lucky was a skill she had. She always moved at night, and she had an amazing sense of direction. She always knew where she was.

And she had help, too. Not everyone was in favor of slavery. Many thousands of people hated slavery, so they set up something called the Underground Railroad to help slaves escape bondage. The Underground Railroad was a series of safe houses that escapees could move to, night after night. They would be given food, money, instructions, and directions to help them make their way into free territory. Many thousands of people risked their livelihoods and their lives to help slaves.

And you know what? Harriet didn't stay in Freedomland for long. She went back to Maryland to help other slaves escape. At first, she went back for her family, but then it was for anyone who wanted to leave. She went back many dozens of times and helped as many as one hundred slaves. It was dangerous, and Harriet always walked, always at night, but she never thought of herself. She kept up her work.

When the Civil War started, Harriet worked as a spy for the Union army. As a black person, it was easy for her to act like a slave. Sometimes she simply pretended she was running an errand for her mistress, and no one asked any questions. Harriet's luck held. It's like God was with her.

Here's something Harriet did. In South Carolina, she led about three hundred Union soldiers on something called the Combahee River Raid. First, she spied. She walked up the river from the sea, pretending to be a slave. She saw the Confederate fortifications, and she made mental notes about where the troops and guns were. She saw that there were plantations filled with slaves.

The next day, the Union troops attacked. They knew exactly where the Southerners were—and they stayed away. Instead, they destroyed plantations and freed almost seven hundred slaves. The slaves were crowding onto the boats, shouting and singing for joy, desperate to get away from bondage. Harriet and the Union commander made sure there were enough boats for everyone. Harriet led those slaves to freedom.

Fact or legend? Tell me what you think.

It's historical fact. Harriet really did do all the things I told you. She lived to be ninety-one years old.

But you know what? I bet we could change Harriet into legend. You know how?

By telling a story about her. That's how you create legends: you tell stories. Let's try it. So what if we said:

The night before the Combahee raid, Harriet has a vivid vision. She's floating over the river, and she sees, in her mind's eye, the plantations filled with desperate slaves. She sees that they are unprotected, that the Confederate fortifications are far away. The Combahee River twists and winds through that part of South Carolina, but Harriet knows exactly where to go.

She knows!

The next day, she tells Captain Thompson about her dream. "I know where they are. We can save hundreds and hundreds of people." Captain Thompson's men are leery. Fight the Southerners just because this strange black woman says they should? No way.

But Thompson is convinced. There's something about Harriet that makes him believe her.

"Let's go."

They make their way up the twisting river in three boats. The river seems to peter out, and there are many false streams, but Harriet, true to her word, knows exactly where to go. She leads. They get to one plantation, then another, and another. The few Confederate soldiers run off. There's no way they're going to fight Harriet.

Hundreds of slaves run to the gunboats. "Thank you! Thank you for saving us." Harriet and Captain Thompson make sure there's room for everyone. Some of the soldiers establish fortifications while boats are brought up. Then they withdraw. Harriet has saved more than seven hundred slaves!

Now, is there any evidence for any of this? There is not. But it makes a terrific story, don't you think? Through stories, legends are made.

Story Points: "Legend or History?"

George Washington

- ★ Background: Washington was a great man, the father of our country, president, plantation (and slave) owner, etc.
- ★ At age fourteen, young George received a hatchet in lieu of a toy. George was delighted.
- ★ In a fit of exuberance, George chopped down one of his father's treasured cherry trees. Gulp.
- ★ Father confronts him. "I cannot tell a lie."

Lincoln #1

- ★ Background: Lincoln was our greatest president, led the country through the Civil War, delivered the Gettysburg Address, and ended slavery.
- ★ Background: Stephen Douglas was a pro-slave Senate candidate, and was very popular and powerful.
- ★ Lincoln challenges Douglas to a series of debates. At first, Douglas says no, but then he agrees. They travel around Illinois, debating—a huge event.
- ★ Lincoln lost the election but assembled his speeches into a best-selling book, which turned him into a national figure and helped him to win the presidency in 1860.

Lincoln #2

- ★ Lincoln—the famous "Rail Splitter"—got into a rail-splitting contest.
- ★ Lincoln built a fence right up a cliff, and he won. He used the money to buy the complete works of Shakespeare.

Harriet Tubman

- ★ Background: Harriet was a slave, from Maryland, born 1822. Slavery was a pernicious institution. Many people were against it, and they formed the Underground Railroad.
- ★ Harriet received a bad head wound when she was hit by a rock.

This gave her intense visions, a sense that she was chosen by God.

★ Harriet escaped. She had an unerring sense of direction and always knew where she was.

★ She went back to help family and friends escape, again and again, at great personal danger. Even after the passage of the Fugitive Slave Act, Harriet went back into slave territory again and again. She could act like a slave.

★ During the Civil War, Harriet served as a Union spy.

★ She helped plan the Combahee River Raid in South Carolina: she scouted the area and knew where the Confederate soldiers were stationed. The Northerners attacked undefended plantations and freed more than seven hundred slaves at very little loss of life.

★ This raid is turned into a legend by adding the following story: we name the Federal commander (Capt. Thompson) and give Harriet a vivid dream about rescuing slaves. She tells the dream to Thompson. Inspired by her intensity, he makes the raid and saves the slaves.

Sacagawea

This is the story of the Louis and Clark Expedition of 1804 and their adventures with the amazing, larger-than-life, and incredibly resourceful Sacagawea, the fifteen-year-old Shoshone woman who served as the expedition's interpreter.

President Thomas Jefferson commissioned Army Captains William Clark and Meriwether Lewis to explore the new Louisiana Purchase. Lewis and Clark made their way to the scrappy frontier town of St. Louis (at the time, pop. 500), hired a crew, and then paddled up the Missouri River, finally wintering in Mandan, North Dakota.

There, they met Sacagawea, wife of Toussaint Charbonneau, a French trapper. They invited the two of them to accompany them west, so that Sacagawea could translate.

One remarkable thing about the Lewis and Clark Expedition is that there was very little violence between the Americans and the Native Americans. Conflict, yes, there was plenty of that, but almost no actual fighting. Thus, it's possible to tell a child about the first encounter in the West between Americans and Natives and not have to deal with a horrific legacy of betrayal and murder. This also means that the tale of Lewis and Clark, and their astonishing adventure, makes primo bedtime material.

It's a long story and, as with most history, the plot is complex. Thus, somewhat older children, starting perhaps at age five, would appreciate it more fully. Still, there is nothing violent or overly scary in it, so if your younger child is interested, give it a go.

I've indicated one possible stopping point in the text.

Night One

"You've got to find out what lies to the west. It's dangerous, that's for sure. It won't be easy, but the country wants to know, has to know: what's out there?"

This was President Thomas Jefferson talking to Meriwether Lewis, telling Lewis that he wanted him to explore the new Louisiana Purchase.

Have you heard of the Louisiana Purchase? It was millions of square miles of new territory, stretching from Louisiana north to Minnesota and then west to the Pacific. No one knew what was there. Mastodons? Easy-to-climb mountains? Ancient civilizations? This is what the so-called scholars at the time thought. It was up to Meriwether Lewis to find out.

The first thing Lewis did was to hire his friend William Clark. They declared themselves co-captains, equals. They made the rounds to formal parties in Washington, you know, drinking tea and punch—all the ladies dressed up, sweating under layers of thick clothing (the men, too).

Then, finally, Lewis and Clark took off.

What an adventure!

The captains went across the country. They had lots of equipment, as you can imagine. They moved slowly. Week after week passed.

They found bluffs, virgin forests teeming with animals, and bands of Native Americans. Were they friendly? The landscape was astonishing.

They reached the Mississippi and headed upstream, paddling hard. They would be going upstream now for at least a year. They reached St. Louis. There they assembled a team of explorers: twenty-nine total.

It took a special kind of person to do this, to set out into terra incognita. Men like this really don't exist anymore. They were young, courageous, with an amazing spirit.

Don't you wish you could do it? I do. I'd like to think I could. I like my computer, our TV, the car, the mall, and the grocery store, but there's something amazing about what these folks did. I'm envious.

They went through what is now Kansas City, and Omaha, into the Dakotas. Always moving upstream, paddling hard. Sometimes they had to land their boats and drag them along the river.

They reached what we now call the High Plains. The Plains teemed with game: deer, antelope, partridges, ducks, and geese.

Ah, but the biggest and best game was the buffalo. There were herds of buffalo that stretched as far as you could see—thousands of animals. You could watch as the

Storytelling Tip:

This is important: Lewis and Clark were moving through mostly unexplored (for Europeans) land. Remembering that your youthful charge really wants to enter the world of the story—to be transported—you might consider taking this further. Describe, for example, a campsite, and an encounter the explorers have with a band of natives. Or maybe they meet a young explorer. The wonderful John Colter perhaps. He's heard about their mission and really wants to sign up. He's entranced by the romance—and by the danger. Naturally, you'd have to make this up, and this might violate the historical validity of the story. But it would be poetically, if not literally, true.

breeze carried your scent through the herd: the buffalo got spooked and ran.

It was paradise.

The explorers met Native Americans. This was the first recorded meeting between the Lakota (what Europeans came to call the Sioux) and the US explorers. The encounters were often very unfriendly. The natives demanded more and bigger gifts. There was always the possibility of a fight.

Winter came. The explorers built a fort in western North Dakota. They called it Fort Mandan. They were now at the extreme western edge of the known world. They knew about the Rocky Mountains, but beyond that, nothing.

And then they met the great Sacagawea.

You know how old Sacagawea was? Fifteen. People started through life at a young age in those days. And even though she was young, Sacagawea had lived an amazing life. She was a Shoshone. The Shoshone live in the mountains, in what we now call Idaho. But Sacagawea was kidnapped at age thirteen and brought over the mountains to the plains. There, she was sold to a French trapper named Toussaint Charbonneau. How about that for a name? When the explorers met her, Sacagawea was pregnant with her first child.

When the explorers heard that Sacagawea was Shoshone and was from the mountains, they asked her and Charbonneau to be their interpreters. The two agreed.

That winter, Sacagawea gave birth to a baby boy: Jean-Baptiste Charbonneau. When spring came, they set out, and Sacagawea brought her baby along.

Here is the image we have of this woman: traveling in a canoe, young, quiet, carrying her child in a sling, quietly guiding the explorers, and making suggestions. She kept everyone calm.

She impressed the natives they met. After all, they reasoned, here are the explorers with a woman carrying a baby. They can't be here to make war. This was one of Sacagawea's main contributions: she persuaded everyone to take things easy.

The explorers loved her.

Especially Captain Clark. Some people have suggested that there might have been a romantic relationship between them, but there's no reason to believe that. They were simply two people who respected each other a great deal. Clark came to care greatly about the boy, Jean-Baptiste—more about this in a minute.

Once, one of the canoes tipped over, and Sacagawea moved fast, recovering most of the goods—which included the precious journals. In tribute, the explorers named a nearby river after her: the Sacagawea River, a name it still carries.

The explorers met their first grizzly bear—a "griz," as they say out west. They had heard of these bears from natives, but they pooh-poohed the stories. Nothing could be that big, or that scary. Ha! The bullets from their guns literally bounced off the bear's forehead. He got mad. "Oh, no!" A big chase happened, and all the explorers jumped into the river to escape the bear.

They reached the Great Falls of the Missouri and started up into the mountains.

Wow. It turned out that whoever said the western mountains would be easy to climb was way wrong. Have you ever seen pictures of the Rockies up there? The Tetons? I'll show you some tomorrow. Those are serious

Storytelling Tip:

Our intrepid explorers have reached the Continental Divide. This might be a good place to leave them for the night. But, as I've said before, the story divisions are arbitrary.

mountains. The passes are high. And since they had left the Great Plains behind, game was scarce. The explorers were starving, reduced to eating candles.

They met some natives, and these people were not friendly; they were stern and unmoved by the explorer's plight.

Until Sacagawea recognized one of the women: they had been kidnapped together. The woman had been able to escape and return to the mountains. They hugged, and cried, and said, "Oh, I thought for sure you were dead." Sacagawea showed the woman her baby and introduced her to Charbonneau. Pretty soon everyone was smiling: Sacagawea's back. The natives sold the explorers some horses.

Once again, Sacagawea saved the day.

Night Two

Sacagawea and the expedition headed toward the Pacific Ocean. They were going downstream, for the first time, down the Snake River to the huge Columbia, always down, down. They sighted Mount Hood—this meant that they were finally in explored territory, as other explorers, moving inland from the Pacific, had noted this huge mountain. Finally, they reached the great Pacific.

As Clark wrote in his journal, "Oh, joy!" They had done it.

It was time to make another winter camp. They voted on where to build it. Sacagawea was given a vote, and so was York, Clark's slave. This was the first time that a Native American and an enslaved person of color were given the right to vote. It was a huge moment—though, at the time they didn't realize it. They wintered in Oregon, close to what is now Astoria, Oregon, at Fort Clatsop. The fort was damp, and the area was chilly and rainy, but they were right by the ocean, and they had plenty to eat.

Spring came, and you know what they did? They returned, this time paddling up the Columbia. When they got to the mountains they took a different route—Sacagawea showed the way. They made it to the Missouri again, and it was downstream from there.

William Clark spoke to Charbonneau and Sacagawea. He had a proposition: he wanted to adopt their son, Jean-Baptiste, and see to his schooling, if they were willing. They said they would think about it.

The explorers paddled hard, anxious to return. They did in September. Two years, four months, ten days had passed. They were home.

Except for one guy, John Colter. He met some explorers on the way back, and even though he hadn't been in anything like civilization for more than two years, he chose to go back upstream with the explorers. Colter and his partners became the first Europeans to visit Yellowstone Park. He tried to tell the world about the sulphur springs and the geysers he had seen, but no one believed him.

This is the way some of these people lived: exploring was all they wanted to do.

Charbonneau and Sacagawea stayed in St. Louis for a few years. Then, they decided to take Clark up on his offer, and he adopted Jean-Baptiste.

What a life this boy had. He went to a boarding school in America. Then he went to Europe, raised children, went back west, guided Mormons, and ran a hotel—living large in that nineteenth century way.

Storytelling Tip:

Interested in this subject? If so, you must read Undaunted Courage: The Story of Lewis and Clark and the Opening of the American West, *by Stephen Ambrose. It's an easy read that's not hard to find (available on Kindle), and the story Ambrose tells is boffo.*

Storytelling Tip:

One possible expansion here: talk about the mountain men, those Europeans who explored the vast west, with particular interest in the mountains. I recommend Tales of the Mountain Men *by Lamarr Underwood, or check out the very good Robert Redford movie,* Jeremiah Johnson.

Sacagawea, meanwhile, got homesick. She and Charbonneau traveled back to the Shoshones, and she had another baby.

What happened to her?

We're not really sure. Most historians believe that Sacagawea caught a fever and died at age twenty-four. But some people believe she lived with the Comanches and died in 1884—she would have been in her nineties. We'll never know for sure.

Sacagawea has become one of the most famous Americans ever as the young native woman who guided and translated for the great Lewis and Clark. There are rivers, statues, markers, and highways named after her. There's even a dollar coin with her image on it. On the coin, she's carrying Jean-Baptiste—the first biracial person to appear on American money.

Would the expedition have reached the Pacific without Sacagawea? I doubt it.

Tall Tales

A tall tale contains exaggerated and impossible story elements, presented realistically, as if the teller is giving a genuine portrait of a real individual. Tall tales are good-natured, intended to entertain and to make us laugh. In myths, the fantastical elements are a natural part of the story. In tall tales, they are the whole point.

Tall tales often have some basis in fact. There really was a French voyageur named Paul Bonjean—the genesis, quite probably, for Paul Bunyan. But it's unlikely that Bonjean strapped huge pats of butter to his feet and went skating around a hot rink-sized griddle in order to prep it for a sea of flapjack batter. Or that he had a giant blue ox called Babe and a lovely twenty-foot-tall girlfriend named Lucette. Bunyan is a completely legendary figure who lives on in tall tales (and as a kitschy, though quite impressive, statue in Brainerd, Minnesota).

There really was a strange religious fanatic named John Chapman, whose larger-than-life apple-tree planting exploits caused him to become known as Johnny Appleseed. Exaggerated stories about Johnny Appleseed abound.

Tall tales were often created in the nineteenth century, quite deliberately, by the powerful dime-novel industry. These short, inexpensive (though they did cost more than a dime), and tremendously popular paperbacks took heroes of the frontier and made from them wildly hyperbolized yarns. Take "Here Dan'l Boon Kilt A Bar 1802" for example. This succinct bit of info was carved, supposedly, into a "Kaintuck" tree. Based on this, Boone (bear-slayer, warrior, and explorer) became a dime-novel hero. Others included Davy Crockett (who died thrillingly, from a dime novel perspective, at the Alamo), Jesse James (a vicious murderer transformed into a working class hero), Casey Jones and John Henry (railroad men extraordinaire), etc. Sometimes the tall tale subjects were completely fictional, e.g., Fearless Fred Fosdick. Given this provenance, it is unsurprising that tall tales are most often set on the nineteenth century American frontier.

The good-natured, humorous, and optimistic intent of tall tales makes them perfect for bedtime stories.

Big Bertha

Here's a yarn entirely created by moi, a tall tale featuring a female protagonist (most of these stories feature men). There is no violence, and there's very little physical danger.

But there is lots of physical action. Big Bertha might thus make a nice lead-in, for younger listeners, to more "mature" and challenging fairy tales.

Big Bertha is written using nineteenth-century-isms: "buffler" for "buffaloes," "Californy," "them cabbages was a-crawlin' with bugs," etc. This, I believe, reinforces the tall-tale flavor of the material, but if you're uncomfortable with this, feel free to adjust your telling accordingly.

But don't fergit: this here's a tall tale, so y'all have fun, and make sure to 'joy yoreselves.

The story is followed by ideas for more Big Bertha stories, in case your child likes the story and wants to hear more. Big Bertha could easily become a series.

Here's a story that happens back in the days of the covered wagons, when folks was a-moving west to git gold and git aholt of some good cheap land — welcome to the nineteenth century. Back when men were men, women were women, and children were children (in the traditional paradigm). Well, I guess it's the same way nowadays, but back then it was even more so.

Anyway, the person this story's about, Bertha, was a big-boned gal from Kokomo, Indiana.

Now, when I say "big," I don't mean large — you know, six or so feet, coupla hundred pounds. Overweight? Heck no. I mean, Bertha was big: eight feet tall, three hundred fifty pounds, and I'll tell you the God's honest truth, there wasn't an ounce a fat on that gal.

Give ya an example. One time, Big Bertha was out in the field tending to the cows. You know them haystacks, the big round kind that nowadays they move with tractors and fork lifts? Bertha had one under each arm. A man was passing along the road. He stopped and said, "Say, there, big fella." People were always thinking Bertha was a man. "Do you know where the Fort Wayne road is?"

Bertha turned.

"Whoa," the man said. Bertha was awful scary to look at full on. The man took a step away.

Bertha took no offense. She was like that. She just picked up a bull and used him as a pointer. "Thataway!"

Bertha wasn't stupid neither. She was all the time thinking deep thoughts. *I wonder why the sky is blue*, she'd ask herself. Or she'd be out in the field a-picking rocks — you know you gotta do that in the spring before you plant. Bertha'd be holding a rock about the size of an equipment shed: *I wonder how old this rock is*. And she'd think and think for hours. People'd ride their wagons past, and they'd think she was a large tree.

Then Bertha fell in love.

It's true. She formed an attachment to a young man called Philaster Q. Perkins — Philly, fer short, which Philly was. He couldn'a stood much more'n five feet, and he couldn'a weighed much more'n a hunnert pounds. The two of 'em looked funny, to say the least, walking down the street, tryna to hold hands.

"Gosh, Philly, I sure do love the heck outta you."

"Oh, Bertha. Likewise."

"Honey bunch."

"Snuggle bunny."

They were sweet.

But all was not rosy in Kokomo.

One night, Philaster come to Bertha's house. It was late. Almost eight o'clock.

Philly knocked on the door. *Knock, knock, knock. Knock, knock, knock. Knock! Knock! Knock!* Bertha was a deep sleeper.

She opened the door, seen him standing there. "What are you doing up?" Then she saw his blotchy, tear-streaked, careworn kisser. "Why are you crying?"

"It's my pop, Jedediah. He's a-going to Californy. Gonna muck for gold."

"Muck . . . ?"

"Look, dig, sluice, find — whatever — gold. It's like some kind of strange fever come over him: gold fever."

"When's he gonna leave?"

"Tonight."

"Tonight?"

"He's a man possessed."

Before Bertha had a chance to take this in, Philaster gave her a desperate hug. "Bye, Bertha! Bye! I'll always love you."

And with that, he disappeared, running into the night.

"Bye, Philly."

The next day, Bertha started to thinking it had all been a terrible dream, so she went by the Perkins place, sure she'd see Phil milking the cow.

But the place was deserted. A broken shutter was banging the old house. The front gate was open, creaking in the wind. The Perkinses were gone.

Gone.

Bertha bust out crying.

And when Bertha cried, she really cried. Salty tears sprayed out of her eyes like water through a hose. There were pools of salt water around the house, and pretty soon, the pools formed themselves into a moat.

Bertha was inconsolable. She went through the motions, but ever'body knew she was in big trouble. All you had to do was look at her wobbly corn rows. Her cabbages was a-crawling with bugs because Bertha didn't wanna de-worm them.

Then one day, in late fall, November, a man stopped by, holding a newspaper. "Bertha! Hey, Bertha!" He stood by the salt moat. "Bertha!"

Bertha came out. She was disheveled; she couldn't be bothered to comb her hair or put on fresh clothes. "What?"

"Have you heard about the Perkins Party?"

"The Perkins Party?"

"They were trying to take a shortcut to Californy, through the Sierry Nevady mountains. Got stuck in a snowstorm, in a mountain pass—ten feet a' snow. No one

Storytelling Tip:

*At the risk of being repetitive:
you're going to do this howl at,
at the most, 10 percent. You're
going to keep your voice sweet
and sleep-inducing. You're not
going to break any windows.*

can get to 'em."

Bertha splashed through the moat, grabbed the newspaper away from the man, and read it: *The Rocky Mountain News*, 1850, three days old.

"It's a dern shame," the man said, shaking his head.

Bertha threw back her head and howled. "Phillllllllllly!"

The front porch peeled off the house and flew across the road, like it had been flung by a giant. The man jumped back, holding his hat. "Whoa."

"The farm's yourn," Bertha said.

"Mine?"

"Take good care a' the cows! And deworm them cabbages!"

And you know what Bertha did?

She run.

She run and she run.

She was a strong runner, as you can imagine. This was a woman who could juggle cows and scarf a batch of flapjacks made with a dozen eggs.

"Phillllllllllly!"

It was like a shock wave. Miles away, people would hold their ears. "What the heck was that?"

Big Bertha got herself into an easy lope. Every step was a quarter mile. She took great lungfuls of fresh prairie air and let 'em go with a teary howl. "Phillllllllllly!"

She commenced to running faster—longer, quicker strides, a mile each. Two miles. Three. Wagon trains, zip. Gone. Trains. Zip, gone! Rivers? No problem, Bertha jumped 'em.

She came to the great herds of buffler, and you know what she did? That's right, she jumped, leapt! Ka-boom, and them bufflers was behind her.

Then she came to the Rocky Mountains. She decided to take a rest. It was pr'near noon. Bertha was startin' to breathe hard.

But while she was restin', she commenced to thinking of poor little skinny Philaster, her sweetie poochie pie, trapped in a snowbank, his poor beautiful young life leaking away — icicles in his hair, shivering, lips turning blue.

Bertha ran straight up them mountains. Up, up, up, she ran. And you know what she did when she got to the top?

She jumped.

That's right. She jumped as far as she could, and she was a-shooting through the sky, legs a-kicking, arms a-flailing. Folks looked up and said, "What the heck is that?"

Bertha landed in the desert. She ran, five miles per stride — through the Utah Desert, then over another set of mountains, to the Great Salt Desert, the Mojave Desert.

Finally, she come to the Sierry Nevady Mountains.

And there was a lot of snow — a lot, at least a dozen feet deep. This slowed Bertha down considerable. Ten foot deep, twelve foot, fifteen foot.

Finally, she just burrowed. She was a vole, an eight foot weasel, always tunneling up, up, up. Up, up, up. Up, up —

Whoa.

Suddenly, there was nothing. Bertha almost fell into the void. She stuck her head outta the snow and looked around.

She was on the edge of a cliff. Everywhere she looked, the world was frozen and snowy. Nothing moved.

Somewhere, she told herself, somewhere in that frozen frigid emptiness, was Philaster Q. Perkins, the man she loved. The man she loved more than the sun, stars, and moon put together.

"Phillllly. . . !"

She listened. Nothing. She tried it again: "Phillllllllllll-ly . . . !"

Then she heard it, very faint. Almost like she imagined it: "Bertha?"

But she hadn't imagined it. Bertha'd know that beautiful voice anywhere.

She looked around. Saw a big tree. She went to it, and yanked it out by the roots. She sat on it and pulled the front up like a toboggan.

And then down she went.

Faster, faster, faster. Down, down, down. The cold wind was whipping Bertha's hair. Her ears was froze solid, and still she went down, and still she went faster. She woulda whooped with a wild, crazed joy if she weren't so darned worried about her honey bunch. Bertha started spinning around. Down, down, down. Faster, faster, faster.

She landed on both feet in the middle of a running river.

A man approached her. He was a-shivering so hard he was a-startin' to blur. "B-B-B-B-B-Bertha?"

"Philly."

"B-B-B-B-B-Bertha."

She wanted to hug him.

"B-b-b-b-better n-n-n-n-not. I'm f-f-f-f- froze s-s-s-s-s —"

"Solid?"

"Y-y-y-y-y-y — that's right."

"Where is everybody?"

"Holed up in that there c-c-c-c-c-cave. We wouldn'a made it another n-n-n-n-n-night."

"I have some pemmican."

"What's p-p-p-p-p-pemmican?"

"Dried nuts and berries, mixed up with bear fat."

"Y-y-y-y-y-y-y-yum." Philaster ate some pemmican, and then he took it to the cave and shared with the other frozen sojourners. They all felt a lot better.

"Well, c'mon," Bertha said. "It's getting dark."

Bertha picked up the tree and used it to clear a path through the twenty-foot snowdrifts. Bertha was a veritable whirligig, leading the shivering pioneers down out of that frozen valley.

Finally, they came to an inn with a roaring fire. There, they had some nice soup and hot baths.

When he was done bathing, Philly looked around. "Where's Bertha?" he cried. "Is she gone?"

Everyone shrugged.

Philaster ran outside. "Bertha!"

"Over here, Philly."

Philaster found Bertha, crying. "What's wrong?"

"It hurts, Philly. Hurts bad."

"What hurts?"

"I'm never gonna see you again. You and your pa, Jedediah, are gonna go off to the gold fields of Californy, and you're gonna forget all about poor me."

"No."

"You will."

Philaster went and found his father. "Pop, I'm twenty-one years old. I'm a full-fledged grown-up adult person of age, and I'm here to tell you that Bertha and me, well, we're gonna get ourselves hitched."

Jedediah cleared his throat. "Philaster, it was my fault we got trapped in that snow-filled valley. I was in too big a hurry to get to the gold. But I see now the error of my ways. Thanks to Bertha, we survived. So, assuredly, you have my permission to marry her."

> Philaster turned to Big Bertha. "I love you more'n the stars in heaven."
>
> "Oh, Philly. I love you more'n the moon in the night sky."
>
> "Oh, Bertha."
>
> The next day, Big Bertha slung skinny Philly up on her brawny shoulders, and she walked off in nice easy strides: a quarter mile each.
>
> There they go.

And thus the story ends.

Or does it? If your child likes this kind of tall tale, certainly there can be more stories about Big Bertha and skinny Philaster. Maybe Philly is exceptionally smart. Perhaps subsequent stories can use Philly's brains and Bertha's complementary brawns to resolve conflict. Indeed, you might spin a series of stories, very similar to the countless tall tales — like those of Daniel Boone, Paul Bunyan, or Casey Jones — that have become a permanent and vital part of American culture. You can tell your child that these stories are larger-than-life, as American as apple pie — and you are the only ones who share them. He or she will adore this.

Here are a few modest ideas:

We have established in this story that Philaster's father, Jedediah, is something of a, well, a screw-up. So this could maybe be a regular part of a Bertha and Philly story line: rescuing old Jed. Maybe he:

★ Gets trapped in a gold mine, and Bertha has to pull apart all the fallen stone. Maybe she keeps the shaft from collapsing, while Philaster leads Jed and the other miners to safety.

★ Falls in with a bunch of men who turn out to be terrible outlaws. Bertha moves fast, swatting their bullets away and disarming them, while Philaster lassoes them in place (maybe proficiency with a rope is Philaster's big skill—in addition, of course, to being super-smart).

★ Jed falls asleep without adequately putting out his campfire. A big forest fire ensues. Bertha put it out by inhaling the water of a river and spitting it out, hose-like, onto the fire.

Or maybe Philaster is running for president. It's a snap: he rides on Bertha's massive shoulders, and they travel around the country. Phil stands up and gives stirring speeches. Ah, but the bad guys, trying to take over the presidency, kidnap Philaster and put him in a barrel and send him down the river, toward Niagara Falls.

Bertha sees the barrel. "Philly!"

She goes under the falls. The water's pounding down on her, flattening her. It's too much. Philaster's gonna die. But at the last minute, just as the barrel hurtles over the falls, Bertha leaps up, through the pounding water, catches the barrel, and saves her beloved.

What if Bertha gets in a series of contests with . . . Paul Bunyan? Maybe:

★ They're canoe racing across a big lake, and Philly catches hold of some goose-sized skeeters and hitches 'em to his canoe. Bertha, not to be outdone, paddles harder and wins.

★ Bertha loves flapjacks, but Philly, cantankerous, replaces the baking powder with gunpowder in Bertha's pancake batter. This results in some explosive (and fiery) belching.

★ It's raining really hard, so Bertha swims up the falling rain and blows the clouds away. "There. I turned it off."

If you wish to pursue these stories, and create your own, I would refer you to Part III of this book, which deals with the process of creating your own stories.

Story Points: "Big Bertha"

★ Set up: Bertha's a farmer from Kokomo. She's super-strong and doesn't know her own strength, eats flapjacks like nobody's business, and doesn't need a mule to plow. She's also shy and goofy, and madly in love with skinny little Philaster Q. Perkins. The two of them are an odd couple.

★ Philaster leaves in the middle of the night; his father, Jedediah, has gold fever. Bertha is bereft.

★ Bertha hears that Philaster is trapped in a snow-filled valley in the Sierra Nevada.

★ Bertha travels to the valley in a single day. Have lots of fun with this journey: she runs five miles with every step, leaping over rivers and herds of buffalo, passing wagon trains, flying over mountains, climbing the snowy mountains, tobogganing down, and leading the frozen pioneers to safety.

★ Bertha then returns to her shy, lovelorn self, but Philaster wants to marry her, and grateful Jed agrees.

Big Dave Dangworth

Here's another delightful (and short) tall tale that your children will love.

"Big Dave's coming."

Now, I swear this is true. It happened in a town in the east part of Nebraska, or possibly Arizona—conceivably in Maine. The exact whereabouts are unimportant. It was a morning of a day just like any day. The sun was shining, and there weren't any clouds anywhere. It was severe clear, as the weather guys say.

Then Ole Farmer Kadiddlehoffer ruined it. He came

staggering down Main Street, and his eyes were as big and as round as cow pies.

"Big Dave's coming!"

"What?"

"Big Dave's coming!"

"Who?"

"Big Dave. I heard it from a fella who heard it from another fella, and he personally knows a fella who saw Big Dave, and he's just a coupla miles back. He's coming."

"Big Dave or the fella who saw Big Dave?"

"You think this is funny? I'm tellin' ya, and I ain't gonna say it again: Big Dave Dangworth is a-comin', an' he's pr'near here!" And with that, he keeled over — fainted dead away.

Everybody looked at each other.

"Who's Big Dave?"

"I never heard of him. 'Cept for right now."

"He's coming."

"He is?"

"That's what Kadiddlehoffer said. Then he fainted. 'Big Dave's a-coming.'"

"Is he?"

"I'm only repeating what Kadiddlehoffer said."

This put a damper on the day.

"There!"

Everybody looked up.

Someone was coming.

Holy moley.

This fella had to be ten feet tall if we was an inch, and he was standing on two, not one, but two oversized mean ole mountain lions, five hundred pounds each, and they were a-snarlin' and a-snappin'. And the man was sawin' at 'em with a whip, and as he got closer, they saw that the whip wasn't a real whip—it was a rattlesnake, a huge rattler. The snake was a-growlin', and venom was a-flying off his gleaming fangs. The man was wearing overalls and a wool shirt, and his muscles was bustin' out like corn after a July thunderstorm.

Everybody took off running.

The man rode in. "Where is everybody?" He climbed off the mountain lions. The lions sat down and started preening, you know, licking themselves. The man rolled up his rattlesnake whip and put it around his neck.

He spied a hardware store. "I need a haircut," and with that, he strode on over to the hardware store where they had a display of lawnmowers, fired one up, *brmmmm, brmmmm, brmmmmmmmm,* and gave himself a haircut.

By now, people were peeking out from behind buildings, places like that. "What's he doing?"

"Looks like he's giving himself a haircut with a lawnmower."

"Wow."

"I need a shave, too!" said the man, and he used the lawnmower to give himself a shave. "Mmm," he said, rubbing his smooth chin, "nice and close. Now I need me a snack."

He went into the grocery store and started eatin' the canned goods. He didn't bother opening the cans; he just stuck 'em in his mouth, crunched 'em up, then spat out the metal. "Time for dessert."

He went back into the hardware store and saw the clerk hiding under the counter. "You."

"M-m-m-m-m-m-m-me?"

"Make me a nice sundae."

"A s-s-s-s-s-s-s-sundae?"

"That's right, a sundae."

"B-b-b-b-b-b-b-b-but the-the-the-the-the—"

"Spit it out."

"The restaurant is acr-cro-cro-cross the-the-the— stree-stree-stree—the stree-stree-stree. T."

"You got ten penny nails, right?

The clerk nodded.

"You got prussic acid?"

Clerk nodded again.

"And you got them hockey puck urinal deals? Good. Make me a sundae."

So the clerk put the nails in a bowl, smothered 'em with prussic acid, and topped it off with a hockey puck urinal deal.

The man snarfed the whole thing down. When he was done, he belched. *Brrrrrrrrrrrrrrrrp.*

A ball of prussic acid-hockey puck urinal deal fire flew out of his mouth. The fireball went across the store, and it didn't break the window—heck no, it melted the window. The fireball went across the street, went through the building—poof, the building was gone—then burned up an outhouse (and the clothes of the fella hiding inside), and then hit the hill. And you know what? That fiery belch-ball kept right on going. Far as I know, it went all the way to China.

"That was an outstanding sundae."

The man went outside. He stretched a little bit. A couple pieces of his overalls flew off. Then he took his rattlesnake whip and gave it a few practice cracks. *Smack! Smack!* This woke up the mountain lions.

A man—he was the mayor—came gingerly across the street. Holding his hat. "S-s-s-s-sir?" he stammered.

"Yeah?"

"I just wanted to ask . . . is there anything else we can do for you?"

"Right now?"

The mayor nodded.

"Well, I appreciate the thought, but I'll tell you, I ain't got time."

"You haven't got t-t-t-t-time . . . ?"

"Ain't you heard? Big Dave's a-coming!"

Fables

I n fables, animals talk and inhabit a magic-charged world. Fables are normally quite short—unless fleshed out by a storyteller, as is the case with "City Mouse and Country Mouse," below, in order to savor character and plot.

A fable's distinguishing feature is a clear and often explicitly stated moral. These stories are teaching tools, a way of expressing a deeply held and heartfelt truth for listeners who are, presumably, too young or too inexperienced in the ways of the wicked world.

A fabulist (a wonderful word, which means "a teller of fables") says: Life is complicated and noisy. Sometimes simple truths get lost. Quiet yourself, and listen to this story. You will hear a clear moral. Thus, fables make excellent bedtime stories and provide for marvelous parenting moments.

Ah, but there is a danger: the moralizing can turn the teller into an authority and wreck the crucial give-and-take between teller and tellee that makes bedtime stories so special and so much fun. Stories in the dark depend on equality and independence, and if you too sternly explicate a firm moral, you violate this. So, do tell fables and parables, but be careful with them.

It is impossible to discuss fables without dealing with the famous fabulist Aesop. Aesop lived in Greece in roughly 600–500 BCE. Classical scholars argue vociferously about when Aesop lived and about what kind of person he was—an aristocrat? A slave? Was there a group of story collectors now called Aesop? It has been noted that his stories are very similar to and contemporaneous with stories coming from India. Did the Indians take material from Aesop? Or did Aesop borrow from the Indian tellers? At this distance, we will never know.

Many Aesopian fables have permanently entered our consciousness. We all know the story of the tortoise and the hare, of the grasshopper and the ants. We've heard the expression "sour grapes," and we know what it means to "cry wolf." These fables have become central to the human experience, and we owe it to our young charges to tell bedtime stories derived from Aesop.

What follows is a bedtime story based on one fairly well-known fable by Aesop:

City Mouse and Country Mouse

Here's the text, from a public domain translation by V. S. Vernon Jones (posted at gutenberg.org). Like many—indeed, most—Aesopian fables, "A City Mouse and a Country Mouse" is very short:

> *A City Mouse and a Country Mouse were acquaintances, and the Country Mouse one day invited his friend to come and see him at his home in the fields. The City Mouse came, and they sat down to a dinner of barleycorns and roots, the latter of which had a distinctly earthy flavor. The fare was not much to the taste of the guest, and presently, he broke out with, "My poor dear friend, you live here no better than the ants. Now, you should just see how I fare! My larder is a regular horn of plenty. You must come and stay with me, and I promise you that you shall live on the fat of the land."*

So when he returned to town, he took the Country Mouse with him and showed him into a larder containing flour and oatmeal and figs and honey and dates. The Country Mouse had never seen anything like it and sat down to enjoy the luxuries his friend provided; before they had well begun, the door of the larder opened and someone came in. The two Mice scampered off and hid themselves in a narrow and exceedingly uncomfortable hole. Presently, when all was quiet, they ventured out again; but someone else came in, and off they scuttled again. This was too much for the visitor. "Goodbye," said he, "I'm off. You live in the lap of luxury, I can see, but you are surrounded by dangers; whereas at home, I can enjoy my simple dinner of roots and corn in peace.

Short and sweet: two brief paragraphs. Clearly, a teller of bedtime tales has some major fleshing out to do.

The story does deal with danger: the mice are chased (but never caught) by a cat. This means the story might not be appropriate for the most impressionable children. But it's very sweet and effectively creates a very special world. I would say the story works for—almost—all ages.

A h, merry old England.
Picture it: Well-heeled ladies and gentlemen in waiting. Happy, hard-working, and well-paid country folk enjoying clean, crisp country air. Castles and picturesque villages. Coaches clomping down country roads. Cows and sheep eating English hay. Everybody living on clotted cream and hearty oatmeal. Trains huffing and puffing along winding tracks. Whoo-hoo. Whoo-hoo.

Now, riding on one of those trains, in an old boxcar, was

Storytelling Tip:
Try some train whistles. Remember: SFX work.

a mouse. He was a City Mouse — never been to the country before. He was standing in the open boxcar door, watching the country glide by.

"Oh, dear. This train seems to be moving with distressing rapidity."

It wasn't moving that fast. It's just that our hero, a City Mouse, had never been on a train before, and he wasn't sure what to do. He watched as a village passed by. He spied a sign:

"'Carrington-upon-Covington.' That's it! He lives just outside this village. Oh, dear. But this train is zipping along! What am I to do?"

"Jump," a voice said.

"Oh!" The City Mouse jumped in time to see an Old Rat hidden among the crates and pallets.

"The train ain't going that fast. And if you jump, I won't have to listen to you anymore. Jump."

"You're suggesting that I jump?"

The Old Rat's voice got hard and threatening. Rats can get this way. "Jump."

City Mouse jumped. "Ouch!" He bounced painfully down a grassy knoll. *Bing, bang, bong,* somersaulting along, rolling through the grass, finally coming to rest next to a dirt road.

"Ohhhhhhhh," he said, sitting up painfully, brushing himself off. "Well. That was no fun at all."

He looked around. "Where am I? Cousin lives west of Carrington-upon-Covington, in a deserted old barn on the top of a hill, next to a big oak. Now I wonder . . . "

Just then he heard a horse clopping along the road. *Clop-clop-clop-clop-clop.* He went to the grass at the edge of the road. There, he spied an old horse pulling a farmer and a cart. He stepped out of the grass. "Excuse me, my good fellow, can you tell me where I can find an old barn—?"

"Eek! A mouse!"

And with that, the horse reared up and took off down the road, as fast as his legs could carry him. The farmer held on for dear life. "Whoaaaaaa!"

"Well," the City Mouse humphed. "What was that all about?"

He set off down the road. Pretty soon, he started enjoying himself and the fresh air and grass.

Finally, he rounded a curve, and there it was: a falling apart old barn, on a hill, next to a big oak tree. He hesitated for a minute. "It looks a little . . . ramshackle."

Then he saw Country Mouse hopping out of the barn.

"Cousin!"

"Cousin!"

City Mouse scampered halfway up the hill and Country Mouse scampered down. They hugged. Have you ever seen mice hug? It's really cute. They sit back on their haunches, and then they embrace.

"What have you been up to, Cousin?" City Mouse inquired.

"It's a quiet life here in Carrington-upon-Covington. I take naps. I gather acorns. There's barley outside the mill."

"Yum," the City Mouse said—just to be polite.

"And I have a special treat for you."

"You do? What is it?"

"I'll show you!" and with that, he scampered off toward the barn. City Mouse followed. He went down an old mouse hole. "Down here!" City Mouse followed him down an old cellar. There, Country Mouse uncovered a big pile of roots that he had buried for safekeeping. "There!"

Storytelling Tip:

Hug your child at this point.

"Whatever are those?" City Mouse asked, appalled.

"They're beets!"

"Beets . . . ?"

"I dug 'em up a couple months ago. Don't they look yummy? Beets're a delicacy after they've had a chance to age."

"I'm sure."

So Country Mouse laid out the feast: acorns, barley grains, and the piece de resistance—beets. Country Mouse dug in. *Mm. Yum. Num. Snarf.*

Then he looked up and noticed that City Mouse wasn't eating. "Aren't you hungry, Cousin?"

"I'm starved."

"Well . . . dig in."

"Those acorns are . . . raw."

"Well, yes."

"And the barley grains are dusty."

"They come from the old mill. Lots of dust there."

"And these beets. Cousin, they're old."

"Aged."

"I have an idea."

You wanna guess what City Mouse's idea was?

To the city! "Cousin, I'm gonna feed you some real food. Cheese and cream and smoked salmon and peanut butter and eggs and mincemeat and sausage—everything."

So, they hopped a train. They had to wait for one to stop, but Country Mouse knew the 2:19 always stops in Carrington-upon-Covington to take on mail. They jumped up on a steel wheel—dangerous!—then ran along a rail to an open door. They went inside the boxcar. City Mouse looked around, nervous.

Luckily, they had the boxcar to themselves, and pretty

soon they were banging happily along, enjoying the fine weather, watching the world go by: fields and mansions and villages and streams and cows and sheep and castles and barns. Pretty soon, the villages got bigger and closer together. They saw more and more people on the road. The train went through more crossings. *Whoo-whoo! Whoo-whoo!*

Then they passed a long, smoky building. "What was that?" Country Mouse cried.

"A factory."

"A factory?"

"Where they make stuff. We're getting close to the city."

Another factory went by and then another. Pretty soon, the villages became neighborhoods. Country Mouse could see long streets filled with brick townhouses. He was amazed.

They went over a river! Country Mouse was flabbergasted. Speechless.

"That's the Thames," City Mouse said proudly. "Isn't it something? We're almost home."

Indeed, the train started to slow down. Finally, it stopped.

The two mice hopped off the train and headed through the train yard. They got to a street. It was filled with a jillion pedestrians and carts and clopping horses and tall buildings.

"We'll get crushed!"

"No, we won't," City Mouse replied. "Follow me," and he jumped down a sewer grate.

They followed the sewer. To Country Mouse, it was like a maze. But City Mouse seemed to know where he was going, so Country Mouse followed. Finally, they went up a grate and entered the basement of a fine old house.

"You can't tell from down here, but this is a grand house. They call this neighborhood Mayfair."

"Mayfair."

"Only the best mice live here."

"Uh-huh. Well, I'm famished."

"Well, we can't eat yet," City Mouse said, as if he were speaking to a child. "Silly. It's not night yet. Let's take a nice nap."

So they curled up and immediately fell asleep. Mice can do that.

The next thing Country Mouse knew, City Mouse was shaking him awake. "Time to eat."

"Goodie. I'm starving."

They headed up to the house kitchen. City Mouse moved quietly—"Shh."—keeping to the shadows.

Country Mouse asked, "What's—"

"Shh."

Country Mouse whispered. "What's wrong?"

"We have to be very quiet. There's a cat."

"A cat?"

City Mouse hadn't mentioned that. "Luckily, she's old and half-deaf. But she likes to eat mice."

"She . . . eats mice?" Country Mouse stammered. Gulp.

They moved carefully down the hall. Country Mouse jumped at every shadow, the ticking clock, the creaking old house, and even City Mouse's breathing.

They came to the kitchen. They went to the back of the icebox and climbed up a pipe. They went out on the counter.

City Mouse opened a bin. "Ooh. They got some fresh ones."

"What are they?"

"Dates." He lifted one out of the bin and held it up to the moonlight streaming in through the window. It glistened, brown and rich with sweet oil and sugar. "Have you ever had one?"

Country Mouse shook his head.

"They're imported from Persia. Here, take a bite." But then he heard something. "Someone's coming!"

"I don't hear any—"

"Quick!" He put the date back in the bin, and the two mice hid behind the icebox just as a small boy came in, opened the icebox, and poured himself a nice healthful glass of milk.

"Midnight snack," City Mouse whispered.

The boy left.

"Let's see what's under the wax paper." They crept out along the counter. City Mouse lifted up the wrapping, to reveal a big wheel of Neil's Yard farmhouse cheddar cheese.

"Ohhhhhhhh," he said, swooning. "It doesn't get any better than this." He broke off a big chuck and held it out. "Smell."

Country Mouse smelled. It was incredible. Country Mouse could smell cows and barns and sweet cream and country air, all rolled up into one cheesy odor. He started to salivate.

"It's the master!"

City Mouse grabbed Country Mouse and dragged back to the icebox, just as a man came in. "Hmm," he said. "Who took the wax paper off the cheese?" He broke off a big chunk o' cheese, replaced the waxed paper covering, and then walked away, munching the rich cheese.

"Don't you ever get to eat?" Country Mouse inquired.

He was getting annoyed.

"Of course I do. C'mon, let's have some honey."

"Honey?"

"Haven't you ever had honey? It's the best thing there is."

He led Country Mouse across the counter, past the dates and the cheese. He came to a small jar with a spoon sticking up out of it. As he approached, Country Mouse could smell the honey. It smelt of clover and sunshine and blue sky. And it was sweet, incredibly sweet.

"Wow," Country Mouse exclaimed. The smell was making him feel faint.

"'Wow' is putting it mildly," City Mouse replied as he jumped up on the jar and reached in for a big, sweet, sticky, amazing handful of honey. *Mmmmmmmmmm.*

"Meeeeeeow!" said the cat as she jumped up on the countertop. Country Mouse just stared. He had never seen a cat this close before. "Meeeeeeow!" she repeated.

"Run!" City Mouse cried as he leapt off the counter, heading for the floor. "As fast as you can!"

Country Mouse was frozen in place.

Then the cat opened her mouth. Country Mouse could see her sharp teeth—good for chomping off the heads of mice.

Country Mouse ran.

He jumped off the counter and tried to take off, but his feet were slipping on the polished floor. Luckily, the cat was having the same trouble.

Country Mouse finally took off and ran around a corner and down the hall. The cat was right behind him. She reached out to grab him and almost had him, but Country Mouse ran under a knick-knack case. *Crash!* The cat hit

Storytelling Tip:

Is this image too upsetting, perhaps, for the young and sensitive? If this describes your child, feel free to omit it.

it hard. Country Mouse kept going, turned a corner, and found himself in the living room. Crash! An end-table and a lamp tipped over. He went under a sofa. *Riiiip!* The cat slashed at him and ripped open the couch. Country Mouse kept going. *Crash!* A bookshelf went over, with decorative plates on top.

"Bad cat! Bad!" It was the father—and he had a broom, which he used to whack at the cat. "What do you think you're doing?! Bad!"

"Over here!" It was City Mouse, gesturing frantically from a tiny mouse hole. "In here! Quick!"

Country Mouse scampered into the hole.

Safe. Whew.

"You know what, Cousin?" Country Mouse said. "Those dates looked good, and that rich cheese, sweating milk and salt, looked fantastic—and that sweet honey. Wow, I don't think there's anything as good. But you know what? I think I prefer raw acorns and dusty barley. I'd rather enjoy my simple dinner in peace."

Story Points: "City Mouse and Country Mouse"

The moral—that it's better stay at home with simple, down-home pleasures than to try for the rich but highly dangerous—is simply and straightforwardly stated. The real pleasure of the story comes from the recreation of Merrie Olde England, a land of eternally crisp and perfect weather, hearty dairy products, castles and green fields, happy peasants, the Thames and fancy London homes. That such a land never existed is quite beside the point. Your child will want to be transported there. So make these details vivid.

★ City Mouse is riding the train through the countryside. Describe the train, the fields, the castles, and the quaint village. Lots of useful detail can be developed here.

★ He discovers that there's a big bad Rat on board. He jumps.

★ City Mouse walks along the road, enjoying himself. Describe more details, such as the grass and the fresh air. Also, the horse-scaring incident is useful.

★ City Mouse finds Country Mouse's barn. It's dilapidated, filled with hay and old machinery. There's an old oak tree. Describe their embrace. Tour the barn.

★ The mice eat dinner: raw acorns, dusty barley, and aged (and, to City Mouse, disgusting) beets. Light bulb thought: "To the city!"

★ The mice take a train ride into the city. Villages get bigger and become neighborhood and then factories, the Thames, the teeming city—scary! The mice find the sewer.

★ They follow the sewer to the basement of a fancy house in Mayfair. They nap, waiting for nightfall.

★ In the dark, they make their way to the kitchen. Lovingly describe the food: dates oozing sugar and sweet oil; cheese, sweating salt and milk, smelling of the countryside; indescribable honey. Their dinner is interrupted by visits from the child, Dad, and finally, the cat.

★ Chase! Describe the crashing furniture, the smashing knick-knacks, and the near misses in loving detail. Believe me, your kid will adore it.

★ Country Mouse finally escapes and states the moral: "I prefer raw acorns and dusty barley. I'd rather enjoy my simple dinner in peace."

Stories from Religion

Bedtime presents us with a God-given opportunity to impart religious beliefs and values to our children in a way they will find enjoyable, un-preachy, and palatable. How? As bedtime stories.

Let's face it: Sunday School is often a drag. Taught by well-meaning but inexperienced teachers who don't know how to really engage their young charges, it can be distressingly dull and dry. Kids look wistfully out the window at the shining sun, the sparkling leaves, and the blue sky. They listen to the shouts and laughter of other, luckier, children playing outside.

(Why do so many churches maintain playgrounds next to their Sunday School classrooms? It's cruel and unusual.)

Ah, but darken the bedroom lights and tell these kids stories in the dark, and suddenly, the religious material lives and breathes—excites! They listen, enthusiastically, and the material makes a lasting impression.

The best part? You don't need to subscribe to one single religion (or any religion, for that matter) to take advantage of the grand story fodder religion offers! In the New Testament, we have

Jesus's marvelous parables, the thrilling story of his three event-filled years of preaching and traveling, the beautiful Christmas Story, and of course, the Easter Story—each moment jam-packed with meaning, beauty, and thrilling action.

In the Torah, we find the astonishing Exodus story, with the grand hero Moses leading the Israelites out of their bitter Egyptian exile into Canaan, the glorious land of milk and honey. Is there a better story anywhere? The Old Testament also gives us the stories of Isaac, the Flood, and King David.

And don't forget Mohammed's and Sakyamuni Buddha's struggles against materialism and ignorance. Religion offers arguably the richest vein of story material we have. Mine it.

But know that there is a big caveat: make sure you're telling stories, not abstract theology. This can come later, as your listeners begin to synthesize the stories and assemble them into coherent belief. If religion-themed bedtime stories are a vital part of a child's imaginative life, then Sunday School will take on a substantial new presence.

Also, be sure to mix it up. Don't give the child an exclusive diet of religiousness. You run a serious risk, if you do, of turning the child off, of making religion seem preachy. Tell fairy tales, legends, tall tales, and stories from history. Then toss in an occasional religious story.

Jesus's Parables of the Lost

Jesus's parables are very short, often little more than a sentence or two—much like Aesop's fables. The "meat," so to speak, comes in the parsing, the interpretation of the parables, often very lengthy.

I have done the reverse: I have added quite a lot of detail to the story but kept the theological explication to a bare minimum. My aim here is to familiarize the child with the story in an enjoyable way, trusting that some time in future, the meaning of the parable will be made clear — by a preacher or by you, the child's parents. I have named the characters, which Jesus does not do, and I have endeavored to give the stories narrative pizzazz.

It would be quite possible, and indeed preferable, to do all three stories in a single night. But if you wish, you could break after the second story and perform "The Prodigal Son" on a separate night.

These stories will work for all ages, though the final story, "The Prodigal Son," does touch on physical suffering.

J esus told three stories in which something important is lost and then found. In the first story, it's a lamb:

The Parable of the Lost Lamb

A shepherd in Galilee, Calaphas, who lived in the time of Jesus was walking home with his flock. He was tired — he'd been out with his flock all the previous night and all that day. He'd slept fitfully. Maybe it was because of the moon. It was full, and it cast wild electric moonlight everywhere. (Of course, in those days they didn't have electricity, but you know what I mean; the moonlight charged you up, kept you awake.) The sheep were crazy that night, and the shepherd was constantly getting up and chasing them back to the group. It was tiring, to say the least.

So, Calaphas was walking heavily down the mountain, thinking of home. Actually, to be accurate, he was think-ing of the dinner his wife Hanina was going to prepare: flatbread, hummus, and perfectly brined olives. He led the flock over a shoulder of land, and there, he saw his village in the valley below. He stopped to admire the view as the sheep passed.

But something was wrong. "Wait, wait," he said the

Going up mountains is a powerful biblical theme — examples being: Moses climbing to the top of Sinai for the Commandments, the Sermon on the Mount, and Jesus's burial on the Mount of Olives, etc.

Storytelling Tip:

Remember: Sound Effects "R" Us.

sheep. They stopped, and Calaphas counted, but he knew even before he finished: there was a sheep missing. It was Little Sophie. Sophie was a bit of a wanderer.

"There's one in every flock," he said tiredly.

He turned to the sheep. "I want you all to go home. You know the way from here. See? Down below? You can see the house. Go on. I'll find Sophie and be down as soon as I can."

The sheep headed off, and Calaphas said to himself, "At least, I hope I'll be back."

Calaphas headed up the mountain.

"Hello? Little one? Are you here? Hello!"

It was getting dark, and Calaphas was getting nervous, but he kept climbing.

"Hello? Sophie, where are you? Hello?"

Calaphas kept climbing, up, and up, and up. Soon, he was at the summit. He could look around and see the land of the Hebrews stretching away in all directions. He saw a few villages and a few fires, but mostly it was dark. The stars were wild. They swept across the sky.

"I can't go home without Sophie," Calaphas said to himself. "I can't."

It was full dark now, cold, and windy. Calaphas shivered. He couldn't hear anything. What if the sheep was lost? Dead? Calaphas and Hanina were not wealthy, and they could ill afford to lose an animal. "Hello?" he said again, his heart heavy.

All he could hear was wind.

"Oh, no."

And then: "Baa. Baa. Baa."

He had found Little Sophie! On the peak, sheltering near an outcropping of rock. She ran to Calaphas.

That night Calaphas carried the little sheep through town, triumphantly. "I found her. I found her!"

People came out of their homes, smiling, applauding as Calaphas lifted the lamb high.

"She's back!"

The Parable of the Gold Coin

The second story is about a gold coin.

" . . . seven, eight, nine . . . Oh! There has to be a mistake."

So Magdala counted again and got the same dismal result: only nine coins. One was missing. "What will I do?" she wondered.

She shuddered to think of the trouble she was in. She had to buy seed for planting and hay for the cow. She had to pay the landlord. What if she lost her house? Oh no!

Magdala had a strong impulse to run away. How could she face the landlord—how could she face everyone?

But she didn't run. Instead, she calmly cleaned her house. She moved the furniture away from the wall, she dusted, and she put the furniture back. Slowly, she became calmer—and stronger. "I know I will find it. I know I didn't lose it. I know that no one has stolen it. No one from this village would do that, and besides, why not steal all the coins?" She kept working.

Then, out of the corner of her eye, as she moved the table, she saw something glitter. But when she looked directly at the wall, she couldn't see a thing. She looked away—and she saw the glittering again.

"There!" She fell to her knees and looked in a crack in the wall behind the table. She found the coin.

"It must have fallen!"

Everyone in the village was very surprised when Magdala marched outside, holding the coin up as high as she could.

"I found it!"

The coin shone, beautiful, in the Galilean sunshine.

The Parable of the Prodigal Son

The next thing that was lost was . . . a man, a son. This is called, "The Parable of the Prodigal Son," and it's one of Jesus's loveliest stories — one of his most famous.

Malach owned many hundreds of acres. His land was well watered and fertilized, so his wheat was the best, rich and dark. Bread made from Malach's wheat was the best, crispy and soft. He owned vineyards and vast vegetable gardens. He raised rare breeds of cattle. He was, to put it mildly, wealthy.

But Malach didn't laze about like other rich men, letting the servants and farmhands do the work — no. Malach got up at dawn, rolled up his sleeves, and plowed and fertilized and weeded. He carried feed and harvested until dusk, like the best of his workers.

What Malach loved best — more than all his land, all his livestock, his vineyards, and everything — were his sons. He had two: Niv, the youngest, and Samaal, the oldest. Malach loved Niv and Samaal more than he loved anything in the world.

One morning, Malach was harvesting wheat — threshing, it's called — and he was working hard, scything large swaths, piling the wheat up for the women who would separate out the chaff. It was going to be a hot day; already at dawn, Malach was perspiring.

"Father."

"Oh!" Malach turned, a bit startled. Niv had approached him from the side of his bad ear. "What is it, sweet boy?"

"Father!"

"Yes . . . ?" Malach was getting worried.

"I want . . . I want my share of the estate now."

"Now?"

"Yes, now. I don't want to wait for you to die."

Malach stared at his son. It was as though he were seeing him for the first time. He saw a young man anxious to find his way in this mad world, a man who never be happy "staying on the farm." He knew he couldn't hold onto him, no matter how he might try or how much he would want to.

"Alright," Malach said, "I will give you your inheritance now."

The next morning, Niv set off, headed for the city. He could feel the heaviness of the coins—his inheritance—in his pockets. Gold! All his! He made goofy little dance steps and twirled around.

In the city, he stayed at the best inn he could find, ate sumptuous dinners in fancy restaurants, drank the finest wine, and bought fancy jewelry and clothes made from colorful silk. Everywhere he went he was treated like a lord. "I could definitely get used to this," he said.

After a week or so, he took passage on a sailing boat (he rented a stateroom, naturally) and went to the Orient. His plan was to set himself up in some kind of business on the Silk Road, but somehow, he just never got around to it. The food was too good, the wine was delicious, and life was perfect. Who wanted to work?

Then, one morning, he woke up and his money was gone. His head was thick, and he wasn't sure why: had someone stolen it? Or had he just run out? Well, it didn't matter; he was penniless now, living in the middle of nowhere.

He took a job feeding swine and cleaning out their stalls. It barely paid him enough to eat, and he had to sleep with the pigs.

Then, one morning, he woke up and said to himself, "Home. I want to go home. Home." It was like a veil fell away from his eyes, and home was all he could think about.

But he was a long way from home, and he had no money. So he walked. He found food when he could and went hungry when he couldn't. He hitched rides. When he got to the sea, he had to find a boat that would take him on as a deckhand. He did, but the sea was stormy, and he was constantly seasick. He made it to his homeland, finally, and spent a week walking home. He walked slowly; he was so weak. His clothes were rags, and he had lost weight. He just concentrated on putting one foot in front of the other.

Finally, he made it. He stood on the ridge looking down on Malach's estate. It was a view he seen hundreds of times. But now, it was like he was seeing it for the first time.

"Home."

At first, Malach didn't recognize him. "We don't have any work right now. Come back at harvest time."

"Father," Niv croaked, barely able to speak.

"Did you say . . . ?" He peered at him. "Niv . . . ?"

Niv nodded.

"Oh, my son. My beautiful son."

He tried to take Niv into his arms, but Niv just backed away.

"All I ask is that you take me on as a hired hand. That's all. I don't deserve anything else."

Malach looked at him for a long time. "Niv, it makes my heart soar with joy to see you. You have no idea." He turned to his servants. "Quick! Cook up the fatted calf we have been saving. Tonight we feast!"

The party began. They feasted, serving the best wine, sweet dates, apricots, and everything.

Late in the afternoon, Samaal came home from working in the fields. He heard the music, saw servants carrying in food, and wondered what has going on.

"Father?"

"Your brother is home! Isn't that wonderful? He's safe!"

"What happened to the money?"

"Money?"

"His inheritance."

"Oh. It's gone. But he's safe, that's the important thing—safe!" Malach broke away and went inside to celebrate.

But not Samaal—he stalked off to the orchard, sulking and refusing to eat. He was angry.

After a while, Malach noticed that Samaal wasn't at the feast. He went looking for him.

When he saw Malach, Samaal vented. "I've been faithful to you. I work from morning to night. I ask for nothing—no wages, no special treatment, nothing. All I want from you is respect."

"And that you have."

"I do not! No! Niv comes home in rags after squandering his money, and what do you do? You throw him a party! You slay the fatted calf! It's not fair!"

"Niv is your brother, Samaal."

"So?"

"Don't you understand? Niv was lost, but he's found. He's my son; he's your brother. We celebrate. What else can we do?"

What do you think? Do you sympathize with Samaal? After all, he behaved well, he stayed home and worked, he didn't waste money on food and fancy inns. Why does Niv get a celebration and Samaal gets, well, nothing. And what about all the sheep that didn't go off exploring, the ones who stayed with the flock, who didn't make Calaphas risk life and limb, climbing the mountain at night?

I think Jesus is telling us something about the importance of community: it's important to be part of a group. The natural response when someone strays from the community — like the little lamb — and then returns is to celebrate. It's not wrong. And I believe that Malach's estate will be better, Calaphas's flock will be stronger, as a result of the prodigal's return.

Story Points: "The Parables of the Lost"

The Lost Sheep

★ Calaphas, a shepherd, is tired, but in awe of the beautiful night, the crisp air, and the shining moon.

★ He heads home, thinking of dinner.

★ He notices the missing sheep: "There's one in every flock"; he sends the other sheep home and goes off in search of the lost sheep.

★ He heads up the mountain; it's scary up there, cold and windy.

★ Finally, he hears the bleating of the sheep.

★ Calaphas carries the lost sheep home in triumph; the other villagers come out to applaud the return to the fold.

The Lost Coin

★ Magdala discovers that the gold coin is missing; she panics, thinking of the landlord and her precarious situation.

★ She starts cleaning, forcing herself to be calm.

★ She finds the coin in a crack in the wall.

★ She marches down the street, holding up the shining coin.

The Prodigal Son

★ Describe Malach's beautiful estate: wheatfields, vineyards, and livestock—rich and sumptuous.

★ Malach loves his sons, Niv and Samaal, more than anything.

★ Niv asks Malach for his inheritance now; Malach considers and then says yes.

★ Niv leads the high life: he goes to the city and buys food, wine, and clothes; takes a ship across the sea; travels, thinking he'll set up a business, but never gets around to it; loses his money; and finds himself stranded, penniless.

★ Niv journeys home—working, struggling, and starving. He finds work on a boat, sails over the stormy sea, reaches the city, and finally, walks home.

★ He asks Malach for a job, thinking he deserves nothing else.

★ Malach celebrates: he stages a feast, "slays the fatted calf," and hires musicians.

★ Saamal is upset. Malach tells him, "But he's our son, your brother. Of course we celebrate when he returns home."

Moses and the Exodus: The Greatest Story Ever Told

For many people, "the greatest story ever told" refers to the story of Jesus Christ: his immaculate conception, the drama surrounding his birth (paranoid and homicidal Herod, the frantic flight into Egypt, etc.), followed by Jesus' quiet upbringing in Nazareth, his astonishing flowering as a preacher, becoming the Christ, the grief and horror of his death, followed by exaltation at his rising. Certainly, this is a grand and thrilling epic.

But for my money, the greatest story ever told is that of Moses: raised by the ancient Pharaoh, touched by a fiery God, coming into his own as a nonviolent revolutionary (four thousand years before Gandhi and King), inflicting the Plagues on great Egypt, creating the first Passover, leading the Hebrews into the desert, splitting the Red Sea, taking the Jews into the wilderness, spending forty days on Mount Sinai and returning with the Commandments, and then, in his final hours, at age 120, leading the Israelites into Canaan, the Promised Land.

Is there a better story?

It retains astonishing power. There have been a number of Hollywood tellings, including a recent adaptation, *Exodus: Gods and Kings,* by the uber-talented Ridley Scott.

In the nineteenth century, many archeologists, believers in the Bible, expected to find evidence of the Jewish Exodus, and they did. But contemporary experts haven't been so sure. There is no historical record of the huge demographic shift the Exodus of the Hebrews—two million people, according to many estimates— would have created. There is no evidence in the Sinai Desert of their passing. Moreover, there is plenty of archeological evidence that Jews evolved in Israel, that they didn't arrive suddenly from Egypt or from anywhere else.

So, was there an Exodus?

Historians, theologians, and archeologists will argue this question until the end of time, but does it matter? Do you remember the Native American truism about story veracity? It applies here, emphatically: perhaps in reality there never was an Exodus, but the story of Moses freeing the Israelites is as true as a story can be. I believe every word.

This is a big one — definitely a multi-nighter. I have indicated a few stopping places, but as always, these are only suggestions. If your child folds his tent before a break, by all means, stop.

The tale of Moses and the Exodus contains scary, and even violent, material: the death of the slave driver, the plagues, the Red Sea closing fatally in on Pharaoh's soldiers. This is raw, primal material. It is, possibly, the scariest tale in this book. Its biblical provenance notwithstanding, it might not be appropriate for the youngest children.

The plagues in particular could upset your children. You might eliminate them; I have indicated in the text of the story where they could be cut. But if you do so, a lot would be lost. The feast of Passover, central to contemporary Jewish identity, is derived directly from the plagues of Egypt. Remember, you are with your child.

I considered the matter at some length and finally decided to end the story after the famous parting of the Red Sea. The material after this is fabulous: Moses leading the Israelites into the Sinai wilderness, the manna, the sweet springs, the getting of the Ten Commandments, the golden calf, and the wandering ending with the triumphant entrance into Canaan, the land of milk and honey. But the character of God in this section is problematic. He becomes capricious, vengeful (he demands, for example, that the Hebrews slay 3500 calf worshippers), angry, violent, war-crazed, nasty, and even sneaky. There is theological justification for all of this, but this complicates the material and takes it out of the realm of a simple bedtime narrative. I choose to omit it.

This story is taken from two books of the Old Testament—Exodus and Deuteronomy—with, of course, plenty of embellishments and story embroidering from yours truly.

Here we go:

Night One

Tonight, I'm going to tell you a great, great story. It's one of the oldest stories, too. It happened nearly four thousand years ago, in ancient Egypt.

Egypt was—and still is—built up mostly along the Nile River, which flows from deepest Africa into the Mediterranean Sea. Every year, before the great dam at Aswan was built, the Nile flooded. Egyptians called this the Inundation. It was hugely important, because it made the desert along the Nile come alive. It deposited rich soil, called silt, onto the land around the river. The Egyptians grew their food here. The floods only went inland for a half-mile, maybe a mile, along the river. The rest was empty—they thought—desert.

This so-called "empty" desert will be an important part of this story.

Egypt was a land of monuments. I bet you've seen photographs of: the great pyramids of Giza; or the amazing Sphinx; or the obelisks, hundreds of feet high; tall statues; deep tombs, filled with secret rooms. I'll show you some pictures tomorrow.

Who do you think did all this work? The rulers? Certainly not.

Egyptians? Well, yes, some of them. Many Egyptians were artisans. They carved statues, painted murals, worked in gold, polished jewels, worked as architects or architects' assistants, foremen, etc. A huge percentage of

Storytelling Tip:

But not now. Keep the lights off. But tomorrow, yes, find some of these images. They're all over the Internet. This can be a way of keeping this story alive.

Egypt's economy was devoted to the creation of the monuments, and many thousands of Egyptians found employment this way.

But the grunt work—the hard work—was done by slaves. Hauling huge rocks from quarries deep in the desert, raising pyramids and statues—all of this was done by slave labor. Many of these slaves were Jews, Hebrews.

Most often they were born into bondage, generation after generation. They had to accept whatever meager payment was doled out by the Egyptians. They weren't citizens. They were considered inferior. They had no rights. If the Egyptians chose to decrease rations, they could, and the Hebrews could do nothing.

Now, the leader of the Egyptians was Pharaoh. Pharaoh ruled absolutely. Pharaohs were considered to be gods, literally. So, needless to say, this man had what you might call an inflated opinion of himself—an ego.

And this particular Pharaoh was crazy. I'm serious. Nuts. He was extremely paranoid, and the thing he worried about most, the thing that obsessed him, was the Hebrews. He thought there were too many:

"There are two million, your majesty."

"Two million Jews! Why, they're almost half the population!"

"Indeed. But they're slaves. They have to accept whatever we give them."

"Still, they're dangerous. Don't you agree?"

"Well, yes, of course." Everybody agreed with Pharaoh. You had to.

"I hereby decree that every newborn Hebrew male be . . . immediately drowned, yes, drowned in the Nile."

"Excuse me?"

"You heard me! Every newborn boy!"

This brings us to our hero, a beautiful little baby, born to a Jewish couple, Jacob and Yocheved, living among the Hebrew slaves, in a shack. Their baby had silky hair, clear eyes, and strength—even as a baby you could sense his power. The order came down—"Death to all Hebrew newborns!" But there was no way this baby's parents would allow their new child to be slain.

So, they hid their baby every time the soldiers came banging on their door: *Boom! Boom! Boom!*

But finally, after one particularly close call, Jacob and Yocheved made a heartbreaking decision: they would make a basket of bulrushes, put the baby in it, and hide the basket in the River, and let the baby be found by an Egyptian family. That way he could be raised—safely.

They wove the basket as tight as possible, and then they said good-bye to their son. The parents were crying too hard, so the boy's big sister, Miriam, and his big brother, Aaron, took the basket to the river. Very gently, they let it go. It drifted along for a while.

Then the current caught it. The basket started moving faster, and faster. Miriam followed as best she could, but soon it was out of sight. The weeds and rushes by the river were thick.

And then, Miriam ran into soldiers: they were near one of Pharaoh's palaces. The soldiers forced her away.

But that night, Miriam snuck back. She stayed in the water, away from the soldiers, moving slow and quiet. She was desperate to find out what had happened to her little brother. She kept moving, silently, silently. Soon, dawn broke. Rich light spread across the calm surface of the river. Miriam could see that she was in a little bay. Marble steps rose up out of the water and went to a grand build-ing: Pharaoh's palace. As Miriam watched, a young wom-an with attendants came down the steps. The attendants watched as the girl bathed. You know who this was?

It was Pharaoh's daughter!

Miriam watched from the rushes. She had never seen anyone so rich, with silks, gold jewelry, and handmaidens.

"Did you hear that?" Pharaoh's daughter looked up, frowning.

"Hear what?"

"That!" Pharaoh's daughter splashed quickly through the water to the reeds on the far side of the little harbor. "Be careful!" the attendants cried, but Pharaoh's daugh-ter was undeterred. "Here!" She slowly drew the basket of bulrushes out of the reeds.

"Oh!" Miriam had to clap a hand over her mouth to keep from being heard.

Pharaoh's daughter slowly took the top off the basket. The baby, hungry and cold, was squalling inside. "Ah-wah! Ah-wah!"

Pharaoh's daughter picked the baby up and held him, laughing. "What a pair of lungs this boy has! Isn't he won-derful?"

"Indeed, your majesty," one of the attendants replied, "he certainly is."

"He's delightful. I'm going to name him . . . Moses."

Just then, Miriam burst out of her hiding place. "Your majesty!"

Several of the guards stopped her and started to drag her away.

Pharaoh's daughter said, "Wait. Let her speak."

Miriam blurted, "Your majesty, would you like me to

Storytelling Tip:

There is a passage of time here, and it makes a natural place to break the story – if you so desire.

find a Hebrew woman to help you feed the baby?"

"Yes, that would be helpful."

And you know who Miriam found for the Princess? Yocheved, Moses's mother. So, between Miriam, Yocheved, and Pharaoh's daughter, Moses was well taken care of.

Like Paul Simon's song says, "His eyes were clear as centuries; his silky hair was brown."

This is our hero: Moses.

Night Two

Moses grew up as a member of Pharaoh's household. He knew he would never inherit the throne—he wasn't blood. Still, he had excellent relationships with Pharaoh, his daughter (of course), and with Pharaoh's young son, Ramses. Ramses was the heir to the throne. The two boys were inseparable.

All around Moses huge monuments rose: temples for worshipping the Egyptian gods, statues, obelisks, and sumptuous tombs. Moses helped—he turned out to have a talent for carving small statues.

But Moses was always aware of the poor slaves who were forced to do most of the work for no money, for barely enough food to live, suffering horrific hardships and beatings: the Hebrews. Moses felt a kinship with them, which he didn't understand. His nursemaid, Yocheved (who was really his birth mother), never told him who he really was, nor did Miriam. All he knew was that he had been a foundling. Moses's awareness of the hardships of the Hebrew slaves soured his relationship with Ramses— Ramses couldn't care less about the Hebrews. To him, they were just slaves—expendable.

Then, one day, something broke inside Moses when he heard the horrible sound of a slave overseer's whip: *Cht! Cht! Cht!* Moses rushed outside and saw the man whipping an old Hebrew man who was so weak from hunger he could barely stand up. Moses grabbed his hand.

"What are you doing?" the overseer growled.

"You can't do this!"

"Do what?"

"Beat people like this."

"They aren't people—they're slaves, Hebrews." He spat on the ground. "I can do whatever I want." And with that, he gave the old man a huge crack across the back.

Moses grabbed the whip away.

"Give it back."

"No."

"Give me. My whip."

"You can't . . . you can't . . ."

"I'll kill you."

"You can't kill me. I'm Pharaoh's grandson."

This gave the overseer pause. He squinted at Moses. Then his pride got the better of him. "You're nobody, a foundling. They discovered you in the reeds along the river. Pharaoh won't protect you."

He pulled a dagger.

They fought. It was horrible, a fight in the hot sun. Many people, slaves mostly, gathered to watch, but nobody did anything; they couldn't. Moses had never experienced anything like the hate he felt from the slave driver. He looked to see the man raising the dagger for a death-blow.

"No!"

Moses rolled out of the way as the dagger struck the ground. He kicked blindly, and a lucky blow struck the slave driver's hand. The dagger skittered away. They both scrambled for it.

But Moses found it first.

Moses had never seen a man die before, but he watched the life flow out of the slave driver's face. He pulled away and stood up. He looked at the knife. Blood dripped from it. He let it fall.

The slaves looked at him in wonder. "You killed him."

"I . . . I didn't mean to. It was an accident. He was going to kill me!"

The slaves moved away, afraid of what would happen now.

Except for one man, who approached him. "Moses," he said calmly, "you must leave now. They will execute you for this."

"They won't. They couldn't. I'm Pharaoh's grandson. Besides, he was beating the slaves. I can't . . . I couldn't . . ."

"Don't you know who you are?"

Moses shook his head.

"You're a Hebrew."

"What?"

"I'm your brother, Moses. My name is Aaron. And the woman who was your wet-nurse . . . "

"Yocheved."

"She's your mother."

"No."

"Believe it. Don't you remember? You were a foundling. Discovered by Pharaoh's daughter in the reeds."

"I have . . . memories."

"Your memories are real."

They heard soldiers shouting. "Over there! He slew one of Pharaoh's overseers! Get him!"

"You have to go." Aaron took Moses by the shoulders. "We'll see each other again. I know we will. May God be with you."

"There he is!"

Moses took off, running through the city, the murderous soldiers just behind.

Was God with Moses? I think maybe so. Moses ran, through alleys and down cul-de-sacs, which turned out to have secret doors. Magically, he left the soldiers behind—though he could still hear their angry shouts.

But that wasn't all Moses left behind. His comfortable life in Pharaoh's palace was a thing of the past. He had no idea what the future held, but he believed Aaron. He knew in his bones that he was different, that he was connected to the slaves.

He was a Jew.

Moses found himself in the vast Saharan desert, alone.

Moses was a palace boy. He'd grown up in Pharaoh's household with dozens of slaves to do the cooking, the cleaning, the washing, and everything. He'd never had to do anything. And now, here he was, alone in the desert, the object of a man-hunt. On several occasions, he saw packs of soldiers thundering by. He had no food and just one skin of water. Moses was, for all intents and purposes, dead.

But something, someone, was guiding his footsteps. At first, Moses wasn't aware of it. But then, he began to wonder: what made me go this way? He went uphill, when it would have been easier to go down. He avoided certain trails—he didn't know why. Moses began to have the feeling that he was going somewhere, someplace specific. He wasn't just wandering.

And sure enough, as he staggered up the side of a dune,

nearly dead, he saw it: a wall of rock, rising out of the dead desert. In Egypt, they call these islands of stone wadis. In the middle of this particularly wadi, there was a break, a canyon. Moses headed for the canyon.

It was like entering a different world. It was shadowy, after the burning sun of the desert, and cooler, much cooler. The canyon was narrow and twisty. Moses followed it, deeper, deeper into the wadi. He saw that he was on a well-trod track—many other people had been here. Then he smelled it. Did you know that water has a smell? It does in the dry-as-dust Sahara. Moses rounded a bend . . . .

There.

It was an oasis. There were palm trees and a few meager huts. And in the middle of it . . . could it be?

A miracle! It was a pool of clear, cold, spring-fed water. Moses collapsed and lost consciousness.

"Drink this."

"Wha . . . ?"

"Drink."

Moses blinked. Someone was giving him a small cup of cool tea.

"Small sips only."

Moses peered at the person giving him tea. She was a beautiful young woman. Her skin was dark from the sun, her thick black hair long and braided.

Moses took the cup. The woman's touch was cool and steady. "What . . . what is your name?" Moses asked.

"Zipporah."

Night Three

Thus began the simplest, least eventful, and happiest years of Moses's life: his days as a sheepherder. Moses married the beautiful Zipporah and lived with the quasi-nomadic shepherds, going from oasis to oasis. Moses and Zipporah had a son.

Egypt, with its magnificence (the monuments, the statues, and the sumptuous tombs) and its horror (the slavery of the Hebrews), faded for Moses. It was all in the past. He was content.

But this complacency was not to last, for God came into Moses's life, suddenly.

It began with the famous burning bush. This is one of the most famous events in biblical history. Here's what happened:

Moses was chasing an errant lamb who had broken away from the flock and was climbing Mount Sinai. "Come back!" Moses called. But the lamb kept climbing and climbing. *Baaaaaaaa. Baaaaaaaa.* The path got narrower and steeper. Baaaaaaaa.

Moses rounded a bend.

Then he saw it. A small bush was on fire, burning bright, making a pure light. But here's the strange thing: the fire wasn't consuming the bush. Its leaves were unaffected. The fire didn't make you want to back away. It was inviting. It pulled you closer.

"Moses," a strange voice called.

"What? Who . . . ? What . . . ?"

"I have seen the anguish of the Hebrews in Egypt. They suffer, horribly. I have decided to lead them out of bondage, to the land of milk and honey, in Canaan. I have chosen you, Moses, to lead the Hebrews."

"Me? But . . . I haven't been to Egypt in years."

"You must go to Egypt and ask Pharaoh to let the Hebrews leave."

"He would never do that. He needs slaves for his statues, and his, his . . . "

"You must convince him."

"How can I do that?"

"You will ask your brother to help."

"I haven't seen Aaron in years."

"Throw your staff to the ground."

Moses looked at his staff. It was a simple walking stick, something he had picked up in the desert years before. He shrugged and threw it down.

It turned into a snake! A huge cobra! The snake writhed and slithered on the ground. *Sssssssssssssss.* Moses jumped back. "Oh!"

"Now grab the snake by the tail."

Moses obeyed, carefully picking up the writhing snake by the tail. Suddenly, it turned back into the wooden staff.

"Whoa."

"Do that for Pharaoh. He will know that you speak for me. Go to Egypt, Moses. I am counting on you," and with that, the flames died. The bush was untouched by the fire. Moses gingerly stepped forward and touched one of the bush's leaves. It felt cool.

So Moses left Zipporah and his family for the first time in many years, and made his way across the desert.

He was scared.

And he grew even more scared as he approached the big Egyptian city. It was night, and Moses could feel the suffering of the Hebrews. He smelt the balefires. He could hear weeping. Smoke hung over the city. Things were worse, much worse, than they had been before.

Then he stopped, frightened. Someone was hiding close by. Who? Bandits? "Who's there?" Moses clutched his staff. "Who is it?"

A figure, a man, stepped out of his hiding place in the rocks and approached Moses.

"Stop."

The man stopped. Moses peered at him. "Aaron?"

"Yes."

"My brother."

"Oh!"

Moses embraced his brother. It had been years. Aaron had changed, but blood will always make itself felt.

"Did you come to meet me?"

Aaron nodded.

"How did . . . ? How could you know . . . ?"

"I had a dream. God told me to meet you here. Moses, I know why you've come. To lead us out of this horrible place, to the Promised Land. I've told everyone."

It was true. As Moses and Aaron walked into the city, the Hebrews came out to meet him. "Hail, Moses! Thank God you're here! Hail!" The Hebrews were thin, under-nourished, wearing rags, and sick.

Moses noticed that the city was more magnificent—filled with statues, obelisks, and murals—but all he could really see was the intense suffering of his brethren.

"Let's go see Pharaoh," Moses said.

"He'll never let us in."

"He will. I'm his cousin."

It was true. The man who had been Moses's playmate growing up, Ramses, was Pharaoh now. Moses and Aaron had to wait for hours, but finally, they were ushered into a huge hall, filled with carved columns and servants. At the far end was a throne, and there sat Pharaoh Ramses. He stared at Moses — then stood and embraced him.

"It's true," he said. "You have returned. I would never have believed it."

Moses got right to the point. "Your majesty, you must release the Hebrews."

"What?"

"You must let my people go."

Pharaoh stared at him. Then he laughed. "You're crazy."

"God sent me."

"Which god? Isis? Osiris? The sun king?" The Egyptians worshipped many gods.

"There is only one true God."

"*I* am a god," Pharaoh shouted.

Moses threw down his staff. It immediately turned into a cobra. *Sssssssssss.* Pharaoh jumped back.

Then he summoned his own magicians. They threw down their staffs. They also became snakes! Sssssssss!

"You see, Moses?" Pharaoh said triumphantly. "My men can do the same thing! Ha! You are my cousin, so I won't have you killed, but you must get out of my sight."

Moses had failed.

He went back to where the Hebrews lived. He saw their pleading eyes. *Please help us*, they seemed to say. *We are desperate.*

Moses went into the desert. He prayed. *What can I do? What can I do?*

God spoke. "Moses, never doubt that I am with you. Here is what you must do. See Pharaoh again."

"He'll kill me!"

"Hold your staff over the river. I will be there."

Moses waited for Pharaoh by the river—it was close to the little bay where Moses had been found. He waited and waited. Finally, Pharaoh returned, riding a horse. He had been racing with his chums. Moses stepped into his path. Pharaoh's horse reared up, almost throwing the king.

"Moses! I told you I never wanted to see you again! Guards! Throw this man into the dungeons!"

As the guards approached, Moses extended his staff over the river. "God has sent this sign!"

You know what happened?

The Nile River turned to blood.

"Oh!"

Everyone jumped back, astonished and horrified. Blood! They turned and ran, everyone except Pharaoh.

"Let my people go," Moses said quietly.

"Never," Pharaoh said. "Never!"

Then he followed the guards, leaving Moses alone. Moses looked at the Nile. It was deep red—blood—as far as he could see. He raised his staff. Slowly, slowly, the river became normal again.

Ramses was proud. He would never, he said, give in to Moses's demands. "We need the slaves, he said, "and besides, I am a god!"

Night Four

[First God sent lice—tiny insects that bored into the skin and made everyone, people and animals, itch.

But the lice didn't affect the Hebrews.

And still, Ramses would not give in.

Storytelling Tip:

What follows is the description of the plagues of Egypt. You could, as indicated in the introduction to this story, eliminate this, on the grounds that impressionable children might find it too scary. All the material in brackets ([]) could be cut.

Then God sent frogs, millions of frogs, hopping out of the Nile. They were everywhere!

And still, Ramses would not give in.

And then came flies, buzzing around the humans, making the animals mad with terror, making the cattle and the horses stampede.

And still, Ramses would not give in.

Next, God sent pestilence—sickness. It didn't affect humans, only the animals. Horses and cattle died by the millions. The stench rose over the city, but the animals owned by the Hebrews were not affected.

And still, Ramses would not give in.

Skin boils were next, itchy, bleeding, painful boils that affected the Egyptians—but not the Hebrews. "Please," Pharaoh's advisors pleaded, "please give Moses what he wants."

"I will not!" Ramses would not give in.

Then God sent a cataclysmic storm. Black clouds roiled in and blotted out the sun. It rained and rained. Hail pounded down. Crops died; orchards were flattened.

And still, Ramses would not give in.

Locusts, howling out of the desert, were next. They devoured the food and crops.

And still, Ramses would not give in.

Then darkness fell. The sun disappeared for three days.

Finally, Pharaoh sent for Moses. By now, his advisors were bent from hunger and sickness. They urged Ramses to give in. "I will let your people go," Ramses croaked, "but you must leave your animals, your horses and cattle, behind. I need them to replace the ones who died."

"No," Moses said.

"What?"

"We will leave, and we will take our livestock."

"You will not!"

Ramses would not give in.

Then came the final plague, the worst one of all: the death of every firstborn in every house in Egypt.

God spoke to Moses, "Tell the Israelites to slaughter a lamb and to mark the doors of every house with the lamb's blood. That way I will know that Jews dwell within the house, and I will pass over on my errand of death."

The Jews did as God asked. And indeed, no Hebrews died during the plague. Jews celebrate this miraculous event to this very day. It's called "Pesach" or, in English, "Passover."

The death of all these Egyptians was horrible—and it included Pharaoh's own son. As he held his son's body, Pharaoh said, "Go. I'm done with you."]

Ramses let the Israelites leave.

"We depart at dawn!" Moses cried. "Take only what you can carry! We are going to the Promised Land!"

And so Moses led the ancient Israelites out of Egypt. The Hebrews, their animals, and other slaves: two million people. They walked out of the city, over the mountain pass, and down into the eastern desert. Moses walked at the head of the line. Have you ever seen the photos of Martin Luther King leading the civil rights marchers? It was like that, but multiply it by a thousand. Two million people!

Ah, but Pharaoh wasn't through. A few days after the Hebrews departed, he gathered his advisors. "All of them left? All of them?"

"Yes, your majesty."

"Who allowed that?"

"Well, you did, sire."

"I must have been insane." Pharaoh's advisors looked at each other. They didn't want to say anything. "Who will do our building? Who will mine granite? Who will drag the statues and obelisks?"

The advisors shrugged.

"We must stop them. I don't care what I said. I am a god, and I can do anything I want. If they won't come back, kill them!"

And so, Ramses sent his army after the unarmed Israelites.

Moses, meanwhile, had reached the Red Sea. There, he stopped. What else could he do?

"Moses!" One of his lieutenants ran up to him, out of breath. "It's Pharaoh's army! They're coming, in chariots. They're coming fast!"

"What will we do?"

"I don't know!"

Moses looked at the Israelites, crowded around the sea. They were waiting from him to make a decision.

Then, on the hill overlooking the Red Sea, the first of Pharaoh's charioteers appeared. They watched the Israelites as they waited for their companions to appear.

Moses turned and faced the Red Sea. He looked up at the sky. "Lord, what shall I do? Please don't forsake me now."

Moses felt God's power building inside him. It was the same feeling he got when he talked to the burning bush and to God in the desert, when God told him about the plagues, a feeling that he could do anything.

Moses struck the ground with his staff! *Boom!* Moses raised his arms.

You know what happened?

The Red Sea parted. The water drew back, hundreds of feet high, and left a channel to the other side. The water quivered and shook. The Hebrews could feel its immense power. But they had no choice.

"Hurry!" his lieutenants cried. "To the other side, quick! Quick!"

As more of Pharaoh's army gathered on the pass, the Hebrew hurried through the channel through the Red Sea.

Pharaoh came riding up to the pass overlooking the Red Sea. "The Hebrews are escaping!"

Pharaoh looked. It was true: the last of the Israelites were scrambling through the channel in the parted sea.

"Follow them!"

"But, Pharaoh . . . "

"Follow them!"

Pharaoh watched as his soldiers went thundering down from the pass toward the parted Red Sea.

Moses, on the other side, still felt God's power coursing through his body. "Hurry," his followers cried. "Hurry!" Moses waited patiently. The Egyptian soldiers came closer, closer, closer. Moses could see murderous hatred glinting in their eyes.

Boom! Moses struck the ground with his staff. *Boom!*

He opened his arms.

And the Red Sea closed. The Egyptian soldiers had to swim back to the far side. Moses and his followers were safe. "Thank you, God, for delivering us safely out of Egypt."

The Hebrews had escaped.

Moses led the Israelites into Canaan, the land of milk of honey. But it wasn't an easy journey. Indeed, the Hebrews wandered for forty years. Moses found springs of sweet water in the desert. Nutritious manna fell from the sky. Moses brought the great Ten Commandments down from Mount Sinai — the same place he had encountered the burning bush.

Moses himself never entered Canaan. He sat on Mount Nebo, watching his followers enter the Promised Land. There, he died. He was 120 years old, one of the greatest men in history.

Story Points: "Moses and the Exodus"

These story points don't include the "night" breaks. These are completely arbitrary, after all.

* Introduce ancient Egypt: built along the Nile; dependent on the River's annual floods; filled with magnificent tombs, statues, and pyramids.
* The Hebrew slaves are responsible for Egypt's magnificence; they were horribly mistreated, generation after generation.
* Pharaoh thinks of himself as a god, so he feels he can do anything; he is insane and paranoid, and decides to drown every newborn Hebrew.
* Jacob and his wife, Yocheved, are unwilling to let the Egyptians kill their son; instead, they build a basket and hide him. Their daughter Miriam lets the basket go in the river.
* The basket is discovered by Pharaoh's daughter. Moses is given his name; Miriam, watching, rushes out and suggests Yocheved as a wet-nurse; Pharaoh's daughter agrees, and Moses is saved.
* Moses is raised in Pharaoh's palace; he becomes friends with Ramses, the heir to the throne. He is always horrified at the

treatment of the Hebrew slaves; one day, he accidentally kills an overseer in a fight and is forced to flee.

★ In the desert, Moses meets Zipporah, who saves his life. He marries her, fathers a child, and begins living a happy, contented life far from Egypt.

★ In the burning bush on Mount Sinai, God tells Moses that he has been chosen to lead the Hebrews out of bondage; Moses turns his staff into a snake.

★ Moses travels to the city. He meets his brother, Aaron; Moses and Aaron enter the city; the Hebrews come out to greet him. The city is smoky, filled with weeping people and evidence of the horrors of slavery.

★ Moses and Aaron visit Ramses. Pharaoh, unimpressed with the staff-as-snake, laughs Moses out of the palace. Moses goes to the desert to pray.

★ The plagues come: blood, lice, frogs, flies, animal illness, boils, storms, and darkness; yet Ramses is still defiant. Pharaoh says he'll let the Hebrews go, but they must leave their animals; Moses refuses.

★ The final plague: the death of the Egyptian firstborn. Moses tells the Hebrews to ritually slay lambs and paint their doors with the blood, thus creating the first Passover. Ramses, holding the body of his son, finally agrees to let the Hebrews go.

★ Moses leads the Israelites, two million of them, out of Egypt; they stop at the Red Sea.

★ Pharaoh, insane, has a change of heart: he sends charioteers to stop the Jews.

★ As the Egyptians approach, Moses parts the Red Sea; the Israelites escape.

★ The Israelites wander the wilderness for forty years. Finally, they cross the River Jordan and enter Canaan. Moses watches this glorious event from Mount Nebo and then dies at age 120.

Stories from Personal and Family History

"What was it like, Mom, when you were my age? Dad, tell me something that happened to you when you were going to grade school. How was it different? There were no iPods, no YouTube, and computers were in their infancy. What could you have possibly have done to pass the time? What movies were you going to? What music moved you?"

Children eat this stuff up. They yearn to know that they're part of something greater than they, a living and growing tradition: a family.

Now, you are you, and I am me. I cannot create stories based on your family history. But I can recommend that you read the later chapter on creating your own stories and have a serious go at this. It's not that hard, and your charges will be delighted.

Here are some potential starting places:

Did anything dramatic ever happen to you as a child? Was there a storm, a tornado, or a flood? Did your dad ever have to do anything dramatic? When I was in the second grade, there was a huge fire in our school (and no one was hurt, thanks to extensive and expert fire drills). But I remember asking a nun, as flames exploded through the school roof, "Sister, can I go home?" She burst into tears. My son loved hearing about this.

Did your family ever move? Did you go to a new school? All children can readily identify with a tentative exploration of a new environment, being the new kid in town, the loneliness and isolation of it.

Did you ever get lost? Separated from your family or friends?

Did you get hurt as a child? Break a bone? I fell out of a tree when I was in the fifth grade and broke my wrist. This hurt like the dickens, but it did make for some excellent bedtime story material when I grew up (not that this was any consolation at the time).

How about bullies? Did you ever have to go mano a mano with one? Children love to hear about this. I once got into a huge fight with a kid who was picking on me at a movie. I remember chasing him down the alley. Then I stopped, bloodied but grinning. I'm not proud of this, but my son is.

Did your parents ever have to do something heroic? Or even not-so-heroic? Did the stove or the Christmas tree ever catch fire? Did your dad, mom, or either grandparent ever do anything that brought home how much they loved you?

Don't make the mistake of thinking that your poor life doesn't offer any good story material. It does, believe me. We are all engaged in a great struggle, to find our occupations, our life partners, and our true destinies. As a result, our lives are filled with marvelous stories. Don't be afraid to embellish, to turn the raw material of your life into vivid and vibrant fiction.

You can also move away from the specifics of your life when you tell family history: "I'm gonna tell you about a crazy thing that happened to my great-grandpa during the First World War."

Or, "Something really bizarre happened to Aunt Helen when she was driving through the mountains."

Or, "Your great-great-great-great-grandma came to this country in the hold of a slave ship. We don't know her name, but her spirit, her strength, and her will to survive still runs in our blood."

Many American families are aware of their "crossing ancestor," the great-great-etc.-grandparent who came to this country, from Europe or Asia, in an immigrant ship. Or from Africa in the fetid and crowded cargo hold of a slave ship. To leave your home, voluntarily or not, to travel to a strange new world: what an adventure. These crossers can be the subjects of marvelous stories.

Some families carefully husband their history. Often, there is a "keeper of the flame," someone who has the interest, the passion, and the time to gather and preserve this material. They may have written a book, created a photo album, or simply jotted down a few facts into a notebook. Or maybe they're keeping everything in their heads. If there is such a person in your family, get to know him or her. Make sure they know of your interest. Read the material, look at the photos, and make copies. Ask questions. Write the answers down. Make sure the knowledge gets passed along. It's a shame when these people take this vital knowledge to their graves.

And if there isn't a person like that in your family, become him or her. Start collecting material. Work the Internet: Ancestry.com isn't cheap (perhaps you've seen the fancy prime-time ads), but it can be a useful place to start. Often (and this is especially true if your last name is somewhat unusual), there are organizations you can join.

But if family material is hard to come by, you can always make it up. I'm not being specious. In the oral tradition, embellishment and out-and-out fictionalizing are not frowned upon.

You do need to be politic. "A crazy thing happened to Uncle Phil when his car broke down in Nebraska" will be problematic if there is a chance your child will meet Phil at a family reunion. But if Uncle Phil is dead and buried, well, my advice would be to not hesitate.

Remember the adage: don't let the facts get in the way of a good story.

Found Stories

From Books, Movies, and Plays

Have you ever read a good book, or seen a terrific film or play, and said to yourself, "If only I could share this with my kid."

But it proves impossible. There's no way you can summarize a book or a movie in a way that a young child will find inspiring.

Unless you turn the material into a story in the dark. Then children listen. They thrill. Once again (albeit in a different form), the book has life, the movie finds vitality, and the play lives.

You don't have to give your child the whole book or movie. You can, certainly, if you want to get into multi-night mode. But it would be more than okay to present a small piece of the story in a one-night format. In the following examples, I do both: my "Great Expectations" story is based on the first five chapters of the Dickens masterpiece. It's intended to be told in one night. With Frances Hodgson Burnett's popular *The Secret Garden*, I present the whole story (albeit in a severely edited form) as a multi-nighter. These two stories demonstrate how reading material can be distilled into effective stories in the dark.

An admonishment: you must respect copyright. If the work is protected by copyright (and most contemporary movies, plays and books are), you mustn't publish or publically perform your story (i.e., in front of a paying audience). But in the privacy of your child's dark bedroom, well, anything goes.

Great Expectations

It would be helpful, though optional, for you to have read the first five chapters of this great book before you tell a story based on them. Go to Gutenberg.org and download a copy of the novel for your computer or e-reader. The price is right (it's free), and it will take you at most a half an hour to read the material.

(Consider reading *Great Expectations* in its entirety. It's a nineteenth-century novel, and the style thus tends to be flowery and wordy, but the story thrills. There are a number of set pieces which you could easily tease out and present to your young miss as a bedtime story: Pip's first encounter with the alluring and angry Estella; the great fire that destroys Miss Havisham's ancient wedding cake (and her mansion); the reappearance of Magwitch. It's a grand novel.)

Back to the first five chapters: As you read, you will notice that I have left out a considerable amount of material. There is no reference in my rendering of the second convict, the "young man" who figures so prominently later in the book. We're only doing the first few chapters, so why clutter up the story with extraneous characters? For similar reasons, I have omitted Uncle Pumblechook and the other Gargery family members. The time scheme has been collapsed (one day instead of two). I have endeavored to make the plot as simple and as vivid as possible.

There is very little overt violence here (the convict does grab Pip from behind), but there is danger and a scary chase. It might not work for the very young or for a child with a delicate sensibility.

Have you ever heard of the River Thames in England? It's one of the oldest, most storied rivers in the world. It's seen the struggles of the ancient Britons, the Druids, the Romans, the Anglo-Saxons, and the invading French.

The Thames winds its way through the heart of London, one of the great cities of the world. The city was built around the river. For eons, there have been ferry services and famous bridges built over the river, such as the London Bridge, the brand new Millennium Footbridge, and the Waterloo Bridge. There's a famous old movie called *Waterloo Bridge*. Two movies, actually: a silent movie and then one from the forties. Tomorrow, I'll show you some pictures of the bridges, and maybe we can watch the movie.

This story I'm going to tell doesn't take place in London. We have to go downriver, downstream, down to where the Thames flows into the sea. This is called the Thames Estuary, and here the river gets really wide. Sometimes you can't even see the other side. The water goes up and down. This is called tides.

Oh, look. Here's our guy, walking down the street. His name is Phillip Pirrip. Can you guess what everybody calls him? Pip. That's right. He's about twelve years old, but small for his age. He's walking fast. It's Christmas Eve, and the night is cold. The stars are sweeping across the sky. The tide is low. This exposes the salt marsh. Pip can smell it. It smells sweet and funky at the same time—fishy. Pip turns a corner, and then he sees it: the old church. Nobody knows how old it is—perhaps hundreds of years. Pip walks faster. He's nervous.

You know why? He's not going inside the church. He's going to the churchyard, where the graves are. Pip finds a stone: *Peter and Georgiana Pirrip.* His parents. Pip looks at the graves. He wonders if he should say anything. It's Christmas Eve, after all. But he can't think of anything. After a few minutes, he says to himself, "I better go."

Just then, somebody big and strong and smelly claps a hand over Pip's mouth. Pip's eyes are wide. He can't breathe!

"Keep still," the man hisses. "D'you hear me?"

Pip nods.

The man looks around, making sure no one's around. But the churchyard's deserted. He takes his hand away from Pip's mouth. Pip sucks in a deep breath.

"What's your name?"

"P-P-P-Pip, sir."

"Eh?"

"Pip."

"What kinda name is that?"

"My name."

"Where do you live?"

Pip points back toward the small town.

"Where's your mother?"

Pip points at the gravestone.

"Your mother's buried here? Your father, too?"

Pip nods.

"Well, all right," he says. "Who do you live with?"

"With, with my sister. She's married to Joe Gargery, the blacksmith."

"You live with a blacksmith?"

The man glances down at his legs. Pip follows his gaze. You know what he sees? A chain. A thick chain connecting his two legs. Another chain dangles from his wrist.

"Now, listen to me," the man says, all gruff and rough.

"You know what a file is?"

"Yes, sir."

"You know what vittles is?"

"It's food, sir."

"You bring me a file and some vittles. You bring 'em back here, and you promise never to tell no one you saw me. You do that, and . . . and I'll let you live."

"Oh!"

"But if you breathe a word of this, I'll come and get you. You and blacksmith Joe."

"Please, don't hurt Joe."

"Get home, and get that file and them vittles!"

"Yes, sir!"

Pip heads across the churchyard. He looks back. The man is nowhere to be seen. Maybe he was just a dream. That's it—just a dream.

Then Pip thinks, *Joe!* He starts running. Sprinting as fast as he could go, past the church, into town, up one street, down another, until he comes to the small house he shares with his sister and Joe. Joe!

"Where have you been?!"

"What, what?"

His angry sister repeats, "I asked you where you were!"

"I, I was at the churchyard, visiting our parents."

"Who gave you permission to go?"

"Well . . . no one."

"Joe," she says to her husband, "fetch the Tickler."

"Oh, now, I don't think that's necessary," Joe says. He's a sweet man.

"The Tickler!"

You know what the Tickler is? It's a cane. Can you guess what Pip's sister uses it for?

Ouch.

Joe tries to soothe her. "It's Christmas Eve. I think the boy's right to pay his respects to his parents, them being dead and all."

"Well . . ."

Then they hear it. *Boooom. Booooooom. Booooooom.*

"Hear that?" Joe says, glad to be able to change the subject. "Cannon fire. Sounds like a convict escaped from the Prison Hulks out on the river."

Boooooooom.

Pip starts to shake.

"Look what you've done, Joe. You've scared the poor boy. Let's eat."

Late that night the weather changes. Pip can feel it, lying awake in his tiny sleeping loft. The wind's blowing, and there's a raw, clammy feel to the air.

Pip gets up. He sneaks through the house, moving as slow and as light as he can. He hears Joe and his sister snoring. *Honk-zue. Honk-zue . . . .*

Pip moves into the kitchen. He takes a loaf of bread and a juicy pork pie his sister's made for Christmas dinner.

Now he goes to Joe's toolbox. He opens it. The lid creaks: *eeeeeeeee.* It sounds incredibly loud. Pip stops, wondering if he woke up Joe and sis.

Honk-zue, honk-zue.

Guess not. He opens the lid the rest of the way. He feels around for a file. *Clang. Clank.* He listens again.

Honk-zue, honk-zue.

Pip finds a file. He carefully opens the front door. *Creeeeeeeeak.*

Outside, the fog has rolled in, like pea soup. Pip can barely see ten feet. He keeps moving downhill.

Storytelling Tip:

Too many SFX? Possibly, for you and me, but from the point of view of a five-year-old, there can never be too many sound effects.

Suddenly, there it is: the church spire rising up out of the swirling fog. Pip finds himself in the creepy graveyard. The fog makes it a weird maze. Pip clutches the food and the file.

"Hello? Sir? Are you here? Hello?"

Suddenly, the man rises up from behind a stone, like a zombie.

"Oh!"

"Shh. Did you bring the vittles?"

Pip nods and hands over the bread and the pork pie. The convict grabs the food and takes a hungry bite. Mmm. Mmm. Num. "Good pie." He snarfs it.

The he looks at Pip. "How about a file . . . ?"

Pip hands it over.

The convict takes it, staring at Pip. "You did it. You brought me everything I asked for."

"I said I would."

The convict looks at Pip, in awe, for another moment. Then suddenly, he sits down and starts sawing away at the chain. *Heeee. Heeee. Heeee.* He works fast.

Suddenly, there's shouting and barking dogs. "Over here! The dogs are making a beeline for the church. Follow the dogs."

"Oh, no," Pip says.

The convict looks toward the shouting. Then he says to Pip, "You better go while you can. Go on, go. Or they'll catch you." He starts filing again.

"Go!"

The last thing Pip hears as he runs through the church-yard is the sound of filing.

Pip runs past the sheriff's men and the prison guards—nasty men—but they don't see him because of the fog.

Pip sprints up the street. The guards are shouting. "Down here! We've got him!"

Pip rushes into his house just as Joe and his sister are waking up. "What's happening?"

"The, the convict," Pip stammers.

"Hey," his sister cries, from the kitchen. "The pork pie's gone! And a loaf of bread!"

"Somebody's been in my toolbox," Joe says. "They left the lid open. They took a file!"

They look at Pip.

"It was you," his sister says. "Wasn't it?"

Pip stares. He doesn't know what to say.

"Get the Tickler."

Then there's shouting from outside. Sis and Joe pull their robes close and go out. Pip follows.

The sheriff's men and the guards are leading the shackled convict up the street. His head is bent. People are waking up and pointing. "Good riddance," they say. "Throw away the key!"

The convict looks up—as if by magic—and sees young Pip. He stops. The guards pull at his shackles. "Keep moving, you."

"It were here," he says. "This is the house I broke into. I took a pork pie, a loaf of bread, and a file."

"So it was you!" says Pip's sister.

"It were me."

Pip looks at him, swallowing.

"Me, and me alone."

"C'mon, you," the guard says as they yank the convict away.

The last thing Pip sees through the fog is the convict's eyes, his smiling blue eyes.

Story Points: "Great Expectations"

★ Pip lives in a claustrophobically small house he shares with his stern sister and her husband, Joe.

★ Pip leaves the house and approaches the deserted churchyard.

★ We see the grave of Pip's departed parents. Pip cries, missing them.

★ Suddenly, the convict appears.

★ The convict forces poor Pip to steal food and a file so the convict can escape his chafing chains.

★ Pip goes home. In the middle of the night, he gets up and swipes a meat pie, a loaf of bread, and, from Joe's toolbox, a file.

★ He goes out. Now it's foggy and weird. The church suddenly appears. So does the convict. Pip gives him the food. The convict eats hungrily and then files at his chains. He's amazed that Pip did this for him.

★ Suddenly, dogs and guards appear! The convict runs off.

★ A chase ensues. Pip runs through the foggy town. He hears the chase, but he makes it home.

★ Sister blames Pip for the missing meat pie, etc. Joe sees that Pip is perspiring and his shoes are muddy. Joe's also suspicious.

★ The convict is caught. The deputies lead him past Pip's house. The convict stops. "This is the house where I stole food and this file." Pip is saved. The convict smiles at Pip as the deputies drag him into the fog.

The Secret Garden

Like *Great Expectations*, this marvelous story, by Frances Hodgson Burnett, is set in England, in a very specific and special place: the Yorkshire moors — sweeping and immense, storm-blasted, rain-pelted, with violent explosions of lightning, bursting with strange life, with hardy, independent people speaking a rich and unique dialect.

The Secret Garden also contains another very English motif: the sprawling manor house with locked rooms, twisting corridors going nowhere, and libraries filled with unread books, bizarre knick-knacks, and years of dust. Sounds—weird, other-worldly sounds—carry through the house, as if across a still lake. The master of the manor, Craven, is strange, flighty, and grief-stricken.

And, of course, there are the gardens, stretching this way and that, overgrown—with a mysteriously locked door.

Wonderful.

The Secret Garden thus gives plenty of opportunity for a storyteller to transport the tellee to a vividly new and alien world. Children adore this, so take plenty of time with it.

Our hero, Mary Lennox, is at first an off-putting, snooty, arrogant, and self-centered sourpuss if ever there was one. Don't pull back. Children adore characters like this. The nastier she is in the beginning, the more we will pull for her when she becomes a delight: smart, solicitous, energetic, and genuinely concerned about the welfare of others.

This bedtime story adaptation is extremely loose, as you will quickly discover if you have read or choose to read the Burnett original (which I hope you will). Burnett has written a multi-layered novel, animated by a rich plot and potent symbolism. There is no way I can reproduce it and create a story that can be done in three or so nights. A vast amount of first-rate material has, of necessity, been left out. Still, I believe, as with my take on Dickens, that I have adhered to the spirit of the original.

This is a fairly complicated story, but there is little in it that is frightening—creepy, perhaps yes, but not scary. The story also has a strong female protagonist, which is a very good thing. I think "The Secret Garden" will work for all ages.

Night One

The moor.

Mary Lennox first saw it at night, through the wet windows of the moving carriage. She kept rubbing at the window, trying to get a decent look.

Boom! Thunder crashed, lightning flashed, and she could see it.

Wow.

Do you know what a moor is? There are no trees, but moors are huge and wild, filled with arroyos and canyons, heather, craggy rocks, and rolling hills. They teem with life: birds, deer, foxes, and wonderful flowers. In Yorkshire, England, where this story takes place, the moor has been turned into the North York Moors National Park. It's huge. I'll find some pictures for you tomorrow.

Mary's carriage kept clattering on and on and on. Mary shivered and drew her coat closer.

She was alone.

Mary was English, but she had grown up in India—this was back in the days when the English ran India, what was called the British Raj. Mary's parents had died in a cholera epidemic, and so young Mary had traveled on a ship all the way to England, alone, to live with her Uncle Craven in Yorkshire. She'd never met him, and it was cold in Yorkshire—not like India. She daydreamed, thinking of her old life: servants, sunshine, wild flowers, heat—not like here.

Hya! The driver was lashing at the horses. Boom! More lightning. The rain grew heavier. "I'm not going to cry," she whispered to herself. "I won't cry."

Finally, the carriage arrived. It was past midnight, and still raining, when the driver pulled down the long—very

Here is an opportunity for lots of thrilling SFX.

Storytelling Tip:

One of Ms. Burnett's masterful effects with The Secret Garden *is her evocation of the long-gone Yorkshire accent. This adds great richness and depth to the book. The local characters speak with a unique vocabulary, using "thee," "thou," and "thy." Unfortunately, I'm not English, and I cannot even begin to approximate this accent. So, I've left it out (though this breaks my heart). Perhaps you are more cognizant of it. If you are, then by all means, go for it. In any case, it would be terrific if the teller here could give the local characters some kind of down-home flavor, even though it probably wouldn't be accurate.*

long—driveway to the old house. A small, wiry woman, Mrs. Medlock, came out to help Mary with her cases. The rain pelted down. "Hurry up," Mrs. Medlock snarled, "or we'll catch our deaths."

Mary caught a quick glimpse of a rambling and ancient manor house, with the moor rolling just beyond—like an infinite, rough sea.

Inside, the house was cold and dark. Mrs. Medlock had a small candle, and it threw creepy shadows on the wall. She led Mary down one corridor and up another, rambling constantly: "Late, that driver was. Bah, he's always late, and I don't care if it is spitting rain—I need my sleep. Mr. Craven is here, but he's left particular word that he's not to be disturbed. Not by no one."

"Mr. Craven, my uncle, is here?"

"Aye, but I told you, he's not to be disturbed. Is that clear?"

"Yes, ma'am."

"Here's your room."

She opened the door, and Mary walked in. The room was big and dark, with lots of stained oak and plush red velvet furniture. There was a cold fireplace. Mary shivered and wondered if she could build a fire, but she saw no wood.

"Well, if ye won't be needing anything else?" Without waiting for Mary to answer, she left. "G'night!"

Boom, the door closed, and Mary was alone.

The room was cold. Mary noticed that the bed was large, canopied, and filled with toasty-looking blankets. She threw on her nightdress and hopped in bed.

"I will not cry."

Mary lay awake for a long time before she fell asleep.

She awoke to the sound of the maid cleaning ashes out of the fireplace, tossing them into a metal trash. She was making no attempt to be quiet.

"Excuse me," Mary said, as imperiously as possible, "but do you have to make so much noise?"

"There you are," the maid replied cheerfully. "I thought you would never wake up. My name is Martha Sowerby. You're Mary."

"You may call me Miss Lennox." Mary wasn't used to servants being so forward. "Miss Sowerby, will you bring me a dress, please?"

"I put your dresses in your closet, Mary."

"Bring me one, a white one."

Martha looked at her for a moment. "I don't fetch dresses."

"I'm wearing a nightdress."

"No worries. We're friends."

"We're not friends!" Mary exclaimed, shocked. The nerve of servants here. Friends? Hmph. "Now please bring me a dress."

"No," Martha said cheerfully. "And I'm to remind you that Mr. Craven must not be disturbed, and you are not to go into any of the upstairs rooms without permission," and with that she left.

"Well," Mary said. She got out of bed and got dressed.

The house was even bigger than she'd imagined. The hallways were creaky and shadowy. It seemed like Mary's footsteps boomed. She stopped outside a door and listened—nothing. She put her hand on the knob. *Should I?*

She didn't.

Outside it was cold, but the sun was shining. Mary could see the gate and the weird Yorkshire moor beyond

Okay, okay. I don't really know what sounds – if any – robins make.

it. It looked harmless, but Mary had the sense that it hid great danger. She shuddered.

Mary went into the gardens. Like the house, they seemed to go on forever, without any plan. Mary followed a wall. It went on and on and curved. Mary wondered what was on the other side.

"Oh!"

It was a robin, sitting on top of a wall, tweeting happily away. *Bee-beep! Bee-beep!*

A robin isn't a big deal to us, but little Mary, fresh from India, had never seen one before, and she was delighted. She followed it along as it flew from the wall to a branch, then back to the wall. *Bee-beep! Bee-beep!* Mary giggled.

The robin flew around a curve. Mary ran.

And collided with a gruff old man: Ben Weatherstaff. He was holding a hoe—he'd been clearing old weeds. "Hey," he grumbled. "Watch where you're going, Missy."

"Oh, I'm so sor—" Mary'd been about to apologize, but then she drew herself up. "I beg your pardon. Can you tell me," she asked, gesturing at the robin, "What is that?"

"S'a bird," Weatherstaff said, not looking up. He started hoeing again.

"I know it's a bird. What kind of bird?"

"It's a robin. You must be the new girl."

"I am."

Ben looked her over, then growled, "Bah."

"Are you the gardener?" Ben said nothing. Mary stamped her foot. "You will answer my question, please."

"Yes, Miss. I's the gardener."

"Can you tell me, how do I get to the other side of this wall?"

Weatherstaff looked at her, but this time there was real

fear in his eyes. "You mustn't go there."

"Whyever not?"

"It's locked, by Mr. Craven himself. He's left specific instructions: no one's ever to go in there."

"How long has it been — ?"

"For years! Ten years. You mustn't even think of going in there."

"Who has the key?"

"There's no key!"

And with that, Ben started hoeing madly, ignoring Mary.

Well, she thought, *these people certainly are odd.*

Bee-beep! Bee-beep! It was the robin, sitting in the branches of a tall tree — on the other side of the wall.

That night, as she was drifting off to sleep — just like you — Mary heard something. It was so faint she wasn't even sure she heard it. She went out into the dark corridor. "There it is," she told herself. "I do hear it."

Crying.

Night Two

Mary fell into a routine: Up at eight, when the Yorkshire sun poured in through her windows. Ate breakfast all alone at the big table in the dining room — the same thing every time: cold bacon and oatmeal with clotted cream.

You know what clotted cream is? I've never had any; they only make it in Britain. It's cream that's been reduced and reduced until it's as thick as yogurt and as rich as butter. It can't be good for you, but I bet it's yummy.

Every now and then, Mary would ask Mrs. Medlock, "Is my uncle available today?"

Storytelling Tip:

Time passes now, and that makes this a good stopping point. I'll call this the end of Night One. However, you could certainly soldier on, if Sweetie Pie seems amenable.

"Not today, Miss. He's left word that he's not to be disturbed."

"Oh."

One day, Martha brought her a present. "For me?" Martha nodded. Mary opened it.

It was a skipping rope: a jump rope.

Martha beamed. "Me ma made it."

"Oh," Mary said. She wanted to say, "Even though I'm such a snoot." But she didn't. Instead she said, "Tell your ma thanks."

"Let's try it!"

They jumped. And they giggled and screamed with laughter. The two girls made the old house come alive again.

A few days later, Mrs. Medlock came in as Mary was eating her oatmeal. She peered at Mary.

"Is there something wrong, Mrs. Medlock?"

"Mr. Craven will see you."

"Now? My uncle will see me now?"

"This way."

Mrs. Medlock led Mary down a long corridor, then another, then up two flights of steps, and then down another hall. At the end of it, a double door led into a large room, with a roaring fire. The room was quite warm, and although it was a sunny day, the blinds were pulled.

A thin man, wearing an expensive wool suit, stood facing the fire. He didn't turn around. "Did you bring her?" he asked in a reedy voice.

"Yes, Mr. Craven."

Craven turned to face her.

"Oh." Mary took a step back, instinctively. His face was misshapen, and he had shaved badly. His hair was thinning and gray.

But it was his eyes. They swam, bloodshot and liquid, with pure, unassuageable grief. To look into his eyes was to cry. Mary peered down at the floor. It was all she could do.

"I'm sorry, I've quite forgotten your name."

"Mary, sir. Mary Lennox."

"Mary. Of course. Well. You look . . . a little skinny. I'll have Mrs. Medlock give you clotted cream with your oatmeal."

"She already does, sir."

"Well. I'll have her double your portion."

"Thank you, sir."

"I wish . . . "

"Yes . . . ?"

"I wish I could be a better guardian, but I'm very forgetful and preoccupied, so there it is."

"I see."

"And, well, I want to tell you, also, that I've been called away to town."

"To London?"

"Yes, and after that, I will be traveling on the continent for a few months. I'm afraid I will be unreachable by any means. But, not to worry. Mrs. Medlock will take good care of you."

"Thank you, sir."

"Well. That will be all." With that, he turned back to the fire. Mary and Mrs. Medlock left.

A few days later, Mary was walking by the garden wall. It was warmer now. Spring was coming. Indeed, a few green shoots were sticking up.

Bee-beep! Bee-beep!

The robin! He was perched in the tree on the other side of the wall. Mary followed the wall. "I so wish I could go over there," she said to herself. She rounded a corner.

And there it was. There was a pile of loose dirt.

But that's not what Mary was looking at.

She saw a big hole. It was probably dug by one of the big Yorkshire badgers.

But that's not what she was looking at.

Can you guess?

It was a key.

Mary fell to her knees next to the pile of dirt and drew it out. Yes, it really was a key—rusty and blackened, like it had been buried. "I bet old Mr. Badger uncovered this," Mary said. She looked at the wall. "But where's the lock?"

She slowly followed the wall. It circled and circled. But there was no door.

She came to a place where vines and branches were overgrown, hanging down. "I wonder . . . " she said. She pulled the branches away.

And there it was: a thick wooden door. The hinges were thick with rust.

There was a large keyhole.

Mary looked at the key in her hand.

She put it in the lock. It seemed to fit. She tried to turn it, but it wouldn't move. She used two hands. It still wouldn't budge . . . .

Wait a minute. It turned, just a little. She put her back it into and turned the key with as much strength as her ten-year-old body could muster, which was quite a lot.

The lock snapped open.

Mary caught her breath.

She pushed on the door. *Creeeeeeak.* The door opened.

Mary peered through the door. She couldn't see much, just more vines and branches hanging down. She took a deep breath.

Then pushed her way in.

The secret garden.

It was smaller than she imagined. It was arranged in a circle, with flower beds and a few benches. One of the benches was collapsed, all rotten. The vines on the wall had gotten out of hand. In some places, the vines were growing across the ground, choking out the flowers.

In the middle was a big tree, an apple tree. This was the tree in which the robin had sat chirping away. The tree was old and gnarled. And under the tree was a bench, perfectly preserved, almost as if it were brand new.

Mary noticed that the vines were invading a flower bed. Green shoots were peeking up. Mary fell to her knees, and without really thinking, she started working, pulling the vines and leaves away.

That night, Mary told Martha about the secret garden. She wasn't sure she should—maybe Martha would betray her. After all, Ben Weatherstaff had made it quite clear that no one was allowed to go into the garden—no one.

But Mary couldn't contain herself. She had to tell someone! She rambled on, then said, "I need tools: a spade, or a hoe. I don't even know what they're called. And a small shovel, and a, a, a—"

"A trowel," Martha offered.

"That's it! If I gave you some money, could you buy them for me? I'm not allowed to leave the estate."

Martha didn't say anything. Gulp—Mary started to fear she had said too much, that Martha was going to tell on her.

Storytelling Tip:

Dickon is an odd name, but it's the name that Ms. Burnett assigned to this wonderful character. If you're uncomfortable with it, you might change it to Dillon or simply shorten it to Dick.

Then Martha smiled. "My brother Dickon could buy all that stuff for you."

And he did. The next day, he showed up with spades, two hoes, a trowel, a shovel, clippers—everything.

And you know what else he brought?

A baby fox.

"I found it out on the moor. I'm going to nurse it until it grows up."

"It's adorable!"

And it was, with its little snout, its red coat, and its big bushy tail. Mary couldn't see how the wee thing could even walk.

Mary and Dickon—Martha had duties in the house—worked in the secret garden all day. The sun was high and warm. Spring had come to the moor, and the garden was bursting with life.

That night, she heard it again: crying.

This time, Mary was determined to find out if it was a ghost. She went into the hall and followed the sound, down a corridor and up another. Sometimes it stopped altogether, and Mary had to wait for a long time before the sound started up again. Sometimes it was loud, like wailing. And sometimes you could barely hear it. Up a set of stairs and down another hallway.

Finally, she found it. It was a hidden room. Mary knew it was hidden because there was no door, just a set of fake leather books at the end of a hall. She hesitated, listening.

Then, with new courage, she pushed the hidden door open and walked into a large room. She pulled back the curtains covering a bed.

Who knows what she expected to find?

It was boy, about her age. Tears streamed down his face.

Night Three

"Who are you?" Mary said to the boy.

He didn't reply, he just burrowed into the covers, trying to hide. Mary could hear him wailing.

"I asked you a question," she said, with a sternness she didn't really feel. There was something about this boy that kept her from getting angry. She pulled back the covers, revealing a boy wearing pajamas. He was painfully skinny, and pale. "Don't cry," she said kindly. "Just tell me who you are."

"My n-n-n-n-name is, is, is . . . "

"Yes?"

"C-C-C-Colin."

"Colin."

"Y-Y-Yes."

"Do you live in here?"

Colin nodded.

"I've been here for months. Why haven't I ever met you?"

"I'm not allowed to leave this room."

"Whyever not?"

"There's something wrong with my back."

Mary looked at him. Colin looked a little sickly, maybe, but apart from that . . . "I can't see anything wrong with you."

"I'm a cripple."

Mary noticed that there was a wooden wheelchair next to the bed. "Oh. I see. Well. Why are you here?"

"I'm Mr. Craven's son."

"His son!"

Colin nodded. "He makes me stay here. I think because

he doesn't want anyone to see me."

"You're my cousin!"

"I guess so."

"Who takes care of you?"

"Mrs. Medlock brings me food. She always complains that I'm not much of an eater. I think I'm going to die."

"You'll do no such thing."

"Very soon, I fear."

"I won't permit dying. Or crying. What you should do now is sleep."

"I'm very tired."

"Good. And I'll be back to see you tomorrow." She looked at him, smiling. "We're going to be very good friends."

The next day, Dickon came by to work in the secret garden. Very carefully and quietly, they stole through the house to Colin's room.

They went inside. It was dark. The curtains were pulled. Mary yanked them open. "You need sunlight."

Colin was in bed, blinking. "Who are you?" he said to Dickon.

"Name's Dickon. I brought you something." He pulled open his jacket and brought out the baby fox. He laid him on Colin's bed.

"Ohhhhhhhh," said Colin. "He's wonderful!"

He played with the baby fox as Mary went around the room, opening curtains and windows.

Finally, she faced Colin. "You need to go outside."

"I couldn't."

"You can and you will."

"I'm a cripple."

"I don't believe there's anything wrong with you. And

even if there is, you still need some sun. Now let's get you into the chair."

"Yes, ma'am," Colin said, even though Mary was no older than him.

Very carefully, Mary and Dickon took Colin into the hall, down the stairs. *Creeeeeeeeak.* Down the series of hall-ways to an unobtrusive side door.

Finally, Colin was outside. The sun hit his face, and he blinked, shading his eyes. "Ohhhhhhhhh."

"Something wrong?"

"I'm not used to this."

"Take a deep breath. The air is good for you."

Colin coughed.

"We're going to take you to the secret garden." They wheeled Colin along the old wall, until they came to the door. Mary opened it, and in they went.

They put Colin's chair in the middle of the garden. "Oh, it's beautiful," he said. "Beautiful."

They let Colin hold the baby fox as they got to work. The garden was starting to look nice. The bulbs were grow-ing: tulips, crocuses, baby-bells, lilies-of-the-valley, and hyacinths. The vines, back in their place, were greening up. There were leaves on the trees. Mary and Dickon got caught up in the work.

Mary looked at Colin and saw that tears were streaming down his face. "Oh! Are you all right?"

"I, I better go back to my, my room."

Dickon and Mary took him back.

"I had a wonderful time."

"There's nothing wrong with you."

After that, Dickon and Mary took Colin to the garden every day. His color improved—along with his appetite.

"Today, I asked for more oatmeal. Mrs. Medlock was amazed." He sat in his chair, basking in the sunshine, sometimes wheeling to get Mary or Dickon a tool. He watched as the secret garden took shape.

Then, one day, they noticed Ben Weatherstaff peering over the wall, watching them work. Mary was terrified — after all, Ben had told her to stay away from the garden, in no uncertain terms. She let him into the garden.

Ben stared at Colin, in amazement. "Master Colin . . . ?"

"Yes."

"We thought you was dead."

"Well, I'm not, as you can see. Mr. Craven — my father — hid me away. He told me I was a . . . that I was disabled. But there is nothing wrong with me. This garden is restoring me."

Tears filled old Ben's eyes.

"Mr. Weatherstaff," Mary said, "perhaps you should sit," and she led the old gardener to a bench.

"I never thought it was possible. This garden . . . " He took a deep breath. "Mrs. Craven — Colin's mother — died in this garden."

"In here?" Mary asked.

Ben nodded. "This place was her pride and joy. She spent hours here, me and her. You see, it was my job to keep the place nice. One day, Mrs. Craven was reading under the old apple tree and a branch broke off, fell, and hit her on the head. She hung on for a few days, but then, well, she . . . she . . . "

"Oh, dear."

"No one could tell why it broke. It weren't windy, and the tree ain't that old. It just happened. Mr. Craven went crazy with grief, and one day, he locked up this garden, buried the key, and forbid us to go in." He looked at Mary. "Then you come along."

"My mother died in here?"

"Yessir, Mr. Colin," Ben said, "sitting on that bench there."

Suddenly, there was a commotion in the front of the manor.

Mrs. Medlock appeared. She had a wild, frightened look on her face. "It's Mr. Craven!" she cried.

"Is he back?" Mary asked.

"There's something wrong with him! I've never seen him like this! He's asking for you, it's all he can talk about! 'Mary, Mary, Mary!' Hurry!"

Mary followed Mrs. Medlock to the front of the big house. They found Mr. Craven and, indeed, he had a wild and crazed look on his face. It was rather scary.

He took Mary in his arms. "Is it true, Mary Lennox? That the garden lives again? Is it true?"

"Yes, sir. I've been working in there every day."

"I had a dream! I had a vivid dream about the garden! I could see every inch of it, and the flowers were all in bloom; the vines—the apple tree was budding out with new life. Is it true?"

"Would you like to see?"

Craven stepped back. "I'm frightened." It was true. Mary could see that he was trembling.

"I'll show you."

"No. I'm, I'm frightened."

"You came all this way. You might as well see the garden."

"My wife . . . " He didn't know what else to say.

"Come." Mary took Craven's hand and led him to the

garden.

When they were almost there, she stopped, and said. "I have a surprise for you." She turned and called out. "Colin? Can you hear me?"

"Yes."

"Colin?" Craven said, incredulously.

"Come here, please. Someone wants to say hello."

"But . . ."

"You can. I know you can."

A few moments went by.

Then Colin appeared, coming out of the garden. He was walking—by himself. He was wobbly and staggering (his legs hadn't been used in ages), but he was moving on his own steam.

"Colin?"

"Hello, Papa."

Craven ran to his son and embraced him. "I had no idea! I'm so happy."

"I'm going to live forever!"

Then they turned and walked into the secret garden. It exploded with colorful new life.

"It's beautiful."

Story Points: "The Secret Garden"

Night One

★ Mary, alone, travels to the Yorkshire moor at night. The moor is storm-blasted, wild, vast, and seemingly uninhabited.

★ The carriage reaches the huge and weird manor house—old, creaky, and creepy. Take your time with all this.

★ Weird Mrs. Medlock shows Mary to her large, but cold, room. No

Uncle Craven.

★ Mary meets Martha, the maid. She tries to pull rank, but cheerful Martha shoots her down.

★ Mrs. Medlock keeps telling Mary that Mr. Craven cannot be seen.

★ Mary explores the house and the endless, disorganized gardens.

★ Mary meets gruff and paranoid Ben Weatherstaff. He warns her away from the secret garden.

★ Mary sees the robin, chirping away from the top of a tree inside the secret garden.

★ That night, Mary hears mysterious crying in the house.

Night Two

★ Mary's routine: breakfast and hanging around the huge house alone.

★ Martha presents Mary with a jump rope, and the two girls become friends—their laughter echoes down the empty corridors of the manor house.

★ Finally, after weeks have passed, Mrs. Medlock brings Mary to meet Uncle Craven. It's a strange encounter. Craven is thin, racked with weird emotion. He tells Mary that he is leaving for months and will be incommunicado.

★ Mary, following the robin, finds the key to the secret garden (a badger has uncovered it).

★ Mary enters the garden, explores it, and starts working.

★ Martha's brother, Dickon, brings gardening tools and a baby fox he has found on the moor.

★ That night, Mary hears the crying again, and this time she follows it to a secret room, where she discovers a thin, sickly boy.

Night Three

★ A scene between Mary and the boy, Colin. Colin explains that he's Craven's son (Mary's cousin). He claims he is dying. Mary refuses to accept this.

★ The next day, Dickon comes by to work on the garden. He has the fox. He and Mary sneak into Colin's room. They show him the baby fox. Colin is delighted.

★ Then Mary has an idea: very carefully and quietly, they wheel Colin outside. At first, he is terrified by the sun and the air. They take him to the secret garden. He watches as they work.

★ They take Colin to the garden every day. His strength and appetite improve. He begins to believe Mary when she tells him that there is nothing wrong with him.

★ Old Ben discovers them. Tearfully, he tells the story: Mrs. Craven died in the garden, in a freak accident, and Uncle Craven, mad with grief, shut it up. Ben is amazed that Colin is alive and that the garden is thriving.

★ There is a commotion: Craven has returned. He tells Mary that he had a strangely vivid dream that his wife's old garden was once again coming alive. The dream made him return.

★ Mary admits that she has restored the garden. She offers to show him. She takes him to the entrance. Then says, "Colin?" Colin appears, walking. He wobbles, but he moves on his own, for the first time. Craven is amazed. Colin falls into his arms. "I'm going to live forever!"

★ The secret garden is resplendent.

Fairy Tales

Ah, finally, we've come to it: the premiere type of story in the dark, the most important, the kind children adore and thrive on — the one they crave and need:

Fairy Tales

The old English word *faeries* originally referred to tiny winged creatures — think Tinkerbell — who inhabit a magic parallel world, what the great J.R.R. Tolkein called the "secondary world." These faeries occasionally visit our world, but they rarely make their magical presence known, except to a very select group of ordinary individuals. Faerie tales were stories about these sweet-natured beings. These adorable beings are referred to as sprites, brownies, elves, pixies, leprechauns, etc.

Since the early days of these faeries, the definition of fairy tales has dramatically expanded to include a wide range of styles and plots. Some fairy tales are realistic, and others are completely fantastical. They hold one thing in common: the ordinariness of the hero.

Fairy tale heroes are nice but essentially unremarkable — sweet-natured Dorothy (*The Wizard of Oz*), shy Red Riding Hood, lovable but dumb Jack ("Jack and the Beanstalk"). They encounter something magical, larger than life, and impossible to understand. Often, what they encounter is dangerous and horrifically frightening: ravenous wolves, fiery mountains, or angry giants. Inevitably, though, our intrepid heroes pluck up their courage and forge forward. Fairy tales almost always portray thrilling bravery.

They often involve a journey, too. Sometimes, the journey is close to home and not that far, as when Little Red Riding Hood makes her way through the scary woods—again, courageous—to Grandma's house. Or when Jack climbs the amazing beanstalk growing right outside his kitchen window.

Sometimes the journey takes the hero vast distances, as in Tolkien's three volume masterwork *The Lord of the Rings* (which, as you undoubtedly know, has become a gorgeously rendered twelve-hour film). An ordinary hobbit, amiable Frodo, makes his way past howling orcs and flying dragons ridden by vile death heads, up sheer cliffs guarded by giant spiders, and over battlefields filled with dead soldiers to, finally, fiery Mount Doom.

Fairy tale heroes have a marked propensity to get themselves into trouble. Jack is a dreamer, easily swayed by the shifty salesman selling magic bean seeds. Sometimes their situations make them vulnerable: Hansel and Gretel are newly orphaned, wandering lost through the woods.

But sometimes, the fairy tale hero is simply in the wrong place at the wrong time. The Fisherman snares a dirty old bottle in his net. He rubs it to see if there's anything inside, and bingo, he frees a magical—and dangerous—genie. Dorothy just happens to be in the house when the tornado whisks her off to Oz.

Sometimes there is an explicit invitation to make the journey. The heroes may not fully understand the import of what they are going to do, but they do make a conscious choice. Gandalf the Wizard hands the ring to Frodo and says, "Will you take care of this?" Frodo accepts the ring. Does he understand what "taking care" of the ring will entail? Of course not, but he does make a choice.

Fairy tales—at least the ones we use for stories in the dark—always, always, always have happy endings. (For our children's sake, we'll ignore the gruesome, not-so-happy endings of many folk tales written by Hans Christian Anderson and collected by the famous Grimm Brothers. We're trying to induce sleep, after all, not cause nightmares.) The heroes go through heck, they encounter mighty and deadly enemies, they make friends and allies, and they find resources of courage and cleverness they never thought they possessed. Indeed, often they become hugely powerful. They grow into something they never would have imagined.

And then they come home. They return to their old lives, wiser perhaps, and more confident. But they always come home, and they always live happily ever after.

Young children passionately identify with the heroes of fairy tales. They respond to the ordinariness of a fairy tale hero, because this is how they see themselves: average Joes surrounded by a world they don't really understand, a world populated by people with powers and prowess of which they can only dream. Children know what it means to find the woods frightening, filled with shadows and ravenous wolves, or to be suckered in by a wily and cynical salesman. The heroes of fairy tales act the way a child would.

Moreover, young children, like fairy tale heroes, live in a world charged with magic. Grown-ups look at a running stream and say, "Here we have an example of gravity at work," or they hear thunder and say, "That results from the discharge of static electricity in the rainclouds."

But a child sees the stream, hears the thunder, and says, "The water runs because it's alive, and the thunder is enormous creatures shouting at each other." These are reasonable conclusions, from a child's point of view.

When you tell a child a fairy tale, you are validating their sweet belief in magic. You are saying, yes, this world is indeed filled with power and magic, with strange, scary creatures, with scary woods and deserted cities and haunted houses. You are validating their experience and conferring upon the child, perhaps for the first time ever, real power.

Moreover, and more importantly, you are telling your child: you can face this magic. You can overcome these obstacles. This is a hugely significant message.

This is where the courage of fairy tale heroes comes into play. Children hear a fairy tale and they say: yes, I can be like this. I don't have to be beaten down by the world. Goblins and ogres and orcs can be defeated, if I can stay the course and trust myself. I will stay calm. I will find friends and allies. Courage and the requisite skills will come to me. I will remain true to myself.

This is why children need fairy tales.

Stacy, the Cowardly Crocodile

Yes, yes, I can hear you snickering: "Stacy?"

I will admit that the choice of a character name is a personal one, and if you wish to change it, please feel free. You might, indeed, change the hero's gender: Jason, the Cowardly Crocodile.

Still, I think there's a lot of mileage to be had in making Stacy a member of the female sex and in using one of our more popular twenty-first century names. It gives the piece an unusual oomph and a particular relevance to young listeners. There's a pretty good chance that your child knows a Stacy.

This story, along with the "Huron Creation Myth," is an example of a major storytelling theme: anthropomorphism, the giving of human qualities to animals. The Disney Corporation has built a vast international entertainment empire on anthropomorphism, and you, a teller of stories in the dark, should become conversant with the form. Young children love it.

Another useful theme here: difference. Stacy isn't like the other crocodiles, and they have to learn to accept her. This is a theme to which young children instinctively respond.

What follows is a short, "all-ages" version of the Stacy story. This is followed by a few ideas for expanding the material into longer, multi-night serials. This would be particularly useful if the Stacy stories fly. However, the longer versions up the "danger quotient." And, being longer, they are more complicated, which means the longer stories might not be appropriate for the youngest of the young.

> *S*tacy was a scaredy-croc.
> Don't get me wrong. Stacy was a crocodile, no question. She had big strong jaws, sharp nasty teeth, claws, scales, a big tail, beady eyes, and even a scary crocodile snout.
>
> Those jaws. Whew. Here's the deal with crocodiles: you don't want those jaws to clamp down on you, 'cause unless that croc is feeling particularly mellow—and most crocs never are—they'll clamp down and never let go. One look at Stacy, and any person with half a brain would run, not walk, to dry land and get as far away from Stacy as possible.
>
> But Stacy wasn't mean at all.
>
> "Where are you all going?" she would say. "I just want to have an interesting philosophical discussion. Aw, heck."
>
> All the other crocs made fun of Stacy. "Stacy is a scaredy-croc, Stacy is a scaredy-croc." Needless to say, this made Stacy feel bad, so she usually went to a far-away corner of the swamp where none of the other crocs ever went. She stayed by herself, hiding in the cattails.
>
> "The square root of a triangle is equal to its hypotenuse cubed, divided by pi." *Sniffle, sniffle.*
>
> That was the vibe for Stacy. She didn't want to do all

those crocodile things, like chasing small animals and un-suspecting fish. She wanted to think deep thoughts—and to talk about them. "I believe that stars are huge burning balls of gas, a kazillion miles away."

Some of the swamp birds had figured out that Stacy wouldn't hurt them, so they flew down and landed on her snout. "I dare ya to eat me. I double-dare ya. I double-dog-dare ya." Then they pecked at her nostrils. This always made Stacy sneeze. *Ah-choo!*

Stacy would say, "Everybody hates me," and off she would go to her lonely hiding place.

But it wasn't true that everybody hated Stacy.

She had a friend, a good friend: Jacob. In fact, if it weren't for Jacob, Stacy would have starved. Jacob brought her tasty crocodile morsels: water weeds, rotten fish filets, dead turtles, and various crunchy insects—all that yummy stuff that crocodiles eat. Then Jacob would hang around while Stacy rambled about hypotenuses and priori proofs of existence. Jacob didn't understand a word of this, but he liked the heck out of Stacy. Sometimes, when he could get a word in edgewise, Jacob'd bring her up-to-date on the latest swamp gossip (although Stacy wasn't very interest-ed in this).

He never called her a scaredy-croc.

Then, one very hot summer day in the swamp—

And by the way this story takes place in what we would call Australia, a very hot continent of the other side of the world. Of course, Stacy and Jacob and the other crocs had no idea that they lived in a country called Australia. All they knew was that they lived in a huge swamp, and that was that.

—Stacy was dozing and dreaming about rectangles intersecting with each other. It was so hot, and there were almost no sounds. Usually the birds made a pretty good racket, but today there was the odd insect buzz, and that was more or less that. Stacy lazily opened her eyes, and that's when she saw it.

Know what it was?

A human.

What's that?

Stacy had never seen a person before, living like she did in the isolated swamp. *Oh, my! He's so tall! And so, so black, and he only has two legs, and what's that long stick he's carrying with the really sharp point? Oh. Is he gonna stick me with it? Do I have to whap him with my tail or something? I don't wanna do that! Doesn't he know I'm a scaredy-croc?*

I gotta tell you about this guy. His name was Adoni, and he was what they call an Aboriginal Australian—similar to Native Americans. They lived in Australia for thousands of years before the European settlers came. One of their really cool customs is that boys around age fifteen go on "walkabouts," trips through the wilderness that they take by themselves, as a coming-of-age ritual. That's what Adoni is doing.

Stacy stared at Adoni. She tensed up. Adoni raised his spear, ready to strike. There was a taut moment. Then, Adoni lowered his spear, and Stacy relaxed.

Then, Adoni smiled, a big grin crossing his face.

What is that? Stacy wondered.

Then he did something amazing: he stepped on top of Stacy. He stood there, his knees bent, balancing carefully, still holding the sharp stick—the spear, actually. *He's standing on me,* Stacy said to herself, in amazement.

Then she realized, *He's standing on me!* She heaved her

Storytelling Tip:

Do I have the first idea what Aboriginal Australians would use to make rope? I do not. "Gum tree bark" sounds good, and I do want [insert your child's name here] to think I'm smart, so I'm faking it. She'll never know.

body convulsively upward, and Adoni went flying, flipping up into the air. Stacy splashed off as fast as she could, her big tail crashing, her four legs flailing. As she disappeared into the swamp, she could hear something:

"Ha! Ha! Ha!" and then, "Whoo!"

Adoni was laughing.

He came back the next day. And this time, he brought a rough rope that he'd made himself, out of gum tree bark.

He also had a smooth stick, with the rope attached at either end of it. And he was doing that strange thing with his mouth, and making those weird "Ha, ha, ha" sounds.

But he wasn't, Stacy noticed, carrying the spear.

Stacy backed away, definitely tense. *I'm not gonna let him stand on me.* Adoni edged closer, still smiling.

Stacy stood her ground.

Adoni got closer. And closer. And closer.

Stacy was tense, still, and ready to fight.

Adoni jumped on her.

Stacy immediately started bucking and twisting and splashing, just like a bronco on the prairie. But this time, Adoni didn't flip off and crash into the swamp water. No, he held on, and no matter how violent Stacy's efforts to knock him off got, Adoni stayed on.

Then Stacy felt something very frightening: it was the smooth stick—the bit—slipping into her mouth. As soon as it was in place, Adoni tightened the rope, and Stacy realized that Adoni could make her go right, go left, or go straight, depending on how he held the rope. Soon, he was making her swim right down the middle of the main channel.

"Whoo!" she heard him holler. "Yee-haw!"

Stacy realized, *Hey, he just wants to have fun.* So she stopped fighting and started swimming in earnest, zipping along as fast as she could, zigging and zagging. Adoni was riding and whooping in joy.

Pretty soon, the other crocs, the same ones who had been making fun of Stacy, came out of their hidey-holes and watched this amazing spectacle, of Stacy and — what is he? A human? — roaring through the swamp.

"I had no idea Stacy was so fearless," one of the crocs said.

"Wow," said another croc.

"Whoo!" said Adoni.

Later, Adoni and Stacy said good-bye: she brought him close to a little spot of dry land. He removed the bit and hopped off. They looked at each other, Adoni and Stacy.

Then, Adoni raised one of his hands.

Stacy said to herself, *Is he saying good-bye?*

So she raised her tail.

As Adoni disappeared into the thick jungle, Stacy could hear his, "Ha! Ha! Ha!"

Story Points: "Stacy, the Cowardly Crocodile"

★ Create the world of the swamp in detail: the heat, the cattails, the muddy water, the squawking birds, the swift turtles, and the lazy fish.

★ Describe crocodiles in loving detail: claws, snout, and beady eyes. Emphasize their powerful jaws and carnivorous anger.

★ Then, describe Stacy: she's different, intellectual, gentle, and not nasty at all.

★ Jacob, her friend, visits Stacy, takes care of her, and brings her croc tidbits.

* Adoni shows up. Describe him, and talk about Aboriginal walk-abouts and his affinity for the swamp.
* Tell about the encounter between Adoni and Stacy. He jumps on her, and she throws him, laughing, into the water.
* The next day, Adoni arrives with a "bit" and a tree bark rope. He rides Stacy. She realizes that he's out for fun, so she takes him on a wild ride, astonishing the other crocodiles.

Other "Stacy, the Cowardly Croc" Ideas

Did Wee One like this story? If so, you could very likely get a number of useful stories out of Stacy and Adoni. The central image—fearless Adoni riding Stacy like Charlton Heston on a chariot in Ben Hur—is, in my opinion, highly cool and could be effectively reused. Here are a few other ideas, too:

* Explore the swamp. We've established that Stacy and her fellow crocs live in an out-of-the-way, isolated portion of it. Maybe Adoni shows her human habitation, highways, etc.
* Concoct a rescue mission. Maybe someone from Adoni's village, a girl perhaps, gets lost and injured in the depths of the swamp, and Stacey and Adoni have to find and bring her home. (This would require some quick research on your part: the geography of Australia, life among the Aboriginal inhabitants of that land, etc.).
* Some Bad Guys escape into the Swamp, and Stacey and Adoni help the authorities find and capture them. Protect the wild swamp. This is a highly relevant and charged subject, given rampant deforestation around the world. Maybe our heroes get involved in a drama having to do with protecting part of the swamp from being drained and developed. [This isn't virgin narrative territory; it's been dealt with in the Carl Hiaasen YA novel *Hoot*, the movie *Ferngully* (an animation for children), *The Emerald Forest* (for adults, definitely), and more recently in *Avatar* (for older children and adults). No doubt, there are other examples. You may

want to read a few of these before you tackle the story.]

★   Change the setting. It might be possible to develop a very nice multi-night story around Stacy and Adoni, in which Stacy finds herself lost in a big city, desperate to get back to the safety of the swamp. Maybe she gets chased by poachers, put in a zoo, or stuck in the sewers. Finally, Adoni finds her and leads her home.

Have fun!

Jack and the Beanstalk

I know: Jack and the Big B verges on cliché. It's a story heard so often that many grown-ups can tell it in their sleep. So why am including it? Because it, along with Rip Van Winkle (another cliché), is one of my favorite stories. I love Jack, that ne'er-do-well dreamer. I adore his impetuous courage: "By golly, I'm gonna climb that sucker!" I still get shivers of delicious terror when I think of that beastly ogre (or, as in many tellings, a giant) booming around Cloud Land, howling and drooling, "Fee, fi, fo, fum! I smell the blood of an Englishman!"

Ooh.

And here's a wonderful thing about stories in the dark: it may be a cliché to you, but there's an excellent chance that the Nucleus of All That Is Wonderful in This Cockamamie World has never heard it before. For him, the story is fresh, full of life, pregnant with discovery. He may even think you made it up. So don't hesitate to tell old and "common" tales.

There is no overt violence in this telling. Here, the ogre doesn't fall to his death when Jack chops down the beanstalk (he does in the original version). However, nastiness is discussed. For example, the ogre several times recalls that he eats young children for breakfast. You could eliminate this material if you wish (though it adds flavor and intensity). In my opinion, this "Jack and the

Beanstalk" is appropriate for—almost—any age.

"Jack and the Beanstalk" is a long one-nighter. You could, if you prefer, tell it in two nights. I've indicated in the text a possible breaking place; others could be found.

J ack woke up.

He stretched, yawned, and rolled over. He saw that it was a glorious summer day. The sun streamed into his room; he could hear birdies chirping, bees buzzing, and chickens pecking. "Ah," said Jack to himself, "what a day. I think I'll take the day off and go for a nice, long walk."

But then Jack heard something else. Know what it was?

Crying. Someone was sobbing very softly.

"Oh!" said Jack. "What's going on?" He got up and quickly put on his clothes. Everything was a size too small: it was hard to button his shirt, and his pants were high-waters. He looked more than a little goofy, truth be told, but his Mom couldn't afford to buy new clothes for him.

Jack went out into the kitchen, where he found his mother sobbing quietly. She saw Jack, and tried to stop crying, but it was too late. Jack saw her. "Mom! What's going on?"

"It's Harriet."

"What about Harriet?"

Harriet was their cow.

"She quit giving milk."

"She's dried up?"

"It's been a week now."

Jack was dismayed. "What're we gonna do?" Without Harriet, they had no source of milk and very little income. Mainly, they sold the cheese that they made from Harriet's milk. "Jeez, Mom."

Jack's Mom tried to be strong. "I have an idea. We'll sell Harriet and use the money to start a business."

"Sell Harriet?"

"It's our only chance. Jack, I want you to take Harriet into town right now and sell her for as much money as you can get. We need that money. Don't sell her cheap."

"I won't."

Jack didn't feel very enthusiastic. He wasn't sure he could drive much of a bargain with the sharpies in town. But he went to the barn, tied a lead around Harriet, kissed his Mom goodbye, and headed down the road to Hangnail Falls.

Jack took his time. It was such a nice day, and Jack was nervous about making a deal with the cow guys. Harriet seemed happy to just mosey along, so that's what they did. They moseyed.

They went around a bend and across a little wooden bridge that went over a creek. On the far side of the creek, just sitting on an embankment with his back against a fence post, was a man. His eyes were closed, and he looked like he was asleep, so Jack didn't say anything as he and Harriet clopped by.

"Hello, Jack!"

Jack looked at the man. His eyes were still closed. "How did you know my name?" Jack asked.

"I understand you have a cow for sale."

"How'd you know that?"

The man opened his eyes. They twinkled and shone. He stood up to face Jack, then said, "I understand you're a young man who drives a hard bargain."

Jack drew himself up and said, with as much pride as he could muster, "That's right, I am."

Storytelling Tip:

I hate to do it, but I'm obligated at this point to stop and say: Symbolism! Symbolism! The barren milk cow, a standard part of this story, marks the end of childhood for Jack. The old cow no longer gives milk, and Jack, now an adolescent, wearing too-tight clothing, is forced to change, to take on new responsibilities. Is he up to the challenge?

"How would you like to sell that cow to me?"

"I couldn't take less than fifty pounds for Harriet," Jack said. Fifty pounds, in those days, was a lot of money.

"Good for you, Jack, good for you. I wouldn't sell her for any less myself. She's worth fifty pounds if she's worth a penny. But I wouldn't deign to offer so little money. No, what I'm offering is worth much, much more."

With that, he reached into his coat pocket and took something out. He looked both ways, to make sure that he and Jack were alone.

Then he opened his palm.

"Diamonds!" Jack exclaimed, for they glittered and shone in the sunlight, like jewels.

"Not diamonds," the man said. "Even better: bean seeds."

"Bean seeds?"

"Not just any bean seeds. These are magic."

"Really?"

"Look at 'em, Jack." He rolled them around in his palm. There were five. "Look at them."

Jack stared.

"Tell you what. You take the seeds; I'll take Harriet. If they're not as promised, you come find me in town, and I'll return Harriet to you, no questions asked."

"You will?"

"On my honor."

Jack stared at the magic bean seeds for another moment. Then he said, "Done!"

"You won't regret it, m'boy," and with that he took Harriet's lead, and the two of them strolled off.

Jack couldn't wait to show the seeds to his Mom. He burst into the kitchen. "Mom!"

"Are you back already? How much did you get for Harriet?"

"You'll never guess."

"Twenty pounds? Thirty?" Jack just smiled. "Fifty? You got fifty pounds?! Oh!" She gave Jack a big hug.

"I got something better than money, mother. Look." He opened his palm to reveal the five bean seeds.

"What is this?"

"Bean seeds. Magic bean seeds."

"I don't get it."

"I traded Harriet for these seeds."

Mom looked at him. "You're making a joke."

"No."

"You traded our cow for . . . for seeds?"

"Magic seeds."

"You traded Harriet, the only valuable thing we owned, for five magic bean seeds?! Are you out of your mind, Jack? What are we going to do with five seeds?!"

"Plant 'em. By tomorrow, they'll be—"

Jack's Mom took the seeds out of his and hurled them through the open window.

"Noooooooo!" Jack howled.

"You're a dreamer, Jack. A gullible, good-for-nothing, lazy, worthless, no-account, silly dreamer! Did I mention that you're good for nothing? Because of you, we're gonna starve! Starve!"

"Mom."

"Go to your room—now. For this, there'll be no supper for you, and no water. You think about the enormity of what you did."

And with that, Jack, his head hanging low, marched off to his bedroom. He curled up in the bed, and pretty soon, he was fast asleep.

The next morning, Jack woke up. He rolled over, stretching. "Mmmmmmmmm. What a beautiful day."

Jack jumped out of bed. "I hope Mom isn't mad at me anymore. Maybe she made some pancakes. Yum. Hey."

Jack looked out the window. The sun was shining, but there was a curious shadow over the window.

"Did Mom build a new henhouse or something?"

He ran into the kitchen. "Mom? Mom, are you here?!"

"Out here, Jack."

Jack went outside.

"Whoa."

Outside the kitchen window, right where his mother had thrown the seeds, a beanstalk had grown—an enormous beanstalk, thick as an oak, and reaching, up, up, up into the sky. It was a sunny day, but at the top of the beanstalk, there were clouds, swirling and twisting, swirling and twisting.

"Wow . . ."

Jack touched the stalk. It was woody—strong. He could feel a strange power coursing through it. There were branches growing out of it at regular intervals, like it had been built for climbing.

"What are you going to do?"

Jack looked at his Mom, and then up at the beanstalk. "I'm gonna climb that sucker."

"Jack, no. No!"

Jack jumped onto the stalk and started up. He was scared—this was quite a high beanstalk. But he never wavered. He climbed as though he were born to it.

You know where Jack ended up?

In Cloud Land.

Everything is big in Cloud Land: big corn, big mead-ows, and big houses. Jack spied a house—a big house—and walked right up to the door. He knocked: *Boom! Boom! Boom!* A woman—a big woman—opened the door. Jack was taken aback by her size. She looked down on him, like he was a silly child. "What do you want, little boy?"

Jack played along. He answered, in a squeaky voice, "Um, ma'am? Could you be so kind to give me breakfast?"

"Breakfast!"

"I'm famished."

She looked at him. "Well, you are cute as a button. Come in, but be quick. If he catches you, he'll fry you whole and gobble you up."

"Who?"

"My husband, the ogre. Hurry!"

Jack wasn't keen to be eaten, but he went inside and snarfed a chunk of cheese, a hunk of bread, and a jug of water.

They heard the ogre's echoey footsteps. *Boom! Boom! Boom!*

The wife cried, "It's him! Hide! Hide!"

Jack hid under the oven just as the husband boomed in. He made his huge wife look petite: he was twenty-five feet tall and a thousand pounds of pure muscle. He threw a couple of cows—not Harriet, thank the Lord—down on the table. "Broil these up for my breakfast."

Then he started sniffing. Sniff, sniff. Sniff, sniff. He bel-lowed, in a deep, scary voice:

"Fee-fi-fo-fum!

I smell the blood of an Englishman!

Be he alive, or be he dead,

I'll grind his bones to make my bread."

Storytelling Tip:

You gotta go for broke here. This rhyme, which will come up again, is the centerpiece of the story. The story has a happy ending — this is a fairy tale — but right now, you want the tellee giggling with fear.

Storytelling Tip:

Too scary? You could change it to "that cow you ate yesterday." Or, "all those eggs you ate yesterday. The shells are still in the garbage."

Jack was trembling and whimpering. Ohhhhhhhh.

"Oh, honey, now," the ogre's wife cajoled. "There's nobody here. You're probably just smelling that boy you ate yesterday. His bones are in the garbage."

Sniff, sniff. Sniff, sniff.

"You just sit down, and I'll bring you a nice big breakfast."

The ogre sat down, dumped out a big sack of gold coins on the table, and started counting them while he ate his breakfast. When he was done, he put the coins back in the sack and let go a huge belch: *brrrrrrrrrrack!* And then he fell asleep. He snored: *honk, suuuuuuuuue! Honk, suuuuuuuuue!*

Jack crept out of his hiding place. Jack took the ogre's sack of gold coins and quickly ran back to the beanstalk. Down he went with his booty. He ran to his Mom. "Look!"

"Oh, Jack, Jack. Where did . . . ?"

"I told you those bean seeds were magical."

"I'm sorry I doubted you."

"That's okay, Mom."

Jack and his Mom lived happily on the bag of coins for quite a while.

But the beanstalk called to Jack, and pretty soon, he just had to climb back up and see what was what. Up he went. Up, up, and up.

In Cloud Land, Jack went back to the same house. He said to the ogre's wife, when she answered his knock, "Hello, ma'am. Could you please give me some breakfast?"

"You!"

"I'm hungry, if you don't mind."

"You know, my husband noticed that you took his bag of coins. If he catches you, he'll eat you up for sure. He hasn't had a good human boy in weeks, and he's hungry."

Just then, the ogre came booming around from the barn:
"Fee-fi-fo-fum!
I smell the blood of an Englishman!
Be he alive, or be he dead,
I'll grind his bones to make my bread."
"See what I mean? Quick, under the oven!"
"Where is he?" roared the ogre. "I'm gonna eat him up and spit out his worthless bones!"
"I don't know what you're talking about," the ogre's wife said, mollifyingly. "Why don't you sit down and eat your soup?"
"Get me that goose."
"Yes, dear."
Wifey brought him a ratty-looking goose. The ogre stroked it, kissed it, and cooed at it. Then he said, "Lay."
And you know what that goose did?
It laid a golden egg. The ogre tossed it to his wife. "Take this into Cloud Town and buy me a half-dozen hogs."
"Yes, dear."
The ogre drank off the soup, laid his head down in the table, and fell asleep. *Honk, suuuuuuue.*
After a while, Jack snuck out from under the oven and stuck the goose under his arm. He ran, quick as he could, to the beanstalk. Down he climbed. He showed the goose to his mother. "Look."
"It's . . . an old goose."
"Watch this," Jack said. Then he cleared his throat, smiled, and said, "Lay."
And the goose laid a golden egg.
"Oh, Jack."
"It's not necessary to say anything, Mom."
Jack and his Mom lived very nicely on those golden

Storytelling Tip:

There is a time jump here, and this might be an appropriate place to break and breathe the story – if you wish.

*As previously noted, here we
have an excellent example of the
Rule of Threes: Jack goes up the
beanstalk three times.*

eggs for quite a while. But the beanstalk called to Jack, and pretty soon, he just had to climb back up and see what was what. Up he went. Up, up, and up.

Up in Cloud Land, Jack went back to the ogre's house. Ah, but this time, he was smart enough not to knock on the door. He hid in a bush and waited.

He heard the ogre before he saw him. "Fee-fi-fo-fum!" the ogre called.

"I smell the blood of an Englishman.

Be he alive, or be he dead,

I'll grind his bones to make my bread!"

"If it's that boy," the ogre's wife said, very testy, "who stole your coins and the golden-egg-laying goose, you're welcome to him. I've finished with him. Maybe he's in the oven."

They pulled the oven open, ready to grab Jack, but he wasn't there.

"Hmph," said the ogre's wife, looking around. "He's not here."

"I swear I smell him," growled the ogre.

The ogre sat down and ate his dinner. When he was finished, he called to his wife, "Get me my golden harp." His wife did, and as he drifted off for a nap, he played the harp. It made incredibly sweet music.

"I bet," Jack said to himself, "I could take that harp back to Hangnail Falls and make a fortune playing for people."

Well, pretty soon, the ogre fell asleep. *Honk, suuuuuuue. Honk, suuuuuuue.*

Jack snuck out of his hiding place, making sure the ogre's wife wasn't around. Then he tiptoed into the dining room and gingerly took the ogre's golden harp. He headed for the door.

But it turned out the harp could do more than play beautiful music. It could talk. "Master!" it cried. "Master!"

The ogre woke, saw Jack, and howled in rage.

"Uh-oh," Jack said.

The ogre's wife came in, saw him, and shouted, "Get him!"

"Uh-oh!" Jack cried.

"Fee! Fi! Fo! Fum! I did smell the blood of an Englishman!"

Jack ran as fast as he could. Run, run, run! The ogre thundered after him. He was big, and he was catching up! "Oh, no!"

Jack made it to the beanstalk. He started climbing down. Down, down, down. Fast, fast, fast. The stalk started shaking. Jack looked up. It was the ogre! He was coming down. "Oh, no!" Jack went as fast as he could.

"Mother!" he called, as soon as he got close to the bottom. "The axe! Quickly!"

Mom looked up, saw what was happening, and ran inside for the axe.

She handed it to Jack as soon as he hit the ground, and he started chopping, chopping for dear life. *Chop! Chop! Chop! Chop, chop, chop!*

He dared to look up. The ogre realized what was happening. He knew that if the beanstalk went over, he'd fall from a great height and probably break his head in several places. He started going back up.

Chop, chop, chop went Jack.

Up, up, up went the ogre.

Then, finally, the beanstalk went over. "Timber!" Jack called.

The ogre was dangling over the edge! But slowly he

pulled himself up and jumped back into Cloud Land. He peered down. *Whew. That was close.*

The beanstalk fell. Boom!

Just then a princess was riding by. Her horse, startled by the noise, reared up. *Neiiiiiiiigh!* Jack ran to the horse, grabbed its bit, and calmed it down. "Easy, boy. Easy."

"Whatever was that?" the princess asked.

Jack just smiled. "Would you like to hear me play my harp?"

A month later, they married and lived happily ever after.

Story Points: "Jack and the Beanstalk"

★ Jack wakes up: fourteen or fifteen years old, optimistic, impetuous, and a lover of life.

★ He hears his mother crying. She tells him the old cow, Harriet, has gone dry; she wants Jack to take the cow into town and sell her; it's new responsibility for Jack.

★ Jack heads into town, whistling: it's a fine day, warm and sunny. Establish that we're in Merrie Olde England.

★ Jack meets an old man by the ford. The man talks Jack into selling the cow for five magic bean seeds—they look like diamonds.

★ Jack returns home with the seeds. Mom, angry at his incredulousness, throws the seeds out the window and sends Jack to his room.

★ Jack wakes up to find that an enormous beanstalk has grown, reaching into the clouds. Jack decides to climb it.

★ The first adventure in Cloud Land: Jack goes to the ogre's house, meets the (large) wife, and asks for breakfast; she's reluctant, but Jack's cuteness makes her give in. The ogre comes home—cue the first instance of the "Fee-fi-fo-fum" rhyme. Jack hides; the ogre eats, and then he counts golden coins and falls asleep. Jack steals the coins.

★ Jack's mother says, "I'm sorry I doubted you." Jack gives her the coins. Time passes. Jack decides to climb the beanstalk once again.

★ The second adventure in Cloud Land: Jack returns to the ogre's house; the wife tells him the ogre was angry that he stole the coins. The ogre returns: "Fee-fi-fo-fum." Jack hides. The wife calms the ogre down, tells him there aren't any Englishmen around. The ogre calls for his golden egg-laying goose and then falls asleep; Jack steals the goose and returns home.

★ Jack gives the goose to Mom. Time passes; Jack re-climbs the beanstalk.

★ The third and final adventure in Cloud Land: Jack sneaks into the ogre's house; the wife and ogre return: "Fee-fi-fo-fum." Both look around, but they can't find Jack: "He stole our goose. I've had it with him. I hope you find him." The ogre asks for his golden harp; when Jack tries to steal it, the harp wakes up and cries, "Master!" The ogre and his wife chase Jack and almost catch him, but Jack races down the stalk and chops it down.

★ The falling beanstalk nearly clobbers a passing princess. Jack calms her horse and asks her if she would like to hear him play the harp. They marry and live happily ever after.

Sophie and the Unicorns

Here is a story I created expressly for this book. "Sophie and the Unicorns" is about grief, about Sophie and her father, Martin, coming to terms with the recent accidental death of Sophie's mother.

"Hmm," I said to myself. "Is this really bedtime-story material?"

I decided that, yes, it is. Grief ups the intensity and power of the story. Moreover, death is a subject that many children are avidly interested in . . . and confused about. They have heard their peers discussing it, heard about death at school, at church, and at the park. They want—and need—to explore the subject. Here is an opportunity for this to happen with the comforting presence of the storyteller (you) to offer reassurance and intelligent guidance. There is nothing "mature" about the story; its core, Sophie and her father finding their way into Unicorn Land, will play for all ages. The presence of grief and death requires, perhaps, some maturity on the part of the listener, but not a lot.

Night One

Sophie's neighborhood isn't a slum, but it's a little bit rough. It's like [name a neighborhood in your city that's funky around the edges and has lots of retired folks and people working two jobs; these days, unfortunately, there's no shortage of neighborhoods like this.]. There are lots of steel fences. When you walk down the streets, you can hear the dogs barking, and these aren't little toy terriers and frou-frou dogs. These are Rottweilers and German shepherds and Dobermans. Most houses are pretty well kept, but some have gone to seed, with uncut lawns and, in the winter, un-shoveled sidewalks. Some are boarded up. Sirens blare at night.

Sophie is watching the movers take furniture into the small, empty house where she's going to be living with her father, Martin. This house is smaller than their old place, so they've sold a lot of their stuff. Sophie watches Martin. He seems okay—he even smiles a bit. But his smile seems pasted on. Sophie knows him well, and she can tell. He's unhappy.

Martin writes poetry. He teaches when he can, but he

doesn't have a full-time job. He writes for a neighborhood paper, but that hardly pays.

Later, they have their housewarming supper: mac 'n' cheese from a box with Sprite. Sophie's pretty sure Martin got the food from a food shelf. Times are going to be lean.

That night, Sophie sets up her unicorns. She used to collect them when she was little. She has dozens. Some are big, some tiny. Something makes her put them on a shelf. Maybe it's the neighborhood and her situation. Or maybe her mother's death. But she's compelled to set them up. Sophie looks at them for a long while, as if she's waiting for them to do something—dance, break into song, anything. But they just look back.

A few days later, Sophie starts school.

It's really different from the place she went before, out in the suburbs. The building is old, and the lockers all rattley. There are cops in the halls. The teachers are frazzled and overworked. Classes are large, with thirty plus students.

And the kids—yikes: goths, gangsters, and jocks; low-riding pants and pink hair. Sophie is usually friendly and outgoing. She's a kid who takes the lead, one who quickly assembles a pack of pals. But Sophie finds these kids weird. She hangs back, says nothing, and just watches, trapped in anxiety.

One of the teachers notices. It's an older woman, Mrs. Ashman. Sophie hadn't noticed her right away. She's small and unassuming. But one day, Sophie sees that Mrs. Ashman is peering at her with sharp, appraising eyes and a very charming sort of half-smile.

After class, Mrs. Ashman asks, "Sophie? Why aren't you smiling?"

"Smiling?"

"I can tell, by your eyes, that you want to smile. But you're not. Why?"

"Well, I smile sometimes."

"I've never seen it. Do you smile at home?"

"No," Sophie admitted. Something about this woman made her want to tell the truth. "Never at home. We just moved into a crappy house, and I'm worried about my father. He's not writing, he's not looking for a job, and I'm afraid he's going crazy with grief. My mom died. But that was six months ago, and I'm worried about Daddy."

Mrs. Ashman looks at Sophie for a long time. Then she does an unusual thing, unusual in this uptight day and age: she hugs Sophie. "Whenever you need to talk, I'm here."

After school one day, Sophie passes a butcher shop, a small place where they sell meat. Sophie notices it because it's one of the few businesses still open on the block. Something makes her peer inside. She sees steaks, chicken, etc. But then she notices hotdogs, wound together, hanging behind the old cash register.

Hotdogs! Daddy loves hotdogs.

Maybe, Sophie thinks to herself, this will bring him out of his funk.

She goes into the store. "How much for the hotdogs?" she asks the old man.

"Dollar and a half each."

Sophie pulls money out of her jeans. Four ratty ones and some change. "I can afford three."

The guy wraps them up. "I threw in an extra one," he says, smiling.

"Thanks."

She takes the hot dogs home and cooks them up at supper-time. She remembers that her mom just heated them up with water, so she does that. She doesn't have any buns, just a can of baked beans.

Martin looks at the hotdogs for a long moment.

"I got them at that weird butcher shop on Mulberry. They look good, don't they?"

"They look great. Thanks." He eats a few bites and then pushes the plate away. "I'm sorry."

That night, Sophie snaps awake. Something is pulling on her. She finds a flashlight—it's already in her hand, but she has no memory of picking it up—goes into the kitchen, opens the cellar door, and heads downstairs into the basement. She hasn't visited the cellar yet. The air is stale and mildewy, and there's cobwebs everywhere—ick!—but something makes her go on. She reaches the basement and plays the light around the old furnace, broken shelves, and old lawn mower.

Then, she sees it. A door, lined with bright light. The light makes a dancing, swirling square. Sophie opens the door . . . .

And finds a brightly lit, colorful world, brilliant green trees, enormous flowers, a blue sky with white floating clouds, tame animals, happily buzzing insects, singing birds, and music—lush vibrant music.

Sophie laughs. This is wonderful!

She takes a step forward. She has to visit this place!

But something stops her. She can't move. Something won't let her in.

What? What's going on?

But she can't go in.

The next day, Sophie is walking home from the school bus, and she sees her father, Martin, walking. She starts to call out to him, but something about him makes her stop.

He seems wrapped up in himself, walking fast, hands jammed in his pockets, looking down at the sidewalk. He's angry and self-absorbed.

So Sophie follows him instead. She hangs back, but Martin is so out-of-it that she could be walking right behind him and he'd never know. He just walks, eyes staring downward, never looking at where he is, walking fast.

Sophie gets scared after a while—scared she might get lost, scared of Martin. So she stops and goes home.

Martin comes in a few hours later.

The next night, Sophie tries again. She waits until midnight and then finds the flashlight and goes down into the basement. She moves slowly—she doesn't want to scare the world away.

And it's there, just like before. A wonderful world of vivid color and music, an achy blue sky filled with soft clouds, greener-than-green trees, and enormous flowers—singing flowers!

Sophie laughs.

She tries to go past the threshold. But she can't. Something keeps stopping her. "Oh!" She tries again, and again. She's stopped every time.

Then she sees them: two unicorns, facing her, just on the other side of the door. They're like horses, but they are multi-colored, and their manes dance. They have unicorn horns growing out of their foreheads, and the horns are like candy canes, swirling with color.

"Hello!" Sophie calls out. "Can you hear me? Tell me how I can go through the door!"

"There is a way, Sophie."

"How did you know my name?"

"There is a way."

"Tell me!"

"Sophie?"

Sophie whips around and sees Martin, who's just come down the steps, fastening his ratty old robe. "Oh, Daddy, you scared me."

"What are you doing? It's creepy down here."

"I want to go there so bad."

"Go where?"

"To Unicorn Land! Can't you see it? It's right—" Sophie turns.

And stops. It's gone. There's nothing on the other side of the door but a dank and dusty basement room.

"It's just an old coal bin," Martin points out.

Sophie gingerly steps into the old room. Nothing happens. She snaps on the light, and looks around. The room is empty and very dusty.

"It probably hasn't used in years." Martin looks at her. "Sophie, is something wrong?"

"I'm fine. It's late. We should go to bed."

They ascend the creaky steps.

Night Two

The next night, the moon is full. It shines through Sophie's window and makes her covers glow, magically. She holds her hand up to the light.

And you know what? The light dances around her hand, swirling, multi-colored—just like in Unicorn Land. It makes her hand glow.

Sophie says, "Whoa."

She closes her hand, making a fist. The light disappears. Then she opens her hand: more crazy, weird light.

Storytelling Tip:

*Here, you would hold your own
hand up to whatever light is
coming through the closed drapes
of your child's room.*

"There is a way!"

Sophie gets up. Her white nightdress catches the galloping moonlight. Again, the crazy-giggly light of Unicorn Land dances over the dress. Sophie laughs.

She shakes Martin awake. "Wha . . . ?"

"Daddy, come with me. I have something to show you."

"It's midnight."

"Come!"

Martin peers at her, getting worried. "Is there something wrong?"

Sophie says nothing; she just grabs Martin's hand and pulls him out of his bedroom, down the hall, down the stairs, into the kitchen, and down the creepy steps into the dank basement.

Martin pulls away. "Are you nuts?"

"Maybe."

"What are we doing down here?"

"I think I know the way in."

"The way into what? It's the middle of the night. You're scaring me."

Sophie faces the coal bin door. As before, with Martin, it's dark and very uninviting.

"Take my hand."

"No. You're scaring me."

"Take my hand."

"I won't."

"Martin!"

Martin takes a step back. Sophie's never called him by his first name before.

"Take my hand. We have to be holding hands."

Sophie stands in front of the coal bin door. Martin hesitates, but then joins her. "This is crazy."

Sophie holds out her hand.

Martin takes it.

Unicorn Land appears, with mad colors spinning, wild and wonderful music, birds and sweetly buzzing insects, and the sky achy blue and filled with marvelous white clouds.

"Oh, my," Martin says, awed.

"Let's go," Sophie says.

They step into Unicorn Land.

It's even more beautiful than Sophie imagined. It's perfect: not too hot, not too cold, and not muggy. The air is clear, but there is some kind of indefinable perfume.

Sophie dances, twirling around the trees. Music fades up, music that perfectly fits Sophie's dance. It makes her giggle.

When she finishes, she hears applause. "Thank you, thank you, thank—" She turns, assuming that Martin's doing the clapping. But it's not Martin. You know who it is?

It's the trees!

Sophie laughs again.

"Welcome! Welcome!"

"Who's singing?" Sophie asks.

Martin replies, pointing, "It's the flowers!"

It's true. A bunch of huge flowers with funny people faces are singing:

Welcome, welcome,
We wish to welcome you
To Unicorn Land,
Unicorn Land,
To Unicorn Land.
We know that you'll have fun

Storytelling Tip:

Add your own lyrics. Make up a melody (the one I created was vaguely inspired by the Munchkin song in The Wizard of Oz). *Make up your own song; it's bound to be better than mine.*

In Unicorn Land,
Unicorn Land,
In Unicorn Land!
Stay as long as you want
In Unicorn Land,
Unicorn Land,
In Unicorn Land.

Martin and Sophie explore Unicorn Land, running through forests with the sun shining through impossibly green leaves, past bowers, wonderful bushes, and riotous blooms of singing and laughing flowers.

They go into ravines. In one, they find a cliff of pure gold. Sophie and Martin run their hands over it. It's polished and shiny.

"It's gold."

"It's wonderful."

In another ravine, Martin finds . . . .

"A cave." Martin pulls the hanging moss aside and passes in.

Sophie hesitates, outside. She's a little nervous. She doesn't hear anything and starts to get nervous. "Daddy? Are you okay?" Then she hears:

"Ohhhhhhhh . . . "

Sophie goes in. Martin's standing in front of a chest overflowing with treasure: gold nuggets, coins, jewelry, and precious stones, polished and beautiful.

Martin takes a gold coin and slips it into his pocket.

Sophie frowns, still nervous. "Maybe you shouldn't."

"It's alright."

"How do you know? C'mon, Daddy, I don't like it in here."

They leave. Outside, they find two large unicorns—waiting for them.

"Oh," Sophie says, "we, we didn't know. We didn't mean to take anything."

"We'll give it back," Martin promises.

"Yes, definitely, we'll give it back."

Sophie looks at the animals. They regard her calmly, not saying anything. But they seem to smile, or maybe it's just Sophie's imagination. Something makes Sophie gush, "Mom died—my mom, Martin's wife. We've had to move into a crummy house. We're not sure what to do!" It's a short speech. But it leaves Sophie breathless and spent.

The unicorns say nothing, but they do something: they bend their front legs and meekly touch their heads to the sun-dappled ground.

At first, Sophie thinks they're bowing down in obeisance. But then it hits her. "Daddy! They want us to climb on."

"Then we'd better."

Martin and Sophie gingerly climb onto the unicorns' bare backs. They grip the side of the unicorns with their knees and hold on to the horns. The unicorns start walking, slow at first, but once they're out of the ravine and into the trees, they move faster.

"Isn't this fun?!" exclaims Sophie.

Then they leave the trees, the unicorns galloping through a meadow.

Suddenly, out of nowhere, the unicorns grow wings! Wide and strong, the wings flap a few times, and then . . . .

They fly!

"Ohhhhhhhh!" cry Martin and Sophie.

Up, up, up they go.

Soon, they can see everything: enchanted forests everywhere; meadows filled with blooms of yellow, blue, and red; streams running clear, the water shooting over colored rocks, with little waterfalls, rills, and trills; rivers, deep and strong and dark; and, in the distance, cliffs, and a wine dark sea.

The unicorns swoop and climb, swoop and climb, faster and higher.

Sophie notices that the sky is filled with unicorns. "They're wonderful!"

After a while, the unicorns drop down, gliding back and forth, circling, until finally, they land in a delightful little glade. The unicorns bend their legs and bow down, signaling that they want Sophie and Martin to get off; Sophie and Martin obey.

"That was . . . " Sophie is looking for the right word. "Wonderful. Incredible. Amazing. I want—I want to do it again, ASAP!"

Martin sees it first. "Sophie. Look."

He points to a rock formation, and in the middle of it is a door-sized opening. Through the opening they can see the dark, creepy, cobwebby basement of their house. The two unicorns station themselves on either side of the door, waiting.

"They want us to go through," Martin says.

"I guess." She turns to the unicorns. "But I can come back, right? Can't I? Can't we?"

The unicorns say nothing.

"C'mon." Martin takes Sophie's hand. Sophie gives the unicorns one more yearning look as they walk through the threshold and find themselves back in their dank basement.

Sophie turns around.

And all she can see is the dark coal bin. Unicorn Land is gone. "Oh!"

Then she remembers. "Daddy! The coin! You were going to give it back."

"I forgot." Martin reaches into his pocket and takes out—not a coin, but a folded up piece of paper.

"What happened to it?"

"It's gone. All that's in my pocket is this paper." He unfolds it and looks at it. "It's . . . notes . . . for a poem."

"It was already there."

"No. It wasn't. I haven't done any writing since your mother . . . not since your mother . . . " He looks at it more closely. "It's in my handwriting." Then he quickly folds it up and puts it back in his pocket. "I'll look at it later."

That night, Sophie looks at the moon—still full, still filling her window. "There was a way," she smiled. "There was a way." She added, "There's no way I'll get to sleep tonight."

She immediately fell into a deep sleep.

The next morning, Sophie wakes up and makes her way down to the kitchen for breakfast. She passes her father's writing room and stops. Does she hear something? She leans her head against the door.

She does hear something: fingers dancing quickly over computer keys. She opens the door. "Daddy?"

"Look!" Martin picks up the laptop and shakes it, as if he could make the poem tumble out. "I'm writing something—a poem! You know what's called? 'Unicorns.'"

He stands, goes to Sophie, and puts his hands on her shoulders. "We're going to get through this, you and me."

"I know."

He hugs her.

Story Points: "Sophie and the Unicorns"

Night One

- ★ Sophie moves to a new neighborhood: funky, down-market, and slightly dangerous, with barking dogs.
- ★ Martin's in a funk; they're poor(er). Sophie wishes she could do something.
- ★ Sophie visits the huge new school full of weird kids: goths, punks, and gangstas. Where does she fit in?
- ★ She encounters Mrs. Ashman, the kindly teacher, and the friendly butcher, who gives Sophie an extra hotdog. Sophie discovers the magic door to the coal center and sees Unicorn Land for the first time. Martin appears behind her. Sophie realizes that he can't see the magic land.

Night Two

- ★ Sophie visits Martin's office and discovers that he has written nothing; he's completely blocked.
- ★ That night, looking at the wild full moon in her room, Sophie understands that Martin is the key. She gets him up. He's tired, but he gives in.
- ★ Holding Sophie's hand, Martin sees Unicorn Land for the first time. Together, holding hands, Martin and Sophie cross the threshold.
- ★ Unicorn Land! They explore it fully: the singing trees and flowers, ravines, and treasure-filled caves.
- ★ In a cave, Martin takes a gold coin. He promises to return it.
- ★ They meet two unicorns. Sophie suddenly tells the shimmering animal everything about her mom's death, the new house, Martin's unhappiness, and the impersonal new school.
- ★ The unicorns say nothing, but they bend down, indicating that Sophie and Martin should climb on. They do.
- ★ And they fly! They see this storybook world: forests, streams, lakes, and meadows. Other unicorns join them.

- ★ The unicorns land in front of the magic door; Sophie and Martin can see the dusty coal room in their house. Sophie takes her father's hand, and they pass through the door.
- ★ Sophie remembers the coin. Martin reaches into his pocket and discovers, not the coin, but notes for a new poem.
- ★ The next day, Martin is writing: "Unicorns." He hugs Sophie. "We're going to get through this."

This could be the end of Sophie, Martin, and Unicorn Land. But if your little sweetheart liked the story — if the idea of a secret conduit to a magical, unicorn-filled world has struck a chord — you might consider making up more. Here are some ideas:

- ★ Explore Unicorn Land in more detail. Maybe Martin and Sophie find a castle. Maybe a princess is being held captive by an ogre, ogres, or an evil magician. Martin and Sophie help her escape. A chase ensues!
- ★ Maybe Martin becomes separated from Sophie. But Unicorn Land has given him new resilience, and he's able to find Sophie. Maybe he has to rescue her from a wicked witch. Don't hesitate to borrow story material from a movie featuring a girl whose name begins with D.
- ★ Maybe a denizen of Unicorn Land is trapped in the neighborhood, with plenty of melodrama resulting therefrom.

Ralph, the Sad, Sad Ghost

How appropriate: I'm ending this collection with my first story in the dark. I'm inordinately proud of it. At the time, I was a brand-new teller of bedtime tales, and I went into Michael's room every night without a clear idea — indeed, with no idea at all — of what I was going to come up with. The story reflects this improvisation. It zigs and zags. Sometimes it's a character study of a quiet young man; sometimes it's a satire of present-day school life; sometimes it's a weird, ghostly melodrama. But the story moves well, and my son, bless him, adored every minute. I present it to you here, with all its flaws and energy. Feel free to edit it, restructure it, and add new episodes, however you see fit.

By all standards, this is a fairy tale: Chuck is a regular guy — shy and quiet, newly arrived on Yankee Doodle Lane. He encounters potent magic. The valley is a strange place, deserted and charged. And, of course, the ramshackled haunted house is occupied by an intensely sad and powerful ghost, Ralph.

The story obeys the Rule of Threes in that Chuck visits the haunted house three times. He makes allies: Madeleine — who also provides Chuck with an invitation to travel into Ralph's strange world. They find Nancy (another ally) and bring her to the alley.

And, of course, there is a goofy Bad Guy: Gil Bates.

"Ralph, the Sad, Sad Ghost" is a "multi-nighter," and as always my "Night" divisions are entirely arbitrary and exist mainly to be altered by you, the teller.

Enjoy!

Night One

This is a story that happens at the very edge of a city just like ours, not so long ago. It's a brand-new housing development, and the streets have names like Mary Poppins Boulevard, Seven Hundred Club Drive, and Ronald Reagan Way.

This story's about a kid named . . . Chuck.

Chuck and his Mom bought a house on Yankee Doodle Lane.

The first day after Chuck and his Mom moved into their house, Chuck went for a walk. You think it's hot here? This is nothing. When Chuck went out, the sun filled the sky and pounded down like a white-hot hammer on the dream houses. There was a park, but no trees, and the playground equipment was so hot Chuck couldn't even touch it.

He kept walking. Pretty soon, he came to a barbed-wire fence. On the other side of the fence was a cornfield. This was the very edge of the city. There were no more houses—just corn.

Chuck looked at the corn. It was tall, and the stalks, with their long, twisty leaves, almost looked human, like thin yellow scarecrows.

Chuck said to himself, "I better get home."

And then something came over him. Something mysterious. A power that reached deep within his breast and made him do things he would never under ordinary circumstances do. And he got down on his tummy and scootched under that fence.

Next thing he knew, he was walking down a long row of corn. Dust hung in the air, and it was so hot in the corn it was hard to breathe. The corn stalks made weird, rattly noises. And there were bugs—biting flies. Pretty soon, Chuck was running, faster and faster down the endless row of corn.

Suddenly, there was an explosion of noise. *Honk, honk,*

honk, and the sound of crashing wings. It was a pheasant.

Chuck stood, gasping for breath, his heart pounding.

He saw another fence. He went to it and found himself looking down into a valley — it was big, full of trees, and the air was so hazy Chuck couldn't even see the far side of the valley.

No way am I going down there, and then, you know what happens, don't you?

Something mysterious came over him, and he scootched under that fence.

Down he went, down, down into the valley. The slope was steep, and pretty soon, Chuck was slipping and sliding, branches and brambles whapping his kisser, and then, finally, he was in the valley.

It was nicer and cooler. There was a road, an old road no one used any more with weeds growing all over it. Chuck followed the road to a stream. The bridge was collapsed, so Chuck had to wade through the stream. The water looked yummy, and the day was sticky hot, but, wisely, Chuck didn't drink the water. You should never drink from streams. Know why?

Cows pee in 'em.

Chuck walked on, enjoying the cool air, the dappled shadows, and the tall trees. "It really is like another world down here," he said to himself. It was so quiet and still.

What's that? That smell?

Apples, rotten apples — brown slimy, fizzy, oogy apple ick. Chuck saw an overgrown apple orchard, all filled with vines and brush and big fat flies and bees drunk on the fermented apple juice. And beyond the orchard . . . .

Know what it is?

A house — an old, ramshackle, falling-apart house.

Storytelling Tip:

It's not much of a parenting moment, but it's something . . .

"No way am I going into that house," Chuck told himself, and then, the mysterious power came again, and he was scrambling through the orchard, slipping on the slime, and yanking the vine tangles away from the trees, making a path. He made it to the house, walked up on the porch—*bmp, bmp, bmp*—reached out for the door, and pulled it open.

Eeeeeeeeee . . .

It was dark in the house. When his eyes adjusted, all Chuck could see were vague shapes and old furniture, and then, suddenly, Chuck knew:

I'm not alone.

Know how he knows?

Chuck asks, "What's your name?" But the ghost doesn't say anything, he just keeps [more blowing].

And then, Chuck could feel the ghost crying.

And then, Chuck started crying, too. And then, he started talking, telling the ghost how scared he was of his new house, his creepy neighborhood, and the school he had to go to where he didn't know anyone. Chuck could feel sadness filling him up, like he was a sponge of sadness, and suddenly, *whoomp*. The ghost was gone.

What time is it?

Chuck went out onto the porch.

The sun was going down! *Uh-oh.*

Chuck ran through the orchard, down the road, through the stream, up the steep hillside to the cornfield, and down the cornrows, until finally, finally, he made it back to the city.

Chuck went back to his house. Sweat was pouring off him. *What'm I gonna tell Mom?* he asked himself.

Then he stopped outside Mom's room. All he could hear

Storytelling Tip:

Here, I hit on a brilliant, if I do say so, device: I blew all over Michael's sweaty body. It made him giggle and gave him the chilly sensation of anxious goose bumps. "Again," he begged. Of course, it may not be appropriate for your Bundle of Joy—you might not be in an un-air-conditioned room in the middle of a heat wave, for one thing. But I offer you the option.

was a TV audience laughing.

Chuck went to his room and went to sleep.

Night Two

The next night, Chuck woke up. This was odd, because Chuck—unlike certain children I could but won't mention by name—is a good sleeper. He looked at his clock. 11:59—almost midnight. He got up, walked to his bedroom window, and looked out.

There was a girl sitting on the curb across the street. "Who's that?" Chuck said out loud. "It's midnight." He tried to go back to sleep, but he couldn't. He looked out again. She was still there. "I'm gonna tell her to go home."

He went into the hallway, past his mom's room. He could hear the television in her room, but he knew Mom was asleep.

Outside, the moon was hot. It was one of those moonlit nights where everything glows with power. The sky was so bright it was almost blue.

When Madeleine saw Chuck, she jumped up and dashed to him. "Are you ready to take me to the ghost?"

"Who are you?"

"I seen you go down into the haunted valley. I know you met a ghost. I can talk to ghosts, but I'm scared to do it alone. Come on, while the moon is full. You and your Mom just moved in. She's so sad I could cry. Oh, my name is Madeleine."

Madeleine—Madeleine is what you would call . . . special. Everybody wants to put words on people, it's sort of a modern obsession, and I'm not sure what word you'd put on Madeleine—autistic, or developmentally handicapped.

When I was a kid, we used to call kids "farmers," like being a farmer was their fault. If you reduce someone to a word, you don't see them for who they really are. Madeleine is one of those people you meet from time to time, who live life more intensely than most of us. Sometimes they're a lot of fun. Sometimes they're scary.

Now, what Chuck should have done is he should have said to Madeleine, "You have to go home. This is crazy—we can't go chasing ghosts in the middle of the night." But do you think he did this? No, something mysterious came over Chuck, and he said:

"Okay. Let's go."

Together, Chuck and Madeleine walked down the moon-hot Yankee Doodle Lane. It was windy, the first actual wind Chuck had felt since being in California. It made the shadows dance. Chuck walked fast, and Madeleine struggled to keep up. But she didn't complain.

They came to the cornfield, at the edge of the city. Chuck lifted up the barbed wire so Madeleine could scootch under, and then he scootched himself. They headed down the long rows of tall corn. The cornstalks rattled in the wind, like evil stick men.

They reached the edge of the valley, filled with moonlight. The wind made the trees cavort and gambol like witches.

Chuck and Madeleine went down into Ghost Valley, slipping down the steep valley slope, branches hitting their faces. *Whap-whap-whap-whap.* They came out onto the deserted road in the valley floor. The road was inky black, and there was wind in the trees.

They were moving fast, heading for the house. The moonlight made the valley look weird, charged, and magical.

This is an unusual image, so take your time here and let it get settled.

More blowing would work here, if you're of a mind.

There it was: the house. But it looked different. It glowed. Well, it didn't glow—not exactly. It was more of an emanation, but not light; it was the opposite of light.

Unlight.

Ooh.

The Unlight was black, and it flew off the house in black strands, like crazy weird licorice. The Unlight pulled them in. Chuck and Madeleine hesitated.

Then, they moved toward the house. *Squish-squish-squish* went their feet through the apple slime. It seemed like the house became more and more agitated. They reached the porch, and then the door. *Eeeeeeeee.*

They stepped inside, and they could feel it: the ghost.

Madeleine started saying things like, "How old are you?" and "Gosh, that's quite old," and "Really? Oh, that's horrible!"

Chuck started feeling sad. It was like sadness was a thing, hardening inside him. He had to get rid of it, and if he didn't, he would turn into a sadness statue.

"We've gotta get outta here." This was Madeleine. She started pulling Chuck to the door. "Chuck!"

She dragged him out of the house, and as soon as the night air hit him, Chuck woke up. "What's happening?" Madeleine dragged him through the orchard.

Chuck turned around and looked at the house.

There was Unlight everywhere—undulating out of the house, heading right for Chuck and Madeleine, and when the rays of Unlight hit Chuck, he started turning into a sadness statue again.

Madeleine knocked him down. "Run!"

They ran.

As soon as they hit the road, they ran, feet *slap-slap-slap-*

ping the old asphalt. Chuck could see tracer rounds of Un-light shooting through the sky, silently.

"Hurry!"

They ran down the road, up the slope to the cornfield, and down the cornrows, until, finally, they were back in the city.

Safe.

They lay down in some weeds.

"That is one sad, sad ghost," marveled Madeleine. Then she added, "I know why he's so sad."

"You do?"

"Yes?"

"Why?"

Just then, a police squad car cruised down Oral Roberts Lane. It had its flashing lights on, but no siren. The car stooped, and a middle-aged woman got out.

"Oh, no," Madeleine whispered.

"Who is that?" Chuck asked.

"Madeleine!" the woman cried. "Madeleine, are you here? Madeleine?"

Madeleine gave Chuck a kiss on the cheek. "See you later, Chaz. That ghost really needs our help." Then she stood up and walked toward the woman. "Hi, Mom."

"Madeleine! Where have you been?" She was angry. Then she took Madeleine in her arms. "Oh, Honey, I've been so worried." They got in the cop car and drove off.

Chuck walked home. He stopped outside his Mom's room. He could hear the TV, but he knew she was asleep.

He went to his room and lay down on his bed. *I wonder why the ghost is so sad.*

And then, Chuck fell asleep.

Night Three

A couple days later, Chuck woke to find a slight figure standing at the foot of his bed. You know who it was, don't you? That's right. "Madeleine?"

Chuck snapped on a light.

It really was Madeleine, and she looked fierce, eyes glowing. "I know what we have to do," she whispered.

"What?"

Then she fainted. Her head thunked the floor like a bowling ball.

"Madeleine!"

Chuck rushed to her. Zzzzzzzzzz. Snoring. Chuck slipped a pillow under her head and covered her with a blanket.

He went downstairs. He said to his mom, "I'm feeling sick. I can't go to school today."

His mom put her hand on his forehead. "Oh, Honey, you're burning up. You'd better go back to bed."

Chuck went back to his room. When he heard his mom's car start up and drive off, he went down to the kitchen and made himself a big bowl of Honey Nut Cheerios and milk.

After a while, Madeleine came down rubbing her eyes. "I'm hungry," so Chuck made her a big bowl of Honey Nut Cheerios and milk. As she was eating, she said, "We've gotta find Ralph's sister — his twin sister, Nancy Watson."

"Why?"

"He wants to say goodbye."

"Oh."

"When they were kids, Ralph and Nancy were playing behind the old barn, and Ralph stepped on some old rotten wood, and he was dangling, his feet swinging over empty darkness. Nancy couldn't hold him, and he fell. That's how come he got dead."

"He's terrified his sister blames herself for what happened. It's made him sad, and his sadness has grown and grown. We have to find her, so Ralph can say goodbye. Otherwise his sadness could destroy the city."

Destroy the city? Chuck asked himself. *Is she crazy? I think she must be crazy.*

Madeleine finished her Cheerios. "C'mon."

Chuck followed her.

Outside, they found it was stormy, roiling black clouds all mixed with shooting fingers of Unlight.

"This is getting serious," Madeleine said.

They rode the bus downtown to City Hall. It looked like an evil castle. They found the Hall of Records. The clerk ignored them, so Madeleine waxed cute. "Um, hi. We're doing a special school project, and we want to check the property records for Maple Valley. It's right by our school?"

"Don't bother me, kid. I'm busy."

"Pleeeeeease . . . ?"

Jeepers, Chuck said to himself, *she's good at this.*

"Yeah, okay," and the clerk went off and came back with a super big book, like an atlas.

Chuck and Madeleine took it to a table and looked up Maple Valley. "There. That's the farm. See the orchard, and—Oh no! I don't believe it!"

"What?"

"Do you know who owns Maple Valley now? Gilbert Bates."

"Who's . . . Gilbert Bates?"

"You don't know who he is? Why, Gil Bates owns every TV station in the state. Look, it says he bought the valley from . . . it's hard to read . . . Nancy Watson."

Storytelling Tip:

This is a potentially upsetting image and if your child is young, easily upset, you can omit it. You might simply say, "Ralph died accidentally."

"From Ralph's twin sister."

"Good thinkin', Lincoln."

"My name's Chuck."

"I know. C'mon."

They went to the address they found in the records: 1807 Magnolia Boulevard. In the backyard, they found a diminutive old lady planting tulips. "May I help you, children?"

"We have a message from your brother."

The old lady stood up. She looked at Chuck and Madeleine. Her eyes suddenly brimmed with tears. "How do you know about my brother? I've never spoken of him to anyone. Never! How do you know?"

"We've been talking to him."

"That's not possible. Ralph has been dead for seventy years." Then she looked at the children again. Then she made a decision. "Let me get my jacket."

Off they went.

The sky was darker than ever, with streaks of Unlightning ripping through the clouds. They went to the cornfield and headed down the long cornrows. They made it to the far end of the field, and you know what they found?

A new fence, fifteen feet tall, made of shiny stainless steel, topped with razor wire, and even in the darkness, the razor wire gleamed. It was electrified. Big fat blue sparks danced through the fence. *Zzp. Zzp. Zzp.*

They walked along the fence. Every ten or fifteen feet they came to a sign: "Trespassers Will Be Prosecuted."

"Here, over here!" Madeleine was standing at a small depression. "Whatever you do," she said, "don't touch the fence."

They scooched—carefully—under the fence and went down into the valley. They started walking toward the farmhouse.

Then they heard it.

Animals — big animals running toward them. They could hear the scrape of claws on the asphalt, and hard animal panting — *Ha. Ha. Ha.* They saw their eyes, glowing red in the swirling darkness, coals of hatred.

Dogs, but they were big, as big as horses.

But they didn't attack. They just surrounded Chuck, Madeleine, and Nancy, penning them in. The giant dogs began herding our heroes down the road, toward the haunted house.

Then they saw it.

A machine — a big machine. A huge machine, with antennas and tubes and turbines, and it was sparking big black sparks of Unlight, thrumming and humming and throbbing, and Chuck could taste the Unlight, like pineapple salsa someone forgot to refrigerate for a week.

A man stepped forward, a dweeby little guy, 'bout five-foot-two, with a bald head, weak chin, and walleyes.

"Gil Bates," Madeleine snarled.

Bates laughed. "You trespassers are about to witness a historic moment. I'm going to turn on my Sadness Amplifier. It's going to suck the sadness out of that old farmhouse and feed it directly into my TV stations. Everyone watching TV will be so sad they won't be able to move. I'll control the whole world. If I say, 'Go to war,' they'll go, or, 'Give me all your money,' then they will. Kristen Dunst will become my scullery maid! Ha, ha, ha, ha, ha, ha, ha, ha, ha!"

"It's *Kirsten*, not Kristen," Madeleine said.

"What?"

"You're insane!" This came from Nancy.

"Am I, Nancy? Am I indeed?"

Storytelling Tip:

Another intense image. You could omit it, but I would be willing to bet that your child will adore this. There's no overt violence, and our heroes are able to control the fierce animals.

"How do you know my name?"

"Oh, I know all about you and your ridiculous kid brother Ralph, clumsy little klutz, getting himself killed. And now he's a ghost, generating all this gorgeous sadness. It's mine! Mine!"

He went to the Sadness Amplifier and started entering data into a keyboard. Then he turned to Nancy. "Would you care to do the honors?"

"No."

"Yes."

"No."

Bates growled at the giant dogs, "Grrrrrrrollllllrrrrg," and they detached Nancy from the group and forced her over to the controller. "Just touch Enter, that's all you have to do."

"I won't."

"You will," and he growled at one of the dogs, "Grrrrrr-rollllllrrrrg," and the dog guided Nancy's hand to the keyboard. The dog gently tapped her finger down on Enter.

Nothing.

It doesn't work, Chuck thought to himself.

Then he felt something in his feet: vibrations, picking up speed, building. Then he felt magnetism crawling across his skin, like millions of tiny insects. He looked at Madeleine. Her frizzy hair was stretched straight away from her head.

"Look at the house!" Madeleine cried.

It was exploding with Unlight. Thick strands of it were squirting through the windows, the chimney, and the roof. The house was melting, dissolving into Unlight. The Unlight shot up, high into the air. It formed itself into a huge ball. It hung for a moment, then came shooting down, fast, straight for the Sadness Amplifier.

Bates opened his arms wide. "Come to Daddy!"

Nancy stepped forward.

"Ralph." Nancy's voice was soft, but Chuck could hear it over the thrum of the Amplifier. "Ralph."

The ball of Unlight stopped. It hung in the sky, shimmering. It faced Nancy.

"Ralph."

Light appeared on the surface of the Unlight. It formed the face of a sweet young boy. Nancy reached out her hands. The face came to her. Chuck saw glittering tears on Ralph's cheeks.

"I don't blame myself for what happened. Maybe I did for a while, but that went away years ago. Whenever I think of you now, I feel happy, happy that I had a brother like you at all, even if it was only for a few years. Go home, Ralph. Don't be sad."

The face of Ralph smiled now, the most dazzling happiest smile you ever saw.

Then it slowly dissolved.

Gone.

Chuck heard someone crying. It was Bates. He was kneeling by the Sadness Amplifier. "Hoohoohoohoo!"

Nancy went to him, knelt next to him. "There, there. There, there."

"I loved my sadness."

"I loved mine, too," Nancy said, "but after a while I realized I didn't need it."

Dogs appeared, cute little spaniels and collies. Chuck realized that these were the giant dogs, shrunk down to puppy size. They nudged Bates with their noses. He sobbed, and then he pet them.

> Chuck looked up. The clouds of sadness were gone, and the sky was a deep, achy blue.
>
> "Come along, children," Nancy said. "Let's go get some quarter-pounders."

Story Points: "Ralph, the Sad, Sad Ghost"

Night One

- ★ Create the world: the edge-of-the-city housing development, weirdly deserted; the shimmering heat; the unplayable playground.
- ★ Introduce Chuck: quiet and lonely, but driven to explore.
- ★ Chuck encounters the strange cornfield (at the edge of the city). Something is pulling on him. He goes under the fence and walks down the long rows of human-like corn.
- ★ He reaches the valley; it's hazy and filled with trees. Again, something makes him go down.
- ★ The valley is cooler, but charged with power. Chuck walks along a deserted road.
- ★ He finds the house on the far side of an overgrown apple orchard.
- ★ He goes into the house, encounters the invisible ghost, and is filled with ineffable and creepy sadness. He weeps.
- ★ Chuck runs home, thinking he's in trouble, but Mom hasn't noticed he's been gone.

Night Two

- ★ Chuck wakes up late at night and sees a girl sitting on the curb outside. He meets Madeline, who is autistic or developmentally challenged—take the time to explain this with sensitivity.
- ★ Madeline saw him go visit the house, and she claims she can speak to ghosts. Chuck intends to send her away, but ends up—

something is pulling him — agreeing to visit the ghost.

★ Chuck leads Madeleine to the edge of the valley. The wind is making the trees wave and cavort.

Night Three

★ Madeleine and Chuck descend into the valley.

★ They go to the house.

★ Madeleine, as promised, talks to the ghost. Chuck feels enormous sadness filling him. He weeps and is frozen in place. Madeleine shakes him. "We have to get out of here!"

★ They run away. Chuck sees black strands of sadness — Unlight — shooting out of the house. Madeleine drags him away. They sprint down the valley, up the ravine, and down the rows of corn.

★ Finally, catching their breath by the housing development, Madeleine tells him what she discovered: the ghost's name is Ralph, and his sadness will infect the whole city unless they — Chuck and Madeleine — can find his sister, Nancy. Chuck sees strands of Unlight, still shooting through the sky.

★ "Oh, no." Madeleine sees that her protective mother is riding in a police car, looking for Madeleine. Madeleine leaves the hiding place and goes to her hysterical mom.

★ Chuck goes home.

★ A few days later, Madeleine goes to Chuck. "We have to find Nancy." Chuck makes an excuse, and after his mom goes to work, they set out.

★ They ride the bus downtown, go to City Hall, and find the records. They see that the nasty Gil Bates owns the valley. They find Nancy's address. They visit her, and the three of them set out.

★ They discover a new electric fence, but they find a way under it.

★ In the valley, giant dogs take them to the house. By now, the sky is dark with sadness — Unlight is shooting out of the house.

★ They meet Gil Bates. He has a Sadness Amplifier, and his plan is to take Ralph's sadness and use it to control the world.

★ Nancy steps forward and calls to his brother: he comes flying out of the house, a huge ball of Unlight with the face of a sweet boy on it. Nancy reassures him that she doesn't blame him for anything. She tells him to go home. There is a huge theatrical explosion as he happily leaves.

★ The Unlight is gone. Daylight returns. The giant dogs are puppies again. Gil Bates weeps. Nancy comforts him. "Let's get some quarter-pounders."

Part III

The Greatest Gift

How-To Introduction

I won't fool you: writing for grown-ups is hard. To create a publishable novel, a doable play, or a producible screenplay takes: vast talent; months, often years, of hard work; an unusually original idea (difficult to come by here in the twenty-first century—more about this shortly); time to focus on and develop the project; and a good agent to represent you.

Oh, and luck—a lot of luck.

None of these things are impossible, but neither do they come easily. Anyone who tells you differently is pulling your leg, as they say. A significant cottage industry has sprung up, in which less-than-reputable experts try to sell you on the dubious notion that writing success is simply a matter of finding the right formula (and, of course, buying their book): *Write a Screenplay in 10 Days* or *Let's Write Novels That Sell!*

Beware those exclamation points.

It's all horse you-know-what. I'm a creative writer myself, and I can tell you from painful personal experience that creative writing is a difficult endeavor, and making some kind of living from it? Even more so. Rewarding? Extremely. A life devoted to writing is a rich and wonderful life, but the trials and travails can be overwhelming.

Enough said.

But now, ah yes, let's talk about stories in the dark, bedtime tales custom-designed for your bright and marvelous children. Are these hard to create? No. Complicated and daunting? Not at all. It's not completely easy, but by no means difficult.

Up until now, we've been working with what might be called "found stories": fairy tales, myths, tall tales, religious tales, etc. You may have found these on your own, in your reading. Or perhaps you're adapting stories from movies, plays, or television programs. Or even from scripture, perhaps. You may (I hope, I hope) be taking material from this book. Whatever your source, the basic parameters of the story are already in place.

Still, they do require heightened creativity. You can't read the material (remember: the bedroom is dark). You have to make the stories your own. You'll recall my earnest counsel about the importance of vivid sensual detail. To do this, you must incorporate the story into your being and make it sound as though you are creating it on the spot. Which, in part, you are. Good bedtime stories have a semi-improvised vibe.

Well, why not take the next step and actually make up the story? It's a natural jump.

And an easy one.

Easy? Really?

Definitely. Consider your audience. You're not creating material for the jaded powers-that-be at the New York Public Theater, the greedy editors at Scholastic Publications, or the cynical execs at the despised Disney Studios. You're writing for your child, and she's the easiest audience in the world. She adores you unreservedly (though she might be loathe to admit this). I promise that she will love whatever you come up with.

When you're telling a story in the dark, you already have a lot going for you: your reassuring physical presence, the tellee's complete adoration, her innocence, her intense need for stories, and the dark magic of the room. If, in addition to all this, you're giving your child a brand-new story, a story no one has ever heard, a story brought to life for the first time that night, they will be beyond thrilled.

Don't be surprised to discover pink rose petals strewn in your path.

One final reason to make up your own stories: you are a born storyteller. Believe it. When you go into that bedroom, turn off the lights, and lie down next to your child, you (and the kids) become part of an ancient tradition, one that goes back to the very beginning of time. Storytelling is bred into your human bones. I'm not telling you how to create a brand new talent; I'm giving you a bit of insight, a simple exercise, and an easy "1-2-3 Method" for revitalizing and bringing to the fore a talent that you already possess.

So try it. I think you'll be pleased with how easy it is. I know your child will love it.

The Idea Approach

It is quite possible—many writers do this—to begin work with a simple, barebones, sketchy, and vague notion for a story. At first, these concepts are like a fish in a pool: you catch only a quick glimpse of it before it swims into the deep and disappears. But you know it's there.

Let's discuss this often-maligned and misunderstood term.

Idea

Many people read a book, or see a movie or a play, and say, "Gee, I have an idea, sort of, but mine isn't as pristine, as rich, or as beautifully developed as what I've just seen. It's vague, the characters are one-dimensional clichés, the story's been told a thousand and one times, and I don't know how to pursue it."

This is (he said, as calmly as possible) wrong. You may rest assured that the gorgeous book you just read, that astonishing play, or that exciting movie all began as a raw, poorly developed, and vague ideas—just like yours.

The difference?

Simple: those novelists, screenwriters, playwrights, poets, and memoirists have developed methods whereby they can flesh out barebones story ideas, add vivid characters, and write with style—thus, what starts as a cliché takes on marvelous life. These methods vary from writer to writer, but they are not esoteric. Anyone can emulate them, and if you have the motivation—if you have a child—you can use these methods to create first-rate stories in the dark.

One of the wonders of the creative life (and this is true in many disciplines) is that once you declare yourself to be in the market for an idea, you will find that they come to you, unbidden—sometimes with alarming rapidity, and it's all you can do to write them down.

Similarly, once you are working on something, once you have a specific bedtime tale in mind, ideas for that particular story (or painting, novel, symphony, etc.) will present themselves precipitously.

So get ready.

Ideas from Reading

Reading is a primary source for story ideas. This can work in two ways:

The book you're reading might be given to Precious as a bedtime story. This will very likely heighten your enjoyment of the material (this is one of the grand side effects of stories in the dark). Jot down thoughts on what to leave in and out, and how to tease out a tellable extract from the book. We've seen how the process works with *Great Expectations* and *The Secret Garden*. At one point, I was gobbling up Alan Furst's outstanding series of spy novels set in the early days of WWII. His rendering of the penniless filmmaker Jean Casson is at first casual and then more serious, given his involvement with the French Resistance (*The World at Night*,

Red Gold). But Furst's stories all translated beautifully in Michael's dark bedroom.

But even if you choose not to utilize the book you're reading as story material, you will very likely find that, as you read, ideas for your story are flying at you.

Here's why: when we read, we share to a great extent the vision of a book's author. We enter her heightened imagination, and this intensity often sparks ideas of our own. Again, this will add richness and verve to your reading life.

Similarly, once you have a specific idea that you are pursuing, reading lets you — indeed, it makes you — take your idea further. The story builds and becomes more detailed, richer. The more you read, the more ideas come — better ideas. Your story acquires life.

So, read, read, read!

Ideas from Writing

Here's another excellent method for developing and building ideas: write them down.

It seems obvious, but perhaps you're not aware of how productive and satisfying the act of writing can be. And how sensuous: the scratching of a pen on paper, fingers flying over a keyboard — all this can be marvelously addictive. These physical sensations can spark real ideas.

Writing often puts you in the previously described "creative zone." It nurtures your creative subconscious. When you seat yourself at the coffee house table and pick up your notebook, fire up that computadora, and uncap that fountain pen, your sub-conscious says, "Yippee, now's my time," (or words to that effect). He (or is it a she?) gets to work, and your previously vague idea takes flight.

So, once again: get a notebook. Write. Put your jottings in a file folder. They can be freeform, stream-of-conscious, and messy. Label the folder "bedtime stories." If your idea takes on life and grows, make a new folder, and keep your jottings about that story in it. Does your story have a title? If so, label your file folder accordingly, e.g., "Sophie and The Unicorns." If it lacks a title (and indeed, many of these bedtime stories will never acquire a perfect title), just label the folder by subject latter, e.g., "The Unicorn Story," etc.

Do you have a home office? Maybe keep this material there, and keep it by your chair, available when your reading or DVD-watching provides you with an idea (which it very likely will). Give your notes a place of prominence and honor.

Ideas from Solitude

I know, you're the parent of a young child, and solitude can be a precious commodity. But when your spouse or partner gets home, don't hesitate to let him or her do some child-care while you go forth to seek inspiration. Go for a long walk (you'll make the dog happy). Think, and ideas will come to you.

Questions

Let's assume that you've taken the above advice, and an idea for a story in the dark is taking shape. What might you do to develop it further?

One answer: Express your idea in the form of a question. When you do, the answers can lead to more questions, and the resulting give-and-take can often spark useful growth.

What would happen if . . . ?

This is a good one. Your initial idea may be vague and unformed — many are. You'll recall my analogy about the fish shape receding into the depths. Maybe your first idea is like that. But ask, "What would happen if . . . ?" and things may become clearer and more lucid.

For fun, let's apply this question to "Ralph, the Sad, Sad Ghost": What would happen if . . . a lonely young man discovered a wild, tree-filled valley?

Answer: he would explore it.

This leads to another excellent question: what would happen if . . . the valley were weird, strangely unoccupied, and creepy?

Answer: it might contain a haunted house.

Question: what would happen if . . . the young man went into the house and encountered the ghost?

Answer: the young man might cry.

Cry? Why would the ghost make him cry?

And here we discover one of the greatest story-creating devices: unexpected answers. Don't make the mistake of saying, "Gee, that makes no sense," as you scratch out the unexpected answer. This would be (he said as calmly as possible) a mistake. Weird answers can get you wondering about a character, about a story. Wondering is good. It might mean that a story is falling into place.

I can easily imagine a storyteller lazing about on a warm summer day, lying in the tall grass, nibbling on a clover stem, looking up, watching clouds drift by, and wondering: What would happen if there was a land up in the clouds? What would happen if everyone up there was huge, dozens of feet tall? What would happen if an earthling could, somehow, reach Cloud Land? Hmm. How might someone get up there?

He could climb a magic beanstalk!

Bingo.

Are you jotting this down? Do you have a vague idea to which you can apply this principle? I bet you do.

What's going on here?

This is another useful question. Think of Dorothy in the great *The*

Wizard of Oz. The violent tornado has transported her away from the sepia-toned black-and-white of the Kansas prairie to technicolored Oz. Why are the flowers so big? What gives with the twisty yellow brick road? Who's giggling? How can I get home?

What's going on here?

The answers to these questions create the story: Dorothy is in Munchkin-land, in Oz. Ah, but there is a special place, the Emerald City, and a wizard lives there. If anyone can tell Dorothy how to return home, he can. Off she goes, and the story unfolds.

For example, you may have chosen—taking a cue from the newspaper headlines, a rich source of stories—to create a story about Asian carp. The carp (huge fish, some approaching a hundred pounds) are leaping into the air, high. It's like they're trying to make it to the sun. Why do they do this?

What, in other words, is going on here?

Perhaps you've chosen to spin a story about an Old Guy who likes to go fishing on the mist-shrouded river, piloting a dinghy with an ancient ten-horsepower motor. He enjoys the solitude, the early morning beauty of the waterway. He daydreams and thinks about the past.

Suddenly, giant carp are leaping, banging into him, falling into the boat. Hundreds of them. This is madness! How will he react? What will he do? Try to get away? Try to catch a few?

What's going on here?

As you think about this question, you may find a story taking shape. The carp are taking over the Old Guy's precious river. What does he do? Why is Old Guy seeking solitude? Has his wife recently passed away? Is he an empty-nester? Maybe he befriends a kid that he meets at the boat landing. Maybe he discovers that the kid is alone camping, a runaway. He finds him, discovers his situation—again, what's going on? Maybe he helps him. All this derives from one question: what is going on here?

What happened to this character in the past?

Backstory, as you likely know, is the Hollywood term for all the stuff that's happened to the characters before the adventure begins. The stodgy old creative writing term for backstory is *exposition.* Whatever word you choose to use, backstory is important. It determines who the characters are, what their situations are, what they want, and how they got to the beginning of the story. Almost every character you create should have a backstory.

It's prominent in "Prometheus and the Stealing of Fire." We need to know the humans' backstory: they lack fire, and this makes them fearful and timid. Thus, when they do conquer fire and learn how to make it, we feel how this empowers them. We also need to know that Prometheus is jealous of Zeus's power and that Zeus takes for granted his sway over the humans. Backstory is also crucial in "Ralph, the Sad, Sad Ghost."

The headlines lately are filled with items about what's being called "Arab Spring": the sudden (or so it may seem to Americans) and cataclysmic struggle for democratic rights throughout the Arab world. Libya, Iran, Egypt, Syria (here the struggle is horrifyingly violent).

Let's say you've decided to mine this rich vein of stories. You're spinning a tale about . . . Saniyah, a Libyan girl, making her way through her rubble-strewn, post-war city, breathing, for the first time, the wonderful, post-Khadaffi air of freedom. A sense of her backstory is crucial (even though it might not be a part of her story): what was it like, in her previous life, to live under the heel of the dictator? How did it affect her family? What kind of life was she able to fashion? Thinking about her past will spark ideas for the present story. Maybe Saniyah has been separated from her family, and she's desperate to find them, to make sure they're okay. Maybe she meets a young man? What is his backstory? Was he possibly in the employ of the Khadaffi power structure? Do they meet an injured woman and try to find medical treatment for her? Does this woman perhaps know the young man?

A sense of backstory here is crucial for these characters to come alive.

Of course it's not always necessary. Do we care about Big Dave Dangworth's past? About Big Bertha's? We do not. Still, all characters have a backstory, and by developing this, thinking about it, you grow them—and their stories.

What is this story about?

Or, to employ the old-fashioned creative writing term, greatly enamored by elderly teachers of English Literature, what is the theme?

Many writers work thematically. Some subjects, for a variety of reasons, fascinate them. They have done research and a great deal of original thinking.

For me, I am passionately interested in adoption. I'm an adoptive father. I have written two plays on the subject. I am unabashedly an expert. Still, my attitude toward this large subject grows and evolves, and will always do so. This evolution informs much of my writing.

Here's another example: perhaps you are passionately interested in the subject (i.e., the theme) of bullying. You think long and hard on this, wondering what would make a young person engage in this kind of destructive behavior? What kind of home situation would turn a kid into a bully? Is he, for some reason, afraid of what he would call "sissy" behavior—in other words, is he homophobic? Why? What drives him?

As you think about this subject, a character emerges: a boy, big for his age, pressured to take charge, to be a leader, but unable to translate this into positive behavior. A sense of his home life emerges: a distant (or absent) father, a drunken mother, abuse at a young age, and poverty.

Serious stuff!

But here, if you will permit me an aside, is something you may already be aware of, and if you're not, you should be: children thrive on dark stories. We, as adults, may be afraid of material like this, on the grounds that it's traumatizing. But children are not afraid. They are hyper-aware of issues like bullying, incarcerated parents, alcoholism, depression, suicide, and poverty (the list is long). They need us to help them deal with these subjects.

A story in the dark creates the perfect environment. After all, you are there to offer support, to answer questions, and to say, in effect, "It's alright. You're safe with me. These issues are scary, but together, we can face them." If you don't deal with material like this, you leave your child susceptible to the influence of rumors, inaccurate peer information, the fear-mongering Internet, and Hollywood.

'Nuff said. Let's move on.

Recapping, here are some of the questions you might ask yourself in order to develop a story:

- ★ What would happen if . . . ?
- ★ What's going on here?
- ★ What happened in the past—what's the backstory?
- ★ What is this story about—what's the theme?

It may well be that as you turned these questions around in your mind and discovered answers to them—that a plot has taken shape. If so, count yourself lucky. Go for it. But perhaps these questions, while they deepen the characters and give the situation expansive size, still haven't resulted in a usable story. If so, you will need to create a story.

Story Categories

What follows herewith are some story categories. They are fairly general. You may find that one (or more) of them fits your idea. If so, use them to create your own story in the dark. These ideas and stories can be combined, so don't assume that you must choose only one. The classic *The Count of Monte Cristo*, for example, starts out as an escape plot. Then it involves the pursuit of a valuable object, when the treasure is hunted down. Once the treasure is discovered, *Cristo* becomes a revenge fantasy. There are three stories in this one terrific (if long) novel. And, by the way, there lurk within its pages a number of potentially effective bedtime stories.

Pursuit

One character chases another. This is a fairy tale staple. There's plenty of room for action (which children love). Your hero can be either the chaser or the chasee. Pursuit adds energy to "Jack and the Beanstalk," as the ogre chases Jack to the beanstalk.

Other examples include:

- ★ *Les Miserables*
- ★ The *Terminator* movies
- ★ *Sleepless in Seattle* (a romantic chase)
- ★ *Jaws*
- ★ *Moby Dick*

Mistaken Identity

Someone believes your hero to be someone else. Or they believe, mistakenly, that the hero has committed a heinous crime. It can be very difficult, and likely impossible, to convince the accuser of the hero's innocence. This often jars your hero out of her comfy life and forces her to face some unsettling questions: who am I really? Why can't I face my accusers? What will I do?

Some examples include:

- ★ *The Comedy Of Errors*
- ★ *Cyrano de Bergerac*

* *Being There*
* Charlie Chaplin's *The Great Dictator*

A Valuable Object

Perhaps the object has been lost and must be recovered. Or perhaps it must be protected or even destroyed. The latter, of course, is the story on which J.R.R. Tolkien builds his three-volume masterwork, *The Lord of the Rings*. In *The Secret Garden*, a valuable object (the garden) was been hidden away, and Mary Lennox finds and restores it.

Other examples include:

* *Aladdin and the Lamp*
* The *Indiana Jones* movies

Disguise

Your hero must go "underground," in disguise, in order to find something or someone. Or maybe evil people are chasing him. There's lots of useful mystery here: will he be found out? Will the nastiness of the world he's entering be too much? The wonderful Musketeers are masters of disguise.

Other examples include:

* *Twelfth Night*
* *As You Like It*
* The *Batman* movies
* *Sherlock Holmes* stories

Quest

Here's another fairy tale staple. Our hero is sent into a new world, a world which is often filled with dangers, with evil opponents, and with magic. Our hero must discover how this world works while at the same time he discovers true love. Or fortune. Or perhaps his true identity. Or maybe just the way home. Children readily identify with heroes like this because they so vividly parallel struggles going on in their lives. Jack London's excellent *The Call of the Wild* works this way.

Other examples include:

★ *The Hobbit*
★ *The Lord of the Rings*
★ *Jason and the Golden Fleece*
★ *The Wizard of Oz*

Restitution

A hero has fallen on hard times, and she must recover her rightful place in the world, often with the help of people who see her worth. Cinderella doesn't deserve to be a scullery maid for her nasty stepmother and her ugly stepsisters. She deserves to be a princess.

Other examples include:

★ *Great Expectations*
★ *Annie*
★ *Meet John Doe*

An Unexpected Ally

This refers to a character, often older than our hero, who provides him, unexpectedly, with something—a tool, knowledge—and thus makes the hero's struggle successful. Glinda the Good Witch in *The Wizard of Oz* is a wonderful example. Ditto for the Professor early on in the story. In "Stacy, the Cowardly Crocodile," Stacy finds herself connected with Adoni, an adolescent human—unusual allies, for sure—who shows her something about herself. Moses is allied with God.

Other examples include:

★ The *Star Wars* movies
★ *One Flew Over the Cuckoo's Nest*

Revenge/Forgiveness

One character, usually evil, is seeking revenge, and our hero has to convince him that revenge is pointless—that forgiveness is the best way to live. This process is usually lengthy and normally involves a lot of chasing, hair-raising escapes, etc.

Some examples include:

★ *Hamlet*
★ *Medea*
★ *Death Wish*
★ *The Princess Bride*

Rescue

Someone is in dire distress—lost in the clutches of a dreadful monster, controlled by a vile Bad Guy—and our hero must free him and escape. An analogous situation animates "Ralph, the Sad, Sad Ghost": Ralph must be rescued so that he can, finally, go "home."

Other examples include:

★ *Kidnapped*
★ 24
★ *The Princess Bride*
★ *King Kong*

Escape

Escape stories are similar to a rescue plot, with the (major) difference being that the hero frees himself, finding a way out and the wherewithal to accomplish it.

Some examples include:

★ *Hansel and Gretel*
★ *The Count of Monte Cristo*
★ *Occurrence at Owl Creek Bridge*

Rivalry

Two people, one good and one bad, are vying for the same honor, the same love, or the same goal. The working out of their rivalry forms the plot.

Other examples include:

★ *Mean Girls*
★ *Ben Hur*
★ The *Harry Potter* books and movies

The Underdog

A person, whom everyone assumes is a useless dork, saves the day, comes into her own, and triumphs.

Other examples include:

★ Chuck in "Ralph, the Sad, Sad Ghost"
★ Jack in "Jack and the Beanstalk"
★ *Cinderella*
★ Anything about Joan of Arc

The "Idea Approach" in a Nutshell

Ask productive questions. Let the idea take shape. Often, the physical act of writing moves you forward. Once a situation, characters, etc., are in place, you can begin searching for a plot. It's quite possible to make up your own. You may wish to use one or several of the above storylines.

You might also consult one of the very useful books detailing with "master plots", i.e., stories featured in almost all world literature. The central idea in these books is that all texts, ancient to contemporary, can be reduced to a few basic plots. An excellent example of these books is *20 Master Plots (and How to Build Them)* by Ronald B. Tobias.

Before we move on, I do want to remind you that we are creating bedtime stories for young children. The tales you create will likely be fantastical, filled with strange and delightful magic. There may be some nasty villains, but the courage and heroism of your heroes will counter-balance this, and then some.

In other words, there is a high probability that you will be creating and telling fairy tales. Therefore, it behooves you to familiarize yourself with this form. Check the "Storytelling Resources" section at the end of this book for ideas. Become a connoisseur of fairy tales; it's a delightful (and surprisingly deep) form.

NOTES

The Character Approach

Working directly with ideas is intellectual. It requires that you "think up" plots and themes (and characters to fit them). But you don't have to work like this. There is a more instinctive method. This approach doesn't depend on your being super-intelligent (a break for me).

You can work directly with character.

Creating a character is easy. We all live in the world. We have coworkers, friends, spouses, and family. A love of humanity flows in our bloodstream — after all, we have children.

Come up with an idea for a character. Think about her. Add random details: What does she look like? What does she do? How old is she? What's her backstory? You may very well discover that in this fleshing-out process, everything has neatly fallen into place. Is this a comedy? A drama? Work on the character, and this will become clear. What's the plot? Again, develop the character and find out. What about style? Length? Setting? Everything comes from character.

There is another grand advantage of working with character: originality. If you're working mainly with ideas, you quickly come against an unavoidable fact: here in the twenty-first century, it is very difficult to come up with a genuinely original idea. Everything, or so it seems, has been done and done and done once again.

Ah, but with a character, originality is vastly easier to achieve. No one has ever seen a person quite like this. She is very unique — like you.

The Character Exercise

I call it an exercise, and it is. But you might think of it as a way to get moving on your story in the dark. If you do this exercise fully, and give your character permission to grow, there's an excellent chance that you will be telling your child something special in a very few days.

Here's the exercise: write down everything we need to know about a character.

That's it.

Simple.

If you want to create a laundry list of random characteristics, you can certainly do that. If you're more comfortable writing fully rendered paragraphs, by all means, go for it. There's no right or wrong approach.

This needn't be time-consuming. Five minutes, ten minutes, fifteen — gee, maybe a whole half an hour — will do.

Let's try one. (I know, you're not here, but give me the benefit of the doubt). What's the first thing you might wish to know about a character?

Age? Okay, how old is this person? Twenty-five. Let's write that down, first entry on our list:

★   25 years old

What else would you want to know? Gender? Yes, that would

be significant. Got a gender idea? Female. Write it down, the second item on our list.

★   Female

What does she do? Any ideas? Schoolteacher? Okay.

★   Schoolteacher

At twenty-five, she'd be new to the profession, which could be interesting.

What else? Where does she live? In a mansion? Okay. Let's write it down:

★   Lives in an old mansion

That's definitely interesting. Where did that word come from? "Old." Hmm. An old mansion . . . outside the city? How far is it from school? How old is the house? What does it look like? How does she afford the place? Is she privately wealthy?

Maybe someone gave her the place. Hmm. Maybe she woke up one day to find the key and the deed to the place on her doorstep. Wow.

Oh, we need a name. Dottie? Fine, Dottie it is.

★   Dottie

See how far we've gotten in half a page?

Let's try another character, and just for the sake of contrast, let's explore the opposite gender. Also, let's make him young — in keeping with many of the heroes of stories in the dark.

★   12 years old
★   Male
★   Eddie

What else would you want to know about Eddie? Who he lives with?

★   Lives with his grandma.

This is a left field choice, and it immediately raises interesting questions: Why Grandma? What has happened to Eddie's parents? Perhaps they . . . disappeared? When did that happen? Remember: backstory is important.

How about . . . exactly 364 days ago, on Halloween — hmm. What were Eddie's sainted parents doing? Just . . . walking down the street of a small town? Maybe they were newly arrived in town and just innocently exploring. Then they disappeared. Are they dead? Captured? In a parallel universe? What is up with this town? Ooh, interesting. Remember my earlier emphasis on the importance of weird and unusual juxtapositions. It definitely applies here — very interesting.

That word keeps coming up, and it's important enough to receive its own subheading.

Interesting

Why do we say something is interesting? It may be like the old definition of pornography: "I can't define it, but I know it when I see it." That may be true, but I believe that "interesting," at least to an extent, can be defined, and the definition can be quite useful.

Something is "interesting" when it's illogical, but not too illogical.

Does this compute? There should be some tension in the main premise of a story: I'm willing to buy this, but I want to know more. I really want this to make sense. Tell me more; explore it more fully. This desire for more drives the story.

But what you come up with shouldn't be so illogical that it makes us throw up our hands and say, "I want nothing to do with this silly plot."

It's unusual to say that Eddie lives with his Grandma. Most children live with their parents. Why doesn't Eddie? Hmm. The illogic of this pulls us in. We wonder about Eddie's situation. We ask: why Grandma? But if you said that Eddie lives with worms, we would lose interest. It would be too illogical.

What if we said he lives with wolves? This could work. Illogic such as this has been used effectively before, in *Tarzan*, *The Jungle Book*, etc. It depends on how realistic or how fantastical you want your tale to be. If you're creating a world where boys can be raised by (surprisingly long-lived) wolves, go for it. It's your choice to make.

Let's look at Dottie. It's unexpected that someone would present her with the key and the deed to a moldering old mansion. Illogical, yes, but acceptable, and thus it raises usefully "interesting" questions. Who did this? Why? How will it make her change?

A less-acceptable choice would have Dottie getting the deed to a huge NYC high rise (these are owned by enormous international corporations) or the Brooklyn Bridge.

So, don't be afraid of illogical, out-of-left-field character traits. If they come, let them. They create story. Just make sure they're in line with the tenor of the world in which you see your character living.

Motivation

Another character-based question would be: what motivates this character? In other words, what does this character want?

All characters want something. All characters take action to obtain it. This passion, this motivation to change, this yearning for something better, is what makes these individuals compelling.

Often, characters know what they want. Hansel and Gretel are lost and they want, consciously, to get out of the woods. Little Red Riding Hood wants to reach Grandma's house unscathed.

But just as often, characters don't initially know what they want. In "Ralph, the Sad, Sad Ghost," Chuck is just exploring, randomly. But when he discovers, through Madeleine, that Ralph the ghost needs something, he becomes fiercely focused on getting it for him.

Sometimes characters know, or think they know, what they want, but what they want changes — dramatically. In "Moses and the Exodus," Moses wants initially to be a good friend to Ramses, the Pharaoh-to-be. Then, Moses wants to survive. Then he wants to build a happy life with Zipporah. Then God intervenes and galvanizes Moses into a new and passionately held desire: to free the Israelites. When a character changes what he wants, it's always dramatic and satisfying. It renews our interest in the story.

In our character exercise, what Eddie wants is quite conscious: he wants his parents back. There may be a related sense that Grandma, though her heart's no doubt in the right place, isn't offering the kind of parenting that Eddie needs. Maybe she's slipping into her dotage. But he will likely stay focused.

Dottie's yearnings are less conscious. She has a new teaching job, and this should make her joyful, but for some reason it doesn't. Then the old mansion comes into her life, a talisman. The mansion, she becomes convinced, holds secrets. She just has to find out what they are.

Now she has conscious desires. She will do something to obtain them. What? We just have to keep sketching her, working on the exercise, to discover what this might be.

Obstacles

Not only do characters want something, but when they take action to obtain what they want, they encounter obstacles.

Often, these obstacles are other characters: Bad Guys. Or, just as often, guys in the employ of the main Bad Guy (think of the flying monkeys in *The Wizard of Oz*, or the beefy dogs in "Ralph, the Sad, Sad Ghost").

Sometimes the obstacle-creating characters aren't villains at all. They are regular folk with other agendas that cause them to interfere with our heroes getting what they desire. These characters may be well meaning, even sweet and friendly. But they create obstacles, sometimes vicious obstacles, anyway. An example of this would be Madeleine's mother in "Ralph, the Sad, Sad Ghost." She is by no means evil, but she makes serious problems for our two heroes.

Sometimes, the obstacle is physical. Think of the cold Atlantic Ocean in *Titanic*, the weird lions-and-tigers-and-bears forest in *The Wizard of Oz*, Mount Doom in *The Lord of the Rings*. The presence of the beanstalk creates problems for Jack. You get the idea.

And sometimes the obstacles are internal, part of the make-up of our hero. These are often the most interesting kinds of obstacles because they require that the characters take a long look at themselves and, maybe, effect some kind of meaningful change. Martin in "Sophie and the Unicorns" has to let go of his grief. Dorothy must understand that there's "no place like home." Moses has to overcome his reluctance to inflict the plagues on the Egyptians. Samaal in "The Prodigal Son" has to overcome his (natural) anger at his brother.

Whatever form these obstacles take, they are very useful; they create story.

Supporting Characters

As characters take action to get what they want, they will, very likely, form alliances and friendships with other characters. Pursue these. They make for terrific story. If dialogue happens in the course of this pursuit, so much the better. You will often find that characters don't really come into their own until you get them talking, so anytime you have an opportunity to do this, seize it.

As an example, let's riff on Dottie.

What if she finds another person, a denizen of the old mansion, living in the attic? In the basement? Down a secret corridor? Who knows?

> "Who are you?" Dottie demanded. "You scared me."
>
> "I'm no one."
>
> "You look . . ."
>
> The old man was shivering. Dottie was unsure if it was from fear or from the cold.
>
> "I'm hungry."
>
> It was true. The old man's clothes were hanging on his emaciated frame.
>
> "Come on," Dottie said. "I'll make you a sandwich." She started toward the kitchen. Then she turned, then repeated, with more force than she thought she possessed, "Come on."
>
> Slowly, the old man followed.

What's going to happen when the old man starts wolfing his sandwich in the nice warm kitchen? Will he tell a story about the house? Is he lost? Has he arrived from . . . another dimension? Or maybe he gets Dottie to open up? Who knows?

And the point is, you don't have to know. This is what makes this character approach different from the idea approach, where you intellectualize your way into a story. Here, if you get stuck, no problem; just start working your way into the story from another angle.

Here, off the top of my head, are some story possibilities created by the arrival of the mysterious Old Guy. Maybe:

★ Some friendly (or not-so-friendly?) neighbors stop by the old house to welcome Dottie. The Old Man, now Dottie's ally, warns her about them.

★ He is a sheriff's deputy convinced that there are teenagers vandalizing the house.

★ He is Dottie's great uncle, one she was never allowed to meet because he knows some family secrets.

Keep in mind that this is an exercise. You're not chiseling this stuff into stone. The Old Guy could prove un-useful. Other, better, ideas could emerge. Things change. Change is good.

The Transformation

Keep in mind that as a story evolves, characters will undergo changes and make important discoveries.

The great Joseph Campbell has a high-falutin' way of asking this: what "magic elixir" do our heroes return with? They will have changed. How? Will Eddie find his parents? What will Dottie discover about the mansion and about herself? It needn't be earth-shakingly dramatic, but there must be something.

Is it simply new knowledge, as when Dorothy in *The Wizard of Oz* chants, "There's no place like home"? Or when the heroes in "Ralph, the Sad, Sad Ghost" understand that forgiveness — of oneself — is possible? Or when Martin in "Sophie and the Unicorns" discovers that his adventures in Unicorn Land have allowed him to become unblocked and get back to work?

Or do the heroes bring something solid home? Jack, in "Jack and the Beanstalk," returns with golden coins, a golden-egg laying goose, and a golden harp — major stuff. Big Bertha returns with a marriage, to Philaster.

Or maybe the characters just have fun — think of "Stacy, the Cowardly Crocodile."

There's always something. It may be a real talisman, or new knowledge, or simply the indelible memory of a rattling good time. Whatever it might be, it produces a vivid sense of an ending.

Remember: creating your own character is easy, and it can very quickly get you into rich and compelling story territory. Look how far we got with Dottie in a very short period of time. Create your own character, think about her, and soon, a whole story world will open up. Junior will adore it.

The 1-2-3 Method

I have created what I modestly call my "1-2-3 Method" for quickly creating effective bedtime stories.

I use the term "quickly" advisedly. Please don't imagine that I pooh-pooh this form. I take bedtime stories very seriously indeed. But I know that most tellers have, in addition to demanding children, demanding jobs, spouses, friends, and time-consuming household duties. They lack the time to develop sophisticated and complex stories.

And they don't need to. Tellers of bedtime tales revel in the semi-improvised, shoot-from-the-hip, winging-it spontaneity of the form. You will want to prepare—to a point. You need at least a sense of the story you plan to tell. You may wish to have created some story points to facilitate this. But your planning shouldn't be long and detailed.

Similarly, if you are creating your stories from whole cloth, you want your creation method to be similarly swift and easy. My "1-2-3 Method" involves the asking three straightforward, character-based questions:

1. Who is this character?

Employ the useful character exercise we discussed in the last chapter to develop this person in vivid detail. Determine their appearance, occupation, personality, and background. Has something recently happened?

What kind of world does the character inhabit? Comic? Dramatic? Realistic? Magical? Think about the setting. Is it realistic? Completely made up? Remember, you're creating a story in the dark, and there is an excellent chance that it is a fairy tale, featuring a magic-charged fantasy world.

Finally, ask: what does this character want? Does she know what she wants? Or will she discover it as the story progresses? Will her desires change?

2. What does she do?

What steps does she take to obtain what she wants? What obstacles might she encounter? Are these obstacles external (either physical or embodied in the characters) or internal? Or (more likely) both? Does she form any alliances? Do her goals change? The answers to these questions form the main part of a story's plot.

3. What does she discover?

In what way does the story change her? Permanent friendships? Life lessons learned? What sort of Cambellian "elixir" does she bring back?

That's it.

Will what results from this simple method attract the interest of The New Yorker, or even the most obscure literary journal? Unlikely. Will it work for your child? You betcha.

This is the method I used when I wrote "Sophie and the Unicorns," a story I have included in the Fairy Tales section. If you haven't read the piece, it might be useful for you to take fifteen or twenty minutes to do so now.

The 1-2-3 Method: "Sophie and the Unicorns"

I wrote "Sophie and the Unicorns" in two sittings, taking, I would guess, four hours total. That I was planning to write the material down, so that you could read it, added considerably to my writing time. I needed to make the material coherent and succinct. Were I planning simply to present the story to a child, I'm sure I could have assembled a solid and tellable story in less than an hour.

Let's apply the "1-2-3 Method" to "Sophie and the Unicorns":

Question numero uno: who is this character?

Let's begin with a quick laundry list exercise:

* ★ Female
* ★ 15 years old
* ★ 15, but older than her years

This is slightly illogical. Sophie is a "mature" fifteen. Hmm.

* ★ Lives with her father

Even more illogical. A slew of useful questions are raised here, mostly having to do with Sophie's mother: where is she?

What kind of world does Sophie live in? For this, I had a very vivid mental picture: Sophie and her father have just moved into a "down-market" house in a slightly rough neighborhood. It's small and white, with broken shutters, surrounded by a metal fence and unkempt yard.

All these details emerged rapidly, in, I would guess, about five minutes.

The Big Question: where's Mom?

Has she died? Are Sophie and her father dealing with her (relatively recent) death? Might this be a story about grief, about coming to terms with capital D Death?

Yikes.

I have developed my quandary about this question earlier (in my introduction to the story, pp . 205). Suffice it to say, I decided to soldier on, creating a story about grief, the presence of death, knowing that many children would appreciate—indeed, need—this. It might up the maturity required from tellees, but the reassuring presence of the teller will obviate this to a great extent.

★ Sophie has a collection of unicorns.

This came out of nowhere, but I could see them—girlish toys, some big, some tiny. They harken back to a sweeter, easier time. Still, the unicorns are the first things Sophie unpacks when she moves to her new house. She arranges them on a shelf next to her bed.

Hmm.

Another strong image come to me:

Something jars Sophie awake. She gets up. Something pulls on her. She goes downstairs, finds a flashlight—it's just in her hand; she has no memory of picking it up—goes into the kitchen, opens the cellar door and heads downstairs, into the basement. The air is stale and mildew-y, and there are cobwebs everywhere—ick!—but something makes her go on.

Then she sees it. A door, limned with dancing, swirling light. Sophie giggles—she can't help herself.

She opens the door.

And beholds an amazing world, with soaring trees,

> enormous flowers, a blue sky, floating clouds, tame animals, and singing birds.
>
> Sophie laughs.
>
> Then she tries to step into the world.
>
> But she can't move. Try as she might—and she tries repeatedly—something won't let her in.

Excellent!

Now I know what Sophie wants: to enter Unicorn Land. This brings us to question numero dos: what does Sophie do to get what she wants?

Here, I came up with several actions. I wasn't sure at the time whether they would make it into the "finished" story, but I pursued them, knowing that even if they wound up on the proverbial cutting room floor, they would move the character of Sophie forward. She would be richer as a result. Here's one:

Coming home from school, Sophie sees Martin walking. She starts to call out to him, but something makes her stop. She follows him instead. Martin walks with his head bent down, not looking up, just walking. After a few blocks, Sophie gets nervous—about the strange neighborhood and possibly getting lost—and heads home. Martin returns, hours later, not saying a word.

Another action:

Sophie has an encounter with a sympathetic teacher. The teacher senses that something's up with her and makes a gentle inquiry. They talk in an empty classroom.

Another:

Sophie finds a neighborhood butcher shop selling hotdogs, a food that Sophie and Martin often share. It brings them together. Sophie digs in her jean pockets, but only has enough money to buy three. The butcher throws in a few extra dogs.

Then I had a vivid image: Sophie lying in bed at night, the full moon radiating through the open window. She holds her hand into hot light—and it radiates color, just like the world through the door. Suddenly, it comes to her: Martin is the key.

She jumps up, rushes down the hall, grabs (the very sleepy) Martin's hand, and takes him to the coal room.

And they enter Unicorn Land.

They explore and find: flowers, birds, and animals dancing and gamboling; music; Arroyos, ravines, and caves. Each has its own treasure. And there are unicorns!

They have adventures. Maybe they meet other people. Or, maybe, in the caves, and maybe (taking a cue from Dickens's *A Christmas Carol*) they are able to time travel to events from Martin and Sophie's past and future, or rescue lost princesses. This requires a fair amount of working-out, but it goes a long way toward answering the second question of what Sophie does.

Finally, question numero tres: what does Sophie discover?

Well, she discovers, or more accurately rediscovers, how to have a good time. She deals with her grief. Sophie still feels Mom's absence keenly, but now she can move forward. She becomes, once again, happy.

This story has a significant side character, very nearly as important as Sophie: Martin. Once the basics of the story were in place, I thought about Martin, thought about how his grief was blocking him creatively. His experiences in Unicorn Land allow him to write again, and this gives the story a happy ending.

And that's "Sophie and the Unicorns." 1-2-3.

Let's apply this method to a story that hasn't been developed in this book:

The 1-2-3 Method: "Fritz, the Squirrel"

Question 1: Who is Fritz?

What kind of world does Fritz — the name appeals to me, but give him another if you must — live in? What does he want?

* Fritz is a squirrel — no surprise here.
* Fritz is an arrogant punk. He thinks he's a master scamperer, quicker up a tree than anyone else. Maybe develop a quick story to demonstrate this: Fritz grabs a walnut from a blue jay and evades the jay's efforts to take it back.
* Fritz lives in the Forest, capital F: endless tall trees and mountains — idyllic.

How realistic or fantastical is Fritz's world? It's fairly realistic, contemporary, and recognizable — there's no Unicorn Land–like fantasy.

Ah, but there's one huge difference: in this story, the animals talk — anthropomorphism redux.

Let's get a clearer sense of who Fritz is. This is easily accomplished while you're walking the dog, washing pots and pans, or daydreaming in your home office. What does he look like? (Maybe he has a crooked tooth — a snaggletooth — and he's super-sensitive about it.) Let's listen to him talk (a mile a minute). Let's feed him. (He adores walnuts; I know this for a fact). Maybe come up with a few more scenarios. These may or may not prove useable, but no matter; they're growing the character.

Ooh, here's one:

Fritz falls asleep in a drainpipe (he doesn't know any better; he's a Forest squirrel) and wakes up as the pipe is being loaded onto a truck. The truck takes off, taking Fritz away from his beloved Forest.

Gulp.
And now, Fritz has a heartfelt desire: to go home.

Question 2: What does Fritz do?

Random answers (in the form of story points):

★ On the truck, he watches the world zip by. He's seen dirt roads before, but this is an asphalt highway. Soon, it becomes a freeway, covered with cars.

★ The truck leaves the mountains, descends to a desert, and approaches—wow!—a city. Finally, it slows enough for Fritz to jump off.

★ Fritz finds a park, but city squirrels are tough and nasty and don't have the time of day for a lost and frightened country bumpkin like Fritz. He was King of the Forest, but now he's a hayseed, out of his element.

★ Suddenly, the squirrels scatter.

★ It's Mrs. McGillicuddy, a crazy, squirrel-hating old woman, carrying her despiséd cane. "Take that!" *Whack, whack.* "And that!" *Whack.*

★ Fritz runs.

★ He comes to a downtown street, with cars, pedestrians, and huge buildings. Yikes! Fritz finds a sewer—whew, a refuge. He wanders aimlessly, trying to make sense of his situation.

★ It rains.

★ Aaaagggghhhh! The water quickly rises, and poor Fritz is swept along by the flood, almost drowning, snatching vainly at pawholds. Finally, the water subsides. Now Fritz is truly lost.

★ He meets rats—ugly, vicious-looking creatures with red eyes. But they turn out to be sort of nice, albeit not terribly bright. They lead Fritz to a train yard and form a rat-ramp so he can climb on a boxcar.

★ He rides the boxcar out of the city, into the mountains. It looks familiar—it's a Forest—but he doesn't recognize anything. He's still lost, and his desperation is increasing. At a likely-looking place, he jumps off the train. Yee-ow!

★ Fritz walks, going up, up, up. He's hungry, lost, and forlorn. One night, it snows. Fritz keeps moving, but sometimes he breaks through the snow. Walking is difficult.

★ Near the frozen summit, Fritz meets Wally the bear. Wally is roly-poly and fun-loving. He puts Fritz on his lap and slides down the mountain. What took Fritz days to travel, Wally negotiates in a few (fun-filled) minutes. Yee-ha!

★ At the bottom, Wally goes off to find a cave in which to hibernate. Fritz travels on.

★ He meets a Native American man, a shaman, who understands instinctively where Fritz needs to go. He feeds the skinny, half-starved squirrel, puts him in a pack, and off they go.

★ Finally, Fritz comes home.

Clearly, Fritz's journey home is this story's centerpiece, but do other stuff—come up with other stories. If you think of something else, then go back to develop the idea. This story is probably a multi-nighter, so you will have time and flexibility.

Question 3: What does Fritz discover?

Easy: (to quote Dorothy) "there's no place like home." He no longer takes his Forest life for granted. Fritz has, no doubt, changed, and it takes the other animals a moment before they truly recognize him. But when they do, celebration ensues!

1-2-3.

NOTES

Conclusion

You're ready. You understand the bennies of telling stories in the dark. You know how to set up the child(ren)'s room and how to tell an amazing story. Here's what you have to do:

Find some story material. You don't have to look far. The next time you see a movie or read a book, keep in mind that you're in the market for bedtime stories. I'll bet you'll find that you can utilize a piece of the book or the movie for this purpose.

Quick example: My son Michael and I found that in Jack London's marvelous *The Call of the Wild* there lurked a number of set pieces that did excellent double duty as stories in the dark. We called the stories "Sled Dogs": the opening kidnapping of Buck; the story of Buck being "broken" as a sled dog; his discovery of the joy of running, how to eat salmon, how to find a place to sleep under the snow, becoming the lead dog, etc. Rough stuff, but darn good stories.

Or make up your own!

Create characters, let them live, get 'em talking, mix 'em up with other characters, and, bingo, you'll have something you can present to your sleepy child. Look at the headlines; I bet you'll immediately find some ideas.

And history. One of the glories of parenthood is that ye olde clichés once again have life. The American Revolution may be a snoozer for you—remember those dreary history classes? But

Dearest Darling likely knows nothing about it and will thrill to your take on the subject. Tell the story of Valley Forge, the first Thanksgiving, the Gettysburg Address, or the story of Crazy Horse (and his tribe)'s valiant struggle against the American government. This can be disturbing stuff, but the stories are fab, and remember that you are there to help your child make sense of it all. The early days of Hollywood have much useful story material (read Neil Gabler's outstanding *An Empire of Their Own: How the Jews Invented Hollywood*.) History is story-rich. Use the 1-2-3 Method, and let it come alive.

The newspaper, history, books, movies, anthologies of fairy tales, tall tales, and legends can inspire stories that you can create from whole cloth. Bedtime stories can galvanize your life and your child's life.

Off you go. Give Mr. or Ms. Incredible a kiss for me, and have fun.

Resources for Storytellers

What primary resource does a teller of bedtime stories require? A child! Or children! And this, I'm guessing, you already have. All you need to do is some reading. Or maybe some light creating. Assemble the bare bones of a story, turn off the bedroom lights — this is crucial — and tell away.

Once you become accomplished at this (which will take you no time at all), you will very likely wish to explore this wonderful form further. One of the first discoveries you will make is that storytelling is by no means a minor art form. Every American city boasts a "scene": coffee shops, bars, small theaters, churches, etc., where storytellers hold forth, working their rough magic. Often, there are headliners, with (relative) unknowns warming the audience up, preparing them for the main event. Sometimes tellers all get the same "billing." No one takes the lead. Everyone gets the same attention.

And sometimes — gulp — the event is "open mike." Anyone with chutzpah and a story to tell can take the stage.

How do you find this stuff? Well, work the Internet. Every storytelling group has a site, a Facebook page, and a robust mailing list. I live in Minneapolis. I Googled "storytelling resources minnesota" and lots of cool stuff came up: a site for Story Arts of Minnesota; a site and a Facebook page for Two Chairs Telling, a regular event at a local theater called Bryant Lake Bowl (a bowling alley rehabbed into a theater, a bar, and a restaurant; you can also bowl); even a site for storytelling focused on healthcare. And I was just skimming the surface. Do the same for your town. Go to the performances. Get on—very important—the mailing lists. Become a fan.

Or, if you prefer, dust off your producer's hat and produce your own storytelling shows. Performing venues aren't terribly hard to find; there are plenty of coffeehouses or churches that will jump at the chance to host a few events. Find tellers. It's easier than you might think. Become one yourself. Spread the word through social media. People will come.

You will also want to become familiar with:

The National Storytelling Festival

This is premiere storytelling event in the US, and it is held on the first full weekend in October in Jonesborough, allegedly the oldest town in Tennessee. As many as 10,000 people attend, filling tents, churches, and street corners, soaking up the nineteenth century atmosphere, visiting the nearby Smokey Mountains, and glorying in the autumn weather. Attend. I promise you will have a grand time. This is a popular event, so reserve your hotel room—or your campsite—well in advance.

National Storytelling Network

For more specific information, visit storynet.org. An offshoot of the International Storytelling Center (which produces the National Storytelling Festival), the National Storytelling Network is chock-full of resources. They offer membership, a searchable database of storytellers, and storytelling conferences. They host storytelling events. There is also a blog: blog.storynet.org. (Blogs, by the way, are an excellent way to find resources, performances, and storytelling groups in your area).

Storyteller Magazine

Published five times per year, this is a publication filled with marvelous material, stories, and information. Subscribe, or find it in your local library.

Story Source Books

There are many, many books of bedtime stories; an Amazon search reveals dozens upon dozens. But these stories are designed to be read out loud, with the lights on and with the distracting (to me) sensibility of the author in the room. This goes against the grain of what we're trying to do. We want to tell, not read. We want to utilize the charged magic of the darkened bedroom. Still, these books of bedtime tales can be a good resource for material. You might discover some that you enjoy and that provide good fodder for in-the-dark stories.

Along these lines, there are a number of story sources I highly recommend:

The Andrew Lang Books

Lang, whose dates are 1844–1912, was a tireless collector of folk and fairy tales. These he published in a series of "colorful" volumes: *The Blue Fairy Book* (the first and best known), *The Red Fairy Book*, *The Pink Fairy Book*, etc. Lang was also one of the major popularizers of the Arabian Nights material and well as the Homer myths. In Lang's wonderful work you will find a wealth of fairy tales and folk material. Some of it is familiar, some completely unknown. His work is in the public domain and his books can be downloaded, for free, at gutenberg.org. Read him on your Nook or Kindle or, less satisfyingly, on your PC. But read him.

The Annotated Classic Fairy Tales, edited and introduced by Maria Tatar

This volume of fairy tales is terrific. As with Lang, some are stories familiar (to the point of being clichés) and some will be brand new. All are excellent.

A Treasury of American Folklore edited by B. A. Botkin

This is one of the most enjoyable books ever penned. Everyone should own it. You don't have to read it straight through; you can dip into it wherever you want. It is an outstanding source of first-rate story material.

Here are some books about storytelling, often written by professional tellers, i.e., people whose real talent lies on the stage, not at the writing desk. Still, they can be an excellent resource.

The Storytelling Coach by Doug Lipman

Mr. Lipman uses the principals of storytelling to increase communication skills. A useful book for storytellers, and anyone who wants to become a more effective speaker, listener, communicator.

Books by Margaret Read MacDonald

Ms. MacDonald is a prolific author and an internationally famous storyteller. Check out her website: margaretreadmacdonald.com. Explore her Amazon page. Lurking in her work is quite likely some useful material.

Creative Storytelling: Choosing, Inventing, and Sharing Tales for Children by Jack Maguire

This is an excellent book, incisively written and filled with terrific stories. Unfortunately, it's out of print. Still, you may be able to locate a copy online. And someone should reissue it; it's wonderful.

The Way of the Storyteller by Ruth Sawyer

This is the bible of storytelling resources—a beautiful analysis of the art and source for marvelous stories. It is still in print and well worth finding.

The Art of the Storyteller by Marie Shedlock

This resource is a classic, and it is downloadable for no charge at gutenberg.org

Books on Creativity

Here are some book on the creative process and on structuring stories. This is an idiosyncratic subject. Some people may find these books useful; some may not. See if they work for you.

The Artist's Way: A Spiritual Path to Higher Creativity by Julia Cameron

This book offers a lovely look at the creative process, with an emphasis on personal growth. Excellent.

Writing Down the Bones: Freeing The Writer Within and *Wild Mind: Living The Writer's Life* by Natalie Goldberg

Here are two excellent books on the writing process—a tad self-referential, but good.

The Hero with a Thousand Faces by Joseph Campbell

This is a marvelous work, based on Campbell's years of research into the universal structure of folk tales. In this book, Campbell details the stages of what he calls "the hero's journey." If you're telling your child a multi-night fairy tale, you will very likely find

Campbell to be very helpful. Campbell died in 1987, but he remains a major presence in the storytelling culture, and this is an excellent introduction to his work. Read it, then rent and watch the Bill Moyers PBS interview.

The Writer's Journey: Mythic Structure for Writers by Christopher Vogler

Self-published but widely available, this book utilizes Campbell's work and sets forth an eminently practical method for giving a story larger-than-life structure. The book is intended for screenwriters (and refers to movies only), but the ideas developed apply to other forms as well, including bedtime stories. I find the book to be invaluable; you may as well. Try to find the 2nd edition; in the 3rd, Vogler pads shamelessly.

The Uses of Enchantment: The Meaning and Importance of Fairy Tales by Bruno Bettelheim

Bettelheim, who died in 1990, was a highly regarded psychotherapist who (allegedly) mistreated his patients, didn't believe in autism, and was a Holocaust survivor and a successful PBS spokesman. He has become a controversial figure. Bettelheim was not a great writer, and the book is dense — a slog, frankly. Still, *The Uses of Enchantment* remains a passionate paeans to the power of fairy tales. I recommend it.

About the Author

John is a widely produced and award-winning playwright. His plays include *Minnesota Moon, Standing On My Knees, Killers, The Voice of the Prairie, The Ecstasy of St. Theresa, Clara's Play, The Summer Moon, God Fire*, et al. Producing theaters have included: The Manhattan Theatre Cub, Wisdom Bridge, Actors Theatre of Louisville, Oregon Shakespeare Co., Old Globe, South Coast Rep, Steppenwolf, ACT/Seattle, and many others. John has won fellowships from the Bush Foundation, the McKnight Foundation, the Rockefeller Foundation, and the National Endowment for the Arts. *The Summer Moon* won the Kennedy Center Award for Drama.

In the past twelve years, John has written many plays for young audiences including *Sideways Stories From Wayside School, The Magic Bicycle, Jason and the Golden Fleece, Pharaoh Serket and The Lost Stone of Fire, Johnny Tremain*, and others. Producing theaters have included Seattle Children's Theatre, South Coat Rep, The Arden, Nashville Children's, Oregon Children's, First Stage Milwaukee, et al. John's latest at Seattle Children's (his 6th), *Art Dog*, opened in April of 2014.

John has also written YA novels, including *Smartass and Deep River* (in-progress, in collaboration with David Grant) and screenplays (Amblin' Entertainment, Shadow-Catcher, etc). John is presently writing an immersive adaptation of *Crime and Punishment*, with Live Action Set.

He writes theater reviews for HowWasTheShow.com and lives in Minneapolis with his wife Mary and their son Michael.

About Familius

Welcome to a place where mothers are celebrated, not compared. Where heart is at the center of our families, and family at the center of our homes. Where boo boos are still kissed, cake beaters are still licked, and mistakes are still okay. Welcome to a place where books — and family — are beautiful. Familius: a book publisher dedicated to helping families be happy.

Visit Our Website: www.familius.com

Our website is a different kind of place. Get inspired, read articles, discover books, watch videos, connect with our family experts, download books and apps and audiobooks, and along the way, discover how values and happy family life go together.

Join Our Family

There are lots of ways to connect with us! Subscribe to our newsletters at www.familius.com to receive uplifting daily inspiration, essays from our Pater Familius, a free ebook every month, and the first word on special discounts and Familius news.

Become an Expert

Familius authors and other established writers interested in helping families be happy are invited to join our family and contribute online content. If you have something important to say on the family, join our expert community by applying at:

www.familius.com/apply-to-become-a-familius-expert

Get Bulk Discounts

If you feel a few friends and family might benefit from what you've read, let us know and we'll be happy to provide you with quantity discounts. Simply email us at specialorders@familius.com.

Website: www.familius.com
Facebook: www.facebook.com/paterfamilius
Twitter: @familiustalk, @paterfamilius1
Pinterest: www.pinterest.com/familius

The most important work

you ever do will be within the

walls of your own home.

CPSIA information can be obtained
at www.ICGtesting.com
Printed in the USA
FSOW03n1505120215
5150FS

9 781939 629586